For

Alex, Caroline, Michael,

Rachel, Thea and Vicki

Cover painting by Montague Dawson
(1890-1973)

Pages 6 - 7: *Mayflower* II sailing into New York Harbor in 1957.
Picture courtesy of B.Anthony Stewart - National Geographic Image Collection

The

Wicked

Pilgrim

by Randal Charlton

Published by

© Three Sisters Publishing Limited 2019

Email: threesisterspublishing@gmail.com

ISBN 978-1-7336204-1-3

A portion of revenues from all sales will be devoted to supporting Anglo American exchange scholarships. For further information on the scholarships go to ***www.charltonfoundation.org***

THE AUTHOR

Randal Charlton has had a long and varied career in journalism and business.

In 2011, he was winner of a national Purpose Prize in the USA for his work in helping to rebuild the Detroit economy. In 2007, he won the National Heimlich award for medical research. He has been recognized as an Entrepreneur of the Year, and won three national prizes in the U.K. for technical journalism.

Randal has given numerous talks about the valuable contribution that older adults can make to economic growth, including a TED talk about the importance of confidence in business success. Aside from his lifelong interest in journalism, Randal has been CEO of two public companies, and confesses to being a serial entrepreneur. He lived the first half of his life in England, and moved to the United States in 1987, bringing with him a passion for education that he shares with his father, the subject of this biography. For the last 20 years, Randal has made Michigan his home, and worked in Detroit, a city that he loves.

U.S.NAVY
JOLLY VAL
NEW YORK

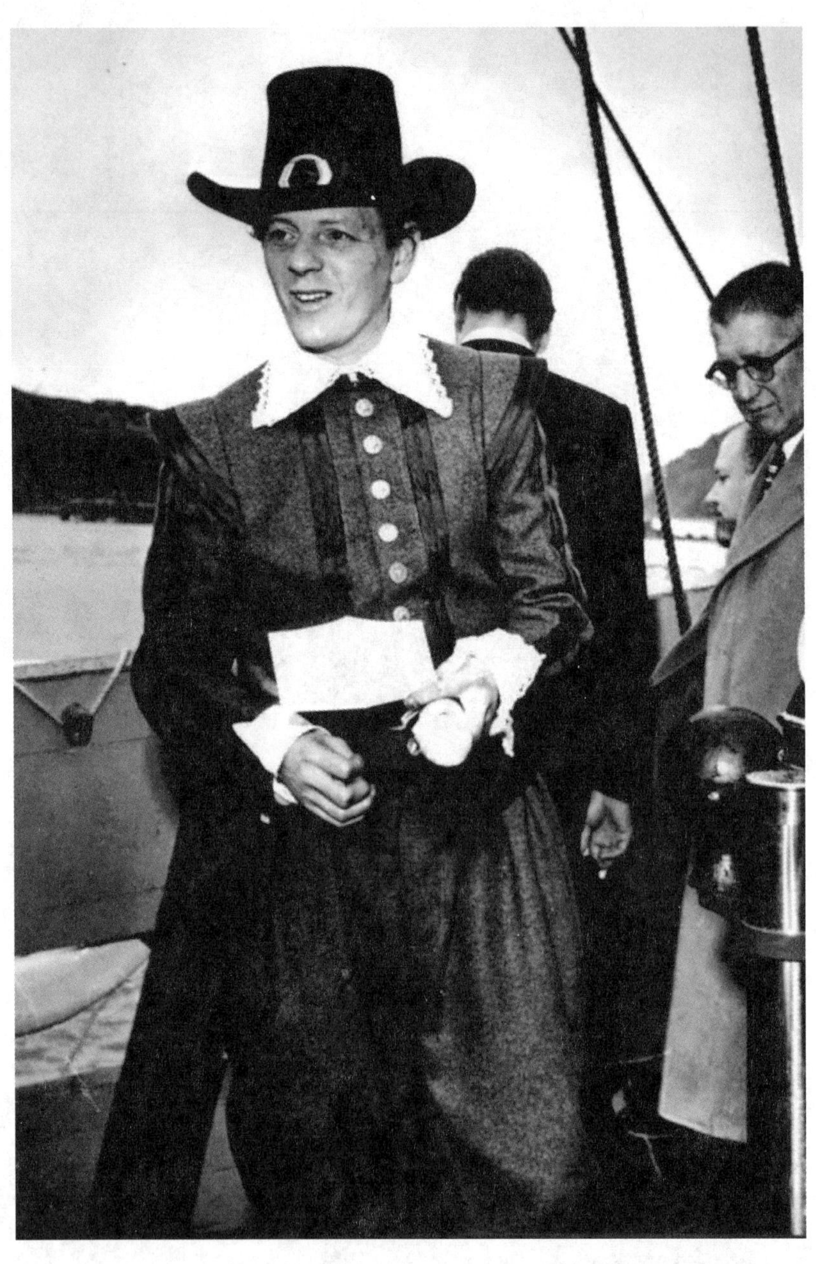

Warwick Charlton, the man who gave America a piece of its history.

"No person has ever been honored for what he received. Honor has been the reward for what he gave."

Calvin Coolidge
Citizen of the Commonwealth of Massachusetts and President of the United States of America.

THE GIFT

On September 12th, 1957, at the law offices of Lothrop Withington in Boston, Massachusetts, an Englishman, Warwick Charlton, put his signature to a document completing the transfer to American ownership of the only asset he possessed. That asset was a unique and extremely valuable replica of the *Mayflower,* the original ship that carried the first settlers to North America in 1620.

Mayflower II was meticulously accurate in every detail down to the inkwells in the captain's cabin. It was an extraordinary gift to the wealthiest nation on earth from an individual, who, at the time was effectively broke. He had no regular source of income, no house, no car, and virtually no cash in the bank.

BILL OF SALE

To all to whom these presents may come, greeting:

Know ye, that The Mayflower Foundation, Incorporated, a corporation duly organized and existing under the laws of the State of Connecticut, owner of the sailing ship called the "Mayflower II", of the burden of 260.12 tons, or thereabouts, in consideration of the sum of $1.00 to it in hand paid, the receipt whereof is hereby acknowledged, have bargained and sold, and by these presents do bargain and sell, unto Plimoth Plantation, Inc., a corporation duly organized and existing under the laws of the Commonwealth of Massachusetts, the said sailing ship, together with the mast, bowsprit, sails, boats, anchors, cables and other appurtenances thereto appertaining and belonging.

To have and to hold the said sailing ship and the appurtenances thereunto belonging unto the said Plimoth Plantation, Inc., its successors and assigns, to its and their sole and only proper use, benefit and behoof forever.

And further The Mayflower Foundation, Incorporated, does hereby promise, covenant and agree for itself, its successors and assigns, that it is the sole owner of said sailing ship, that this Bill of Sale is intended to transfer unconditionally the entire interest in said ship and the appurtenances thereunto belonging, and that it will warrant and defend the title to said sailing ship, and the appurtenances aforesaid, against all and every person and persons whomsoever.

IN WITNESS WHEREOF, the said The Mayflower Foundation, Incorporated, has caused these presents to be executed and its corporate seal to be hereunto affixed by its officers thereunto duly authorized this 16th day of September, 1957.

The Mayflower Foundation Incorporated

Title: Incorporator and Director
W. CHARLTON

Title: Incorporator and Director
J. LOWE

Personally appeared before me the above-named officers of The Mayflower Foundation, Incorporated, and acknowledged the foregoing Bill of Sale to be the free act and deed of said corporation.

Notary Public.
NOTARY PUBLIC,
LONDON, ENGLAND.

The transfer of *Mayflower II* to *Plimoth Plantation* for the nominal sum of $1.

CLASS OF SERVICE
This is a fast message unless its deferred character is indicated by the proper symbol.

WESTERN UNION

TELEGRAM

W. P. MARSHALL, PRESIDENT

SYMBOLS
DL=Day Letter
NL=Night Letter
LT=International Letter Telegram

1201 1957 NOV 25 PM 6 50

The filing time shown in the date line on domestic telegrams is STANDARD TIME at point of origin. Time of receipt is STANDARD TIME at point of destination

131.

.BC465 1

3 CDU633 43 PD INTL FR=CD WYE VIA RCA 25 2138=
HORNBLOWER=
75 FEDERALST BSN=
TODAY I HAND OVER MAYFLOWER TWO TO YOUR SAFE KEEPING STOP MAY SHE BE A REMINDER TO THE PEOPLE OF OUR TWO COUNTRIES THAT ALTHOUGH THE ATLANTIC OCEAN MAY SEPARATE US IT CAN NEVER KEEP US APART=
WARWICK CHARLTON=(

THE COMPANY WILL APPRECIATE SUGGESTIONS FROM ITS PATRONS CONCERNING ITS SERVICE

Telegram from Warwick Charlton handing over *Mayflower II* to the care of Henry Hornblower II the President of the *Plimoth Plantation.*

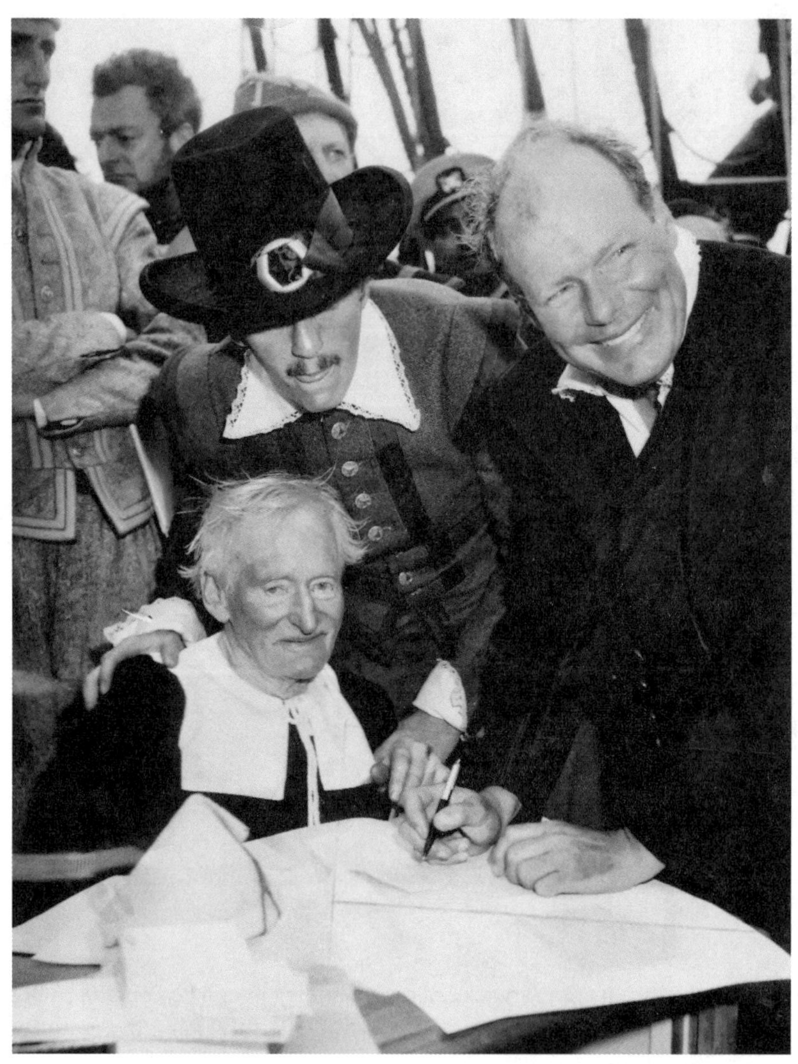

Warwick Charlton's first act on reaching America in 1957, was to stage an historical re-enactment of the signing of the Compact by all the men onboard the first *Mayflower* in 1620.

The compact is regarded as the first evidence on the North American continent of a new democratic approach to government. Warwick looks on intently behind Harry Kemp, the Provincetown poet whom he asked to oversee the ceremony while a smiling Captain Alan Villiers adds his signature.

1957: THE RECEPTION

There was something not quite right about that first day on the shores of America, but blinded by the sheer excitement of the occasion, Warwick Charlton did not see it. There was just a nagging worry at the back of his mind.

Even later, all he could really remember with absolute clarity, was the look on a young boy's face.

The boy was ten, maybe 12 years old and he was running through the crowd, wide eyed with wonder, his gaze locked on the beautiful little wooden sailing ship. He kept bumping into other spectators in the dense crowd but ran on without apology. Several times the boy had tripped and nearly fallen as he ran along the harbor front but he was unable to take his eyes off *Mayflower II* as she glided into the bay.

Warwick Charlton would never forget the absolute joy on that boy's face as he arrived at Plymouth Harbor on June 13, 1957. It was the end of a journey that had begun many years earlier with a dream of building a replica of the original *Mayflower* that had brought the first settlers to North America in 1620. Now the journey was reaching a climax after 53 days at sea under sail with a captain and crew.

An estimated fifteen thousand people, and enough media to report a major war, were there on June 13, 1957 to greet the *Mayflower II,* and tens of thousands would flock to Plymouth in the days of celebration and welcome that followed.

Warwick had come to give the ship to the American people. He was resplendent in the costume of a seventeenth century military man as he was rowed ashore close to Plymouth Rock with his captain and cabin boy. Warwick surveyed the sea of faces gazing back at him from the shore and thought how different this welcome was from the cold empty coast that awaited the first settlers when they had arrived 337 years earlier at the same spot.

Back then, when 102 adults and children had waded ashore at a place they named Plymouth Rock they had no idea if hostile Indians were hiding in the wooded coastline. One woman was described as so upset by the landscape that she fell overboard and drowned in the harbor. Half of those who made land would die in the first horrific winter.

Three hundred and thirty-seven years later the *Mayflower II* was to be welcomed by Vice President Richard M. Nixon representing U.S. President Eisenhower. The young senator from Massachusetts named Jack Kennedy would drop by to shake everyone's hand. The retiring governor of Massachusetts, Christian Herter, had already presented Warwick with a signed illustration of the *Mayflower II*, praising his vision and important contribution to Anglo-American relations. Eleanor Roosevelt would devote part of her weekly column to celebrating the achievement.

The National Geographic Magazine described the voyage of *Mayflower II* as one of the great adventures of modern times. When, several years earlier, Warwick Charlton conceived the idea of building a replica of the *Mayflower* he had no financial resources. Yet, over time, he raised the funds he needed to complete the ship, an amount that in today's currency would be in the millions of dollars. Then he sailed it to America where, for a time, the world took its eyes off its day-to-day troubles and gloried in a powerful and romantic early chapter of American history, a history that Warwick had brought dramatically to life.

Following the arrival of *Mayflower II* in Plymouth there would be two weeks of celebration attended by an estimated 250,000 people, including a parade led by vice president Nixon.

However, on that first day in Plymouth, there was a restrained formality in the handshakes of some of the officials that greeted Warwick, and then there was confusion concerning where Warwick would sleep that night. All the hotels were full but the committee that had planned the welcome for *Mayflower II* had been working on the accommodation details for the crew for months.

The residents of Plymouth had begged for the opportunity to host one or more of the 33 man crew when they arrived from Plymouth, England. Ronnie Forth, the man in charge of the welcoming committee, had been obliged to disappoint dozens of local home owners.

For some strange reason, no one had been assigned to open their home to Warwick. At the last minute, he was found a four-poster bed in a museum - historic Howland House, just off Main Street. Warwick was unconcerned, in fact he rather liked the idea. In the end, the only interest in Warwick's accommodation came from a lady friend who visited him in the middle of the night. After nearly two months at sea in the company of 32 men and Felix the cat, Warwick welcomed the new company.

Warwick Charlton had been both invigorated and rested by the journey and felt fitter than he had been for years. He was thirty-eight years old, over six feet tall, handsome and possessed a powerful soft baritone voice that had seduced both men and women over the years. He was ready for the next chapter in the *Mayflower* story. He had already made the

Mayflower II the main news of the moment, not just in America but around the world.

The interest that had boiled to the public surface followed years of obsessive promotion of the *Mayflower II*; first the idea of building the ship, then raising the funds, then finding a builder, and a captain and crew. Then a permanent American berth had to be found and plans for the long term developed.

Warwick had never imagined he would have to charm so many people from Lords of the British aristocracy to the leading members of the New York Mafia. And the key to it all had been a relentless media campaign.

Life magazine had been persuaded to put the little ship on its cover. So had the prestigious *Paris Match* in Europe and hundreds of magazines and papers throughout the world, including Argentina, South Africa, Portugal, Rhodesia, Malaysia and Malta had carried stories. Many of these countries had populations with relatively little interest in the United States let alone its history. Yet their media reported on the voyage of the *Mayflower II* as a major world event.

Warwick was determined that the *Mayflower II,* like the Statue of Liberty, would have a permanent role in the living history of America. He was convinced the ship would generate a great deal of money because he believed Americans would be excited at the prospect of walking the decks of the magnificent little symbol which had given birth to their nation.

With his trademark attention to historical detail, Warwick had been listed on the manifest of the *Mayflower II* as "supercargo", a term he had gleaned from his study of sailing ships in the 1600s. It was a term recognized and defined by the British Admiralty which meant he was legally the officer in charge of all commercial concerns of the voyage. This included, but was not limited to, managing the cargo owner's trade, selling the merchandise in ports to which the vessel was sailing, and buying and receiving goods to be carried on the return journey.

In this case, of course, there was to be no return voyage because the ship was to be given to the American people, but he expected to partner with Americans to use the *Mayflower II* exhibition revenues to develop an historical theme park as well as provide funds for other purposes. As far as Warwick was concerned he was, as *the supercargo officer,* to be involved in all such decisions related to income from the *Mayflower II.*

Arrangements had been made for the ship to be on permanent exhibition at Plymouth, Massachusetts. The tourist income was to be used to keep the *Mayflower II* ship-shape with the surplus funds administered by a trust set up to improve Anglo-American relations. Warwick and others whom he chose would represent the English on the board of trustees. There would be educational scholarships which to Warwick, were almost more important than the ship. The *Mayflower II* would put Americans in touch with their history and the ideas of the first settlers who were in search of a new form of government.

Importantly, annual scholarships from surplus revenue would help to establish a permanent modern dialogue between the UK and the US. Warwick also had plenty of other ideas designed to capture the imagination of people on both sides of the Atlantic and he had already lined up some distinguished Englishmen to serve on the management of the Scholarship fund. They included Sir Francis de Guingand, who had become a friend of President Eisenhower during the war while serving as General Montgomery's Chief of Staff.

Sir Francis wrote a letter to President Eisenhower on March 21, 1957 in which he said, *"Through the initiative of Mr. Warwick Charlton, who was a member of the old British Eighth Army in the desert, the [Mayflower] scheme has now reached fruition, and the Mayflower II sails from Plymouth in the second week of April for Plymouth, Mass.*

"It is hoped that there will be considerable surplus revenue available for an endowment to further Anglo-American relations, and I have agreed to become a trustee of this fund. I thought you might be interested in this development."

And yet when Warwick Charlton awoke in the museum on that first morning in America, few people seemed interested in talking to him about his grand ideas. The welcoming party was busy entertaining the crew, and the people who were to be entrusted with the care of the ship were according VIP treatment to the ship's captain. Meanwhile the media, who had fallen in love with Warwick's dream, were waiting with questions that were to give him sleepless nights.

One of Warwick's financial backers wanted him out of the way and the captain, whom Warwick had employed to sail the ship across the Atlantic, wanted nothing more to do with him. Even the crew could not find a good word to say about Warwick as they were fêted in Boston, New York and Miami.

Finally, and more significantly, the people to whom Warwick would entrust the ship were determined to keep him as far away as possible from any involvement in *Mayflower II*'s future.

What caused those who celebrated the gift of *Mayflower II* to do everything they could to distance themselves from Warwick and his partner, John Lowe?

Warwick Charlton died on December 10, 2002. His life before and after *Mayflower II* was packed with adventure in times of both war and peace.

WARWICK CHARLTON

Born
9 March 1918
Chelsea, London

-

Died
10 December 2002 Ringwood, Hampshire

He became involved with some of the great and notorious men of his time and demonstrated high principles as well as a love of mischievous politics, wild projects and scandal.

He endured bankruptcy, disappointment and eventually made money, before being elected to an unpaid position as the Town Crier of a small community in England.

This last job satisfied both his love of history and dressing up. Town Criers, he would point out, were the first bearers of news. However even in his 80s he could not let go of his obsession with *Mayflower II*. As it turns out *Mayflower II* and America cannot let go of him.

HISTORY LESSON

Warwick Charlton's love of history began with a powerful blow to the head at an early age. It came after he had made one of his foolish attempts to attract the attention of one of his peers. As a young boy, he found it particularly difficult to get attention from the people that mattered to him. His parents were both attractive, entertaining and brilliant, but they were

Randal Charlton

Warwick's father, who was described as the last of the Fleet Street Dandies.

He left Warwick a legacy of a taste for catholic living and the friendship of journalists in positions of influence.

far more interested in themselves than their children, Maudie and Warwick.

Warwick's father, Randal Charlton, came from a catholic, military family in the north of England. Randal was nearly 6ft.

5in. tall and chose to dress impeccably, not in the uniform of the army, but in the elegant civilian attire of an Edwardian gentleman. He cut a dashing figure among the more modern conservative dress code of the 1900s as he paraded in long frock coats, brocade waistcoats and top hat, that belonged to a romantic bygone era. Randal became a journalist and author and in 1906 helped to start one new London paper, the ill-fated daily Tribune.

He had a long successful spell on the London Daily Mirror and from 1914 - 1918, throughout the first World War, he contributed to their popular entertainment page. He also worked on the Daily Sketch, Sunday Pictorial and Daily Graphic. One colleague described him as " *...a curious character, vastly tall and impressive, a fine journalist when he chose to be and a man of odd enthusiasms."*

One of those enthusiasms was support for *"The Cry of the Children Campaign"* an attempt to improve the lot of children by enacting laws to keep them from entering public houses before a certain age. He was, apparently, a powerful speaker and his efforts led to the passing of the Children's Act by the Liberal government.

Randal Charlton was *"an astonishing bohemian"* records another former colleague, Bernard Falk. *"(He was) tall, mysterious, unplaceable, promising once to be a first class novelist, next looking like one of the great journalist successes of Fleet Street, finally tailing off into an odd job reporter."*

He was also a drama critic and from time to time he exhibited a love of the dramatic in his own behaviour. At one staff meeting hosted by an embattled newspaper owner who was threatening to close the paper where Randal worked, he is reported to have thrown his lanky frame to the floor to emphasize a point. The incident appears in a book written by Phillip Gibbs. The two men had become friends when they worked on the Tribune, the liberal newspaper that collapsed after two years of publication.

Following the demise of the Tribune, Phillip Gibbs made Randal the center of a fictional book called *Street of Adventure.* It was a very thinly veiled story of the rise and fall of the Tribune. Randal, under the pseudonym of Christopher Codrington, was portrayed as one of the central characters. Phillip Gibbs assumed this would please his friend but Gibbs recounts in his memoirs that Randal was apparently aghast at his fictional portrayal.

Perhaps it was too close to Randal's real-life, exotic behaviour. In any event he retained legal counsel and the two former friends spent money they could ill afford in preparing for a court case. At the last minute before the court hearing, Randal decided to drop the case and the two men buried the hatchet.

Randal produced at least three works of fiction himself - a romantic novel called *Mave* (1906), *The Virgin Widow* (1908) and *The Bewildered Bride* (1908).

Randal's taste for social life was as catholic as his religion and his friends included writers, politicians, prize-fighters, actors, barmaids, actresses, criminals and royalty, including King George V.

Randal died when Warwick was 13 years old and was celebrated in his obituaries as *"The Last of the Fleet Street Dandies."* The New York Times carried a brief obituary noting that he was one of the most well-known figures in the English newspaper industry and had a wide circle of American friends.

Warwick hardly knew him and remembered little more than his last meeting when his father was a 6ft. 5in. 70 lb. skeleton, dying of esophageal cancer at the age of 49. However, many of Randal's Fleet Street friends would be helpful years later to his son in advancing both his journalistic career and his *Mayflower* project.

Randal separated from Warwick's mother "Birdie" after only three years of marriage. She came from a large Russian Jewish immigrant family and, like Randal, had not impressed her family with her choice of a partner. Only one family member, her brother Eric, attended her wedding but there were plenty of journalists on hand to report the event and note that the bride had been appearing with great success in the revue *"Half-Past Eight"* at the Comedy Theater.

Birdie Courtney

Warwick's mother. A classical scholar with a modern approach. She counted many men and women of influence as her friends.

Birdie was the daughter of Elimelech and Rachel Coplans – Jewish immigrants from Lithuania in 1874. Like many other newcomers from Eastern Europe they lived first in Whitechapel, a poor district of East London, before making their home in Kent.

Birdie was born Fagilia Coplans in 1891 in Canterbury, the religious capital of the English protestant church. Fagilia means little bird in Yiddish but she was registered as Fanny Coplans, then became known as Birdie or B and later changed her name again to Barbara.

Birdie's six brothers all studied medicine and if Birdie had been a boy she might have done so too. She was a first class student with a fondness for Latin and Greek and somehow managed to sit the entrance examination to Simon Langton School, known to be one of the best in England. She won a scholarship. However, girls were not expected to pursue an academic career in those days and she was encouraged not to accept.

Perhaps as a way of rebelling, Birdie decided on a stage career, a vocation which was not held in high regard by some, including her parents.

Under the stage name of Birdie Courtney, she rose from the chorus line of George Edwardes "Merry Widow Company" to become a noted actress, sufficiently well regarded to appear in two full page photographic poses in the Tatler and Bystander, the magazine of record for London's high society.

Following her separation and divorce from Randal, Birdie put a premium on retaining her youthful looks and eligibility and packed Warwick and his elder sister Maudie off to private boarding school. Warwick was three years old and his sister Maudie four when they arrived at their first school, a convent run by Catholic nuns. Warwick's first experience of religion was not good. One one occasion, in an effort to control their boisterous new charge who had picked a fight with another boy, the sisters held his hands to the top of a burning stove to show him that hell was hot and literally close at hand.

Warwick learned that opportunities to impress the mother he adored, were not often presented as she concentrated her efforts on her acting career and her affections on at least two extremely rich and powerful men. Admiral Beatty, one of Britain's top naval leaders, became Birdie's lover as did Sir George Ealy, who was chairman of the Midland Bank, one of Britain's largest financial institutions.

At one point the family had two homes: one in London's fashionable Knightsbridge district and later another spacious house in the equally fashionable south coast resort of Hove. Birdie also spent time in Paris where Warwick was occasionally allowed to visit during school holidays. There, in a beautiful apartment on the elegant Champs Elysées, Warwick was enthralled by his mother's exotic circle of friends. They included the Duke de Gees - pretender to the French throne, Lucien Deville - a star of the French theater and Prince Yusupov who had gained notoriety as the assassin of Rasputin - the evil advisor to the Russian czars.

Warwick found that in such company he had to be very interesting or amusing or both to persuade anyone, including his mother, to listen to him. Eventually Birdie married the Honorable Hughes-Onslow, a nephew of the Earl of Onslow, who in addition to his blue blood, was a talented first class cricketer.

As soon as Warwick was old enough, he transferred from the care of the nunnery to Bickerly Hall preparatory school, a boarding school for boys aged between eight and thirteen. An early school report stated Warwick's attitude crisply; *"he resents correction."* Although Warwick's initial experience with religion had not been encouraging he did not forsake spiritual influence immediately. At one point he sought out the chaplain, to ask if God could be persuaded to intervene on a matter of some urgency. Warwick was being punished with beatings on an all too regular basis for his resentment of authority. Was there any way God could postpone the heavy punishment scheduled for the following Sunday evening? The chaplain regretted that the Lord would not stop the beating but he promised to ask him to alleviate the intensity of the pain. *"Did your beating hurt?"* the Chaplain inquired later. Although Warwick had felt the pain as sharply as usual he thought it polite to say *"No."* Secretly he began to wonder if the Chaplain, the Church and God had as much influence over events as they claimed.

The boarding schools of the day operated on three terms a year and the pupils would long for the breaks of three or four weeks to go home to their families. Only those sick and languishing in the sanitarium would remain a moment longer than necessary, but more than once, Warwick was left a lone boarder in the otherwise empty school grounds.

Warwick noticed that boys who became good at sports tended to receive more visits from parents, who would turn up to bask in the reflected glory of their children's achievement at inter-school rugby, cricket and athletic matches. So he took up sports in an attempt to impress his mother and treated each contest as though he were General Sherman marching to Savannah, laying waste to everything in his way.

As often happens, one teacher made a crucial impact on Warwick's life. Mr. Spencer Paine found his resentful, 12 year-old pupil, particularly difficult to control and his frustration bubbled over into violent retaliation in one explosive exchange on a hot summer evening, when he was desperately trying to knock some English history into the heads of his class.

"1066 is an important date in the history of Britain," Mr. Paine reminded his class. *"Now what is the next important date?"* Insolently, Warwick rushed to answer *"1067."* The frustrated Mr. Paine struck Warwick a heavy blow to the head, then recovered his composure and apologized. Later Mr. Paine gave Warwick a massive tome entitled, *"The Decline and Fall of the West."* The young boy was amazed and intensely flattered that his teacher thought that he could actually digest the contents of such a learned treatise.

Warwick quickly forgot the blow and forced himself to plough his way through the book. As he did so, he developed a taste for history that was to become a fierce hunger he could never satisfy. He became fascinated by the great men of history including Napoleon, the emperor of France, and the puritan Oliver Cromwell who deposed the King of England.

His family gave him plenty of time to pursue his new found love of literature. After several years at Bickerly Hall Preparatory school he became a student at Epsom public school in Surrey. Epsom was one of England's top boarding schools, a place where the upper middle classes sent their boys. There they received an education that would permit entry to medical school - which could lead to a comfortable middle class life as a doctor. Warwick's love of reading and his talent for writing had already equipped him to excel in English and History but he showed no interest in science or medicine, which were the special forte of Epsom. His reputation for being a pretty tough competitor grew. At one point he was cautioned for using unnecessary roughness when playing rugby - a tough sport where aggression is normally a behaviour to be congratulated.

He excelled at boxing, where, for a while, he was matched against boys of his own age. Unfortunately, Warwick experienced a spurt of growth at one point which resulted in his being matched against much older, bigger boys. There followed a series of heavy beatings as he was given uninvited lessons on the need for both courage and determination.

Warwick grew up without any understanding of the importance of money or interest in it. Although he may have suffered a very lonely childhood, he was hardly financially deprived. Both before and after the separation of his parents his mother lived in the style of the English upper middle classes. Her brothers, all successful doctors, were around if things got tight. When Warwick was home there was a live-in maid to keep the spacious house in good order.

He received no training in business or even simply managing money, at home or school. In pre-war class-ridden Britain, business was for tradesmen, shopkeepers, families that owned factories and people who were forced to earn a living buying and selling things. There was no concept of business as a detailed subject with its own set of disciplines. There were no college courses to gain a Masters in Business Administration.

Long after Warwick had started to earn a living, like millions of others in pre-war Britain, he had no bank account. He was paid in cash by his employers and had no ideas of owning anything like a car or a house. The concepts of corporations and corporate responsibility were totally foreign to him. Money and the rules connected with its use had no place in his world of ideas and literature. Years later, when some of his backers and the media began to question his handling of the finances of *Mayflower II*, Warwick would find it hard to comprehend what they were talking about.

A BAD START

Warwick Charlton's career in journalism got off to a bad start. After one week in his first big job he was fired and thrown into a state of desperation.

He had always expected to follow in his distinguished father's footsteps and work on Fleet Street, the headquarters of the great national newspapers of Britain. At only nineteen years old, six years after his father's death, Warwick had made a start as a junior reporter on the London Daily Sketch.

He persuaded a friend of his dead father to write a letter of recommendation and at his interview he implied that he had some experience. Lying didn't worry him. He was a fast learner and would soon get the hang of things. After a week on the paper the editors discovered that they had hired a complete novice and promptly dismissed him. Warwick was devastated. However his agitation at his dismissal had nothing to do with his love of journalism or shame at tripping at the first stride in the path of his colorful father's career. He had just met a beautiful dancer and was desperate to impress her.

At 5 ft. 1 in. she was short for a showgirl so she danced at the end of the chorus line but she had an incandescent smile and a classical beauty that Warwick and others believed belonged in the center of the stage. Warwick met 24 year old Lucy Haywood through his elder sister Maudie. Lucy was a classically trained ballerina while Maudie was an energetic but less accomplished performer in the same dance troupe. He immediately told Lucy that he was a national newspaperman and, in case she didn’t believe that a mere 19 year old could hold down such a prominent position, he encouraged her to call him at his office at the *Daily Sketch*.

Now, if Lucy called they would say he didn't work there any more. So Warwick, without the least embarrassment, went back to the Daily Sketch and begged for his job back. The editor was not impressed even when Warwick, close to tears, offered to work for nothing. He was asked to leave the premises.

Warwick refused. He just sat in the corner of the news room and recounted his problem to anyone who would listen.

Eventually, a *Sketch* photographer, Geoffrey Keating, became so amused by Warwick's outrageous reason for wanting his job back, that he spoke to the editor and offered to take young Charlton under his wing. He arranged for him to be paid on a freelance basis for any stories that he produced that were published.

So Warwick was allowed to resume his week long career as a journalist and got to answer the phone when Lucy called a few days later. He tried to marry her almost immediately but his mother prevented the union. The age of consent was 21 and he was still 19. A few days after his 21st birthday they were married in a London registry office.

Years later, Lucy, who was five years older than Warwick, said she never intended to marry him. He just kept insisting. He was tall, charming and handsome and she was very attracted to him but she was not ready to marry and settle down. Her career was blossoming and she had a large number of other admirers - stage door Johnnies they were called. They included a handsome young doctor called Donald Thornton. Thornton was possessed of such a beautiful body and face that he earned money posing nude as an artist's model and was described as "the world's most beautiful man". Whether that was hyperbole or not, he certainly adored Lucy which did nothing to deter

Warwick. A confident Warwick invited Donald to be his best man when they were married in London in 1939.

After the early hiccup at the *Daily Sketch* the words that flowed from Warwick's typewriter secured his position. Journalists worked shifts and he volunteered to take over anybody's shift if they were sick as well as the much hated week-end assignments. He couldn't believe he actually got paid to do what he loved and what he loved to do was to take any story and find a way to make it as big as possible. There was, in any case, a financial imperative to do so because he was paid by the number of lines that appeared in the paper.

On one occasion a gay Austrian actor arrived in town. The actor was due to play a masculine starring role and the theater managers were concerned that he would not attract the public. Warwick persuaded his sister Maudie to go to Marleybone Town Hall and take out a licence to marry the unsuspecting star.

His first story was headlined "Showgirl's love for star actor," followed a day later by the predictable denial , then a third episode with a picture of the star and showgirl above the announcement that they *"were just good friends."* Everyone was delighted including Warwick's editor, the actor and the managers of the theater. Sell-out crowds flocked to see the star who nearly married a local show girl.

Warwick had a natural ability to produce interesting stories from the flimsiest of mundane facts but sometimes he stepped over the mark, as he did when he returned from an investigation of a ghostly apparition with a story that included direct quotes from the ghost.

It was the summer of 1939, and a few months before the outbreak of the Second World War. The war would change millions of peoples' lives, including Warwick's. It would lead to the end of his first marriage, the blossoming of his career in, of all places, the desert, and would herald the beginning of many new friendships.

It would also lead Warwick face-to-face with a bunch of cocky, self-confident, well-equipped soldiers and this encounter would seriously affect his perception of the world. These Yankee fighting men and their leaders would give the journalist an idea, that, for good or ill, would remain an obsession for the rest of his life.

Warwick acquired the skills to build *Mayflower II* on the battlefields and in the brothels of Africa and Asia. He thrived in the organized chaos of war where he perfected his powers of persuasion and learned how to harness the power of the media. Still in his early twenties he discovered he could inspire courage in ordinary men and put fear in the hearts of generals and leaders of governments.

Sitting in a tent in the desert with flies buzzing around him, he tapped out stories, two-fingered on an old Remington typewriter and a few days or weeks later government departments, such as the War Office, and whole countries would change their policies. It was a Masters degree in manufacturing something from nothing; the perfect training in how to build a ship for which no plans existed; to construct it with tools that no one knew how to use; to pay for it without any money; and to find sailors to sail it when no-one in the modern world had previous experience with a ship of its kind.

After the nerve jangling news of the British declaration of war against Germany in September 1939, an eerie calm broke out in

England. There was no cataclysmic event like the Japanese bombing of Pearl Harbor to set off hostilities between Britain and Germany, just the dramatic tones of Winston Churchill on the radio followed by months of mundane, often boring preparations. Ration books were issued, farmers ploughed extra pastures to grow more food and men marched up and down with broomsticks instead of rifles. The period was called the "phony war".

Captain Warwick Charlton

Lessons learned and friends made in the heat of battle would be applied to the *Mayflower* project.

The lack of real action did not prevent Warwick from making the front pages of the *Daily Express*, where he had worked before going off to battle. On the last day of 1939 his wife Lucy gave birth to a son. A few days later Warwick was photographed in his dashing officer's uniform, complete with cap, holding the infant in his arms. Lucy, the mother, was off-camera as if Warwick alone were responsible for creating the child. Warwick's story which made the front page of the paper began: *"What shall I tell my war baby son? Will he know who Hitler was? Will he care? "* The article went on to question whether his son and the children of the next generation would grow up in a free society or if Hitler would prevail and impose dictatorial rule. An ordinary event, the birth of a child, had been turned into a story of universal relevance. Warwick's reputation as a first rate communicator was growing.

Earlier that year he had enlisted as a private in the Royal Fusiliers which was unusual because someone of his middle class, elite school background would normally go straight to officer training camp.

In a matter of months he was promoted three times to the rank of sergeant instructor where he used his deep powerful voice to dramatic effect on the parade ground. Off duty he began to learn for the first time about the lives of the other enlisted men, who were all from working class, cockney backgrounds. "*They had very little to look forward to,"* recalled Warwick. *" Most had no education, no job prospects other than manual work and some lived in homes with no baths or even inside toilets."*

Warwick earned the respect of a few hard cases with a willingness to fight anyone who questioned his orders and was badly cut on the knee in a bayonet fight with a difficult soldier. He declined to report sick which left him with a permanent scar on his leg but the increased respect of his men.

Soon the inevitable happened for this educated fish out of water. He was recommended for officer training. There he would join his old Epsom school friends and other boys from Britain's private school system, who, in this class-ridden country, made up the vast majority of the officer class of the army.

He was called in front of his commanding officer, a man called Rhodes, to be told of his transfer to officers training camp. *"You know Charlton this is a very important step. Most important,"* said Rhodes. Warwick could have simply saluted and left the room but his natural suspicion of authority surfaced. He allowed a smirk to spread across his face.

"What do you find so amusing?" asked the perplexed commander. *"I don't see the importance of becoming an officer, sir!"* As Warwick let out these words he could hear his sergeant escort behind him begin to breathe uneasily. *"The officers in this regiment are a disgrace sir,"* Warwick continued. *"They are drunk half the time, they play games with their men and they set a bad example."*

Warwick couldn't stop himself. The men in ranks were being ruled, rather than led, by a lazy officer class who had acquired their positions through their social background and family wealth. Warwick's commanding officer added a note to his file to the effect that he should not be permitted to pass his exams to become an officer.

Warwick passed anyway - and at the same time earned much needed pocket-money taking the test on behalf of an aristocratic, dim-witted colleague. He was compromising his belief that officers should earn the right to lead, but he desperately needed the money. He had a wife and young son to support.

DRINKING BUDDIES

Eventually Warwick was posted to Cairo, Egypt, the base of operations for the Allies' fight with Germany in North Africa. However, in Cairo, the sound of gunfire was still some way off. To kill time, he put together a small magazine of poems and writings which he published called *"ME."* It caught the attention of Randolph Churchill, the son of Britain's great war leader Winston Churchill. Randolph and Warwick became drinking buddies.

Randolph was responsible for setting up an intelligence unit for the British Army in North Africa and he asked Warwick to start a news service to keep the Eighth Army troops informed.

Randolph Churchill

The son of the British Prime Minister was a close friend of Warwick and supported him in the time of war and later in advancing the *Mayflower* project.

Warwick responded by starting a rash of newspapers and magazines, often with captured or stolen printing presses. The most famous of these was the *Eighth Army News*, which was published daily, and *The Crusader* which was a weekly.

The papers came out on time even though the offices moved often and at each new headquarters new printing presses had to be borrowed or stolen. No one was left in any doubt about Warwick's determination to fight censorship. The slogan that appeared on the top page of every issue was, "A FREE PRESS FOR FREE PEOPLE".

The newspapers contained articles that were often highly critical of wartime leaders including the British government and Warwick soon found himself established as an enemy of those in positions of authority while his papers became morale builders for the troops. When Field Marshall (then General) Bernard Montgomery assumed command of the Eighth Army, Warwick found a patron who understood what his young press secretary was trying to do.

General Bernard Montgomery

A brilliant war general who never lost a battle, but lost his fight with the Government to keep Warwick on his staff.

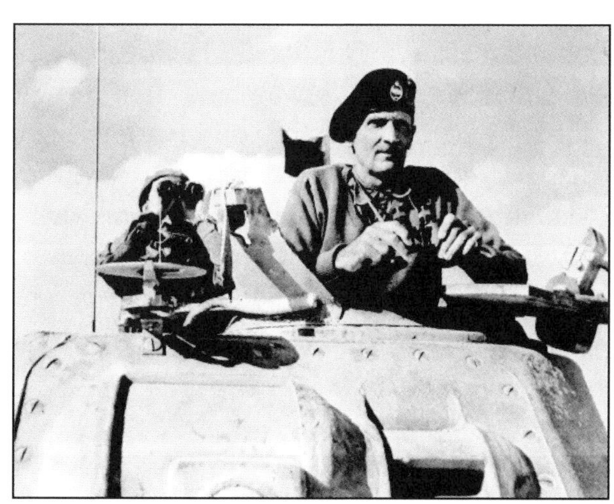

Montgomery took command at a time of crisis, when the Eighth Army had suffered a series of heavy defeats inflicted at the hands of the German Afrika Corps, led by the charismatic Marshall Rommel. Rommel became known as the Desert Fox as he won the admiration of his troops, praise and promotion to Field Marshall by Hitler and the grudging respect of the Allied forces that he was driving back across North Africa towards Cairo.

Desperate to turn things around, The British High Command had recalled their commander General Auchinleck, but his designated replacement, General Gott, was killed just 24 hours after his appointment, when the plane flying him to the battle headquarters, was shot down by enemy fire.

Montgomery was quickly drafted in as a replacement but Warwick and his colleagues were not impressed by the sight of their new commander. He had a slight build, a thin face, pointed nose and pale complexion and when he opened his mouth a high pitched voice completed the impression of an unlikely saviour.

However, below the facade, Montgomery brought to the battle both a mastery of battlefield tactics and a powerful personality, together with a self-awareness that recognized that he had to look the part to gain the confidence of his troops. Above all he had served in the first World War where millions of men were slaughtered, in large part by Generals who committed men to battle, with no thought for the likely casualties. Montgomery understood that the soldiers of the second World War were different; they demanded more from their leaders.

In many ways Montgomery was a revolutionary, a general who recognised the vital importance of keeping his men informed and letting them know the plan for victory.

Montgomery allowed Warwick, who was assigned to the General's personal staff, to give him a make-over. Warwick set out to design a new look for the new commander with the help of Monty's aide-de-camp John Poston, and Geoffrey Keating, the head of the Army Film and Photographic Unit - the same man who had saved Warwick's bacon when he had been fired from his first job at the Daily Sketch.

They tried various different hats and badges before they discovered that the General looked the part in the black beret of the Royal Tank Regiment decorated with two badges - the tank regiment's insignia and a general's insignia. They also asked the General to wear informal sweaters. Monty then allowed his three young sartorial advisors to photograph him in various poses, among troops and using binoculars, including occasions when they were under enemy fire.

"I couldn't believe it ," recalled Warwick. *"At one point shells were dropping left and right but Geoffrey Keating kept clicking his camera and asking Monty to move his pose this way and that and the General calmly ignored the shells and did as requested."*

They settled on one picture of Monty in a tank to be used as a stock photo and it soon appeared in publications all over the world, including *Time* magazine and *Life* magazine. Monty did more than just look the part. He was forever driving among his troop positions and stopping to introduce himself to his troops and communicate his total confidence in the men under his command.

"I'm Monty your new Commander, " He would typically begin to a stunned bunch of soldiers. *"I have studied your track record, there is nothing wrong with you; (defeat and retreat) will now end. Together I will lead you to victory."*

The Eighth Army now had a charismatic straight-talking leader and Monty's combination of military brilliance and his concern for his men rapidly earned their total loyalty. In two months the Eighth Army would re-engage with the German Troops led by the apparently invincible Desert Fox and win a battle which proved to be a turning point of the war in North Africa.

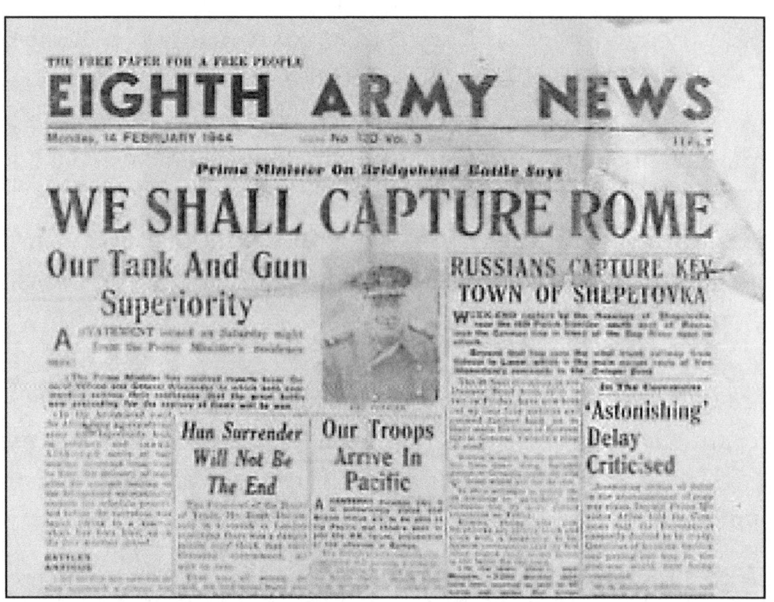

THE FREE PAPER FOR A FREE PEOPLE

EIGHTH ARMY NEWS

Monday, 14 FEBRUARY 1944

Prime Minister On Bridgehead Battle Says

WE SHALL CAPTURE ROME

Our Tank And Gun Superiority

RUSSIANS CAPTURE KEY TOWN OF SHEPETOVKA

Hun Surrender Will Not Be The End

Our Troops Arrive In Pacific

In The Commons

'Astonishing' Delay Criticised

Warwick's *Eighth Army News* was popular with soldiers in the battlefield but caused anxiety among wartime leaders back in London.

Warwick decided he would go to extreme lengths to support and protect his leader, which landed him in serious trouble with both politicians and the War Office back in England, and more than one attempt was made to remove him from Montgomery's staff. Montgomery intervened to save his skin on several occasions but eventually Warwick was brought before two courts-martial. The charges included a decision by Warwick to publish top secret exchanges from the War Office criticising Montgomery's conduct of the North African campaign.

Influential journalists in London caught on to a growing conflict between Montgomery and the war leaders in London. Tom Driberg, who was later to become the chairman of the

Labour party, wrote a story in *Reynolds News* reporting that Montgomery was using Charlton to develop more censor-free papers. Then another piece appeared in the *Daily Herald* written by Hannan Swaffer, a respected national journalist who had been a close friend of Warwick's father Randal.

Swaffer's story posed the question, *"Should the British Forces on the Western Front have a weekly journal free from political censorship? General Montgomery thinks 'Yes'. Sir James Grigg and Lord Croft think 'No'. Who will win?"* Swaffer stated that although London daily papers were flown to the front to supply his men with news, Monty wanted a "Weekly" concerned with spreading community spirit among his men and he wanted Charlton to run it.

However, the British Minister of War objected to Charlton's appointment. Monty sent his chief welfare officer, Colonel Medlicott, home to press his case for Warwick to publish in Europe as well as Africa but the Whitehall war chiefs would not be persuaded. The senior civil servant at the War office, Sir James Grigg, wrote a sneering memo to Monty pointing out that Charlton's friends seemed to consist of Jews, homosexuals and communists. *"If I am to judge Charlton by his friends then I am quite right to veto your employing him."* Warwick's irreverent behaviour, his enthusiasm for drink and women as well as his circle of friends sorely tested Montgomery's loyalty.

Monty had a distinctly un-military opinion of Warwick which he was forced to make public when one of the Whitehall military chiefs, Brian Robertson, paid a visit to the Eighth Army. Robertson was disgusted to find Warwick publishing the *Tripoli Times* from a brothel. Warwick explained that brothels were the best place from which to operate a wartime paper because the news came to you.

The puritanical Robertson was unimpressed and after meeting with Monty, as he was leaving the general's tent, as a throwaway remark he said, *"By the way Sir, I hope I have your approval. I've decided to get rid of Charlton."*
And Monty said *"What?"*
"I've decided to get rid of Charlton, the Editor of the Tripoli Times," Robertson repeated.
"Why do you want to do that?" asked the general.
"Well Sir, he is a bad man." ....There was a silence.
Monty said, *"I don't think he's a bad man. I think he's a funny man."*
Monty was particularly amused when Warwick expressed left wing views that bordered on the revolutionary. On more than one occasion, he wrote threateningly that if social changes were not made after the war, then perhaps the soldiers of the Eighth Army should unite under Montgomery to rekindle the democratic spirit.

One of Warwick's distinguished wartime colleagues Hugh Cudlipp (later Lord Cudlipp, who became the head of the Mirror Group) described him as a maverick, erratic and mischievous, but a man of sustained inventiveness and maniacal energy.

Hugh Cudlipp , left, and **Bill Connor**, two giants of the postwar media Industry, would help Warwick kick start his *Mayflower* project

He also credited Warwick with one of the best headlines ever. Over the front page story of the Eighth Army News, describing the fall of the Italian dictator Benito Mussolini, Warwick's two word headline read:

" BENITO FINITO!"

Sir Francis de Guingand, Monty's Chief of Staff, found Charlton to be *"an odd type."* He wrote in his memoirs, *" On occasion he has to be handled pretty firmly but he certainly delivers the goods. The arrival of the Eighth Army News and Crusader under all sorts of conditions is entirely due to his energy, enthusiasm and resource. He is editor, publisher, leader writer, gossip column contributor and everything else all rolled into one."* Randolph Churchill, the Prime Minister's son, continued a close friendship with Warwick and he connived to arrange for Warwick to meet his father, Winston Churchill.

Sir Francis de Guingand.

Protected the young Warwick during the war and promoted his *Mayflower II* goals to President Eisenhower.

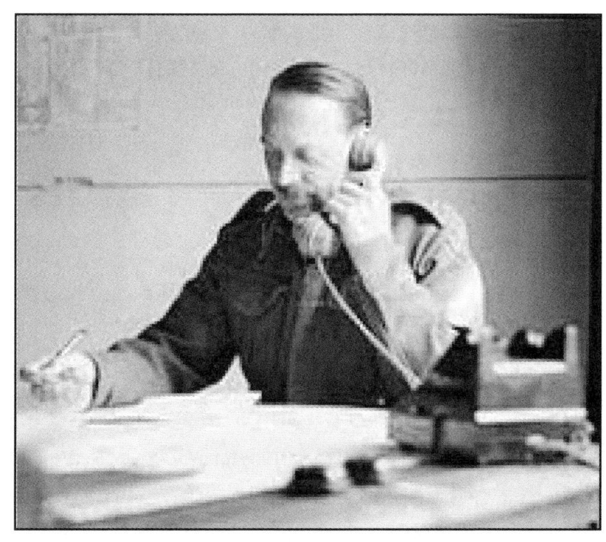

When the Prime Minister flew out to Africa to celebrate the victorious advance of the Eighth Army to Tripoli, Warwick handed a copy of the *Tripoli Times* to Mr Churchill. The ink was still wet on a newspaper containing a complete report of the Prime Minister's visit, although of course it was still in progress.

In Algiers, Churchill asked General Alexander how he kept in touch with events elsewhere in the battlefield. Alexander replied jokingly to a stern faced Churchill, that he got most of his intelligence from the *Eighth Army News.*

TRIPOLI TIMES

NORTH AFRICA'S FIRST ENGLISH DAILY — PRICE TWO LIRE

ITALY OUT

UNCONDITIONAL SURRENDER

BADOGLIO SAYS "WE CAN NO LONGER STRUGGLE AGAINST THE ALLIES"

The BBC announced yesterday evening:
- The Italian Government has surrendered unconditionally.
- The official announcement was made at 5.30 pm by General Eisenhower, the Commander-in-Chief of the Allied Forces.

RUSSIA

TANKS AND GUNS WILL FLOW TO THE FRONT

ALLIES CLOSE GRIP ON LAE

***Tripoli Times*:** Another of the many papers created by Warwick. This one he claimed as the first English language paper in North Africa.

To other observers Warwick displayed a single-mindedness that often bordered on suicidal madness. He made it a rule that his *Eighth Army News* and other papers would be delivered first to those soldiers closest to the sound of gunfire. André Glarner, a distinguished French war correspondent, was one who observed Warwick's hazardous rules about newspaper delivery. Glarmer recalled in a book "*Montmartre to Tripoli*" that in the middle of one particularly fierce tank battle a fifteen hundredweight truck appeared in the thick of the action, laden with copies of "*Eighth Army News*."

While the forces continued to exchange heavy fire, Warwick and his driver were delivering papers which informed the troops " *that the battle was going well.*"

Remarkably, censorship was imposed by Montgomery on only one occasion. The American General Patton was under investigation for slapping a soldier. Warwick wanted to run the story but Monty insisted that there be no reference to the incident in his army papers.

Winston Churchill

Warwick met Britain's wartime leader in North Africa.

Over a decade later Churchill would make a significant contribution to Warwick's *Mayflower* cargo.

TOILET ARRANGEMENTS

Warwick had no doubts about the US contribution to the war efforts, however. He was convinced the whole operation in North Africa, including the British victory, owed itself to American equipment. *"The British tanks were not effective. The British were undergunned,"* he said in a post war interview.

"The Americans quickly learned how to fight. They seemed like rank amateurs when Eisenhower first came to Africa and, at the time, the British were the seasoned troops. The Americans had to be bloodied - literally. Once they were, they quickly became very effective."

Warwick noticed the different toilet arrangements of the British and Americans as a bizarre but telling symbol of the difference between the two armies. The British soldiers were permitted only five pints of water a day for all purposes including drinking.

"The British only bathed when at sea while American troops brought mobile showers." To Warwick and his Tommy mates it was incredible. Most of the British soldiers didn't even have showers at home.

Warwick observed that all armies were a reflection of their supplies and the American troops were no exception. He also admired their *"total generosity."* In a remark that reflected the lack of respect for women in war time, Warwick praised his American friends. *"They even gave me a girl."*, he reported in the news one evening. *"A French girl."* The Americans brought a bacchanalian zest for war that Warwick loved.

He would never forget watching one exhibition they put on at the Sphinx in Cairo. *"Then there was the food they brought, the whisky and the cigarettes. In war, cigarettes were very important to people and to morale."*

Warwick made two great American friends, Slim Arons and Scottie Burgess who both worked for *Yank* magazine. He fell in love with Scottie because he was absolutely open. *"Everything on their paper was well done but they were not as free from censorship as we were. They were exuberant and self-confident and always curious to learn."*

"Only a couple of years before the Americans arrived, we were training with a frightening lack of equipment; using broom sticks because we had insufficient rifles. The British had been on their own for a year against the Germans. We were supplied covertly by Roosevelt but the Germans were sending British ships to the bottom of the sea. Only the physical protection of US Liberty ships kept the German Navy at bay and the British Fleet alive," Warwick said after the war.

The war continued to go very badly for Britain and the Allies with the fall of Tobruk in 1942 to Rommel's North Afrika Corps. Before Montgomery took command, the British Eighth Army had been forced to withdraw across the inhospitable north African desert to El Alamein.

At Montgomery's headquarters some experts told Warwick *" ...that the British army might all have to retreat to the Nile Delta."*

Wendell Wilkie was sent out by Roosevelt after Tobruk, and Warwick went around with him on an inspection to check the battle readiness of the British troops.

"Suddenly jeeps arrived," Warwick recalled. *"Which was a miracle; then American-made Grant and Sherman tanks."*

The Americans provided the Allies with Sherman tanks, which made a crucial difference to the Eighth Army in their battle with Rommel. They were made by the Ford Motor Company and were easy to fix in the harsh desert conditions. *"No one could be in any doubt about American generosity",* said Warwick.

ATTACK! ATTACK!

"It was quite a decision to divert equipment from your own troops to your allies", said Warwick. *" If you were in the Eighth Army at that time, you could not be in any doubt about American generosity. If you look at a map of the war when the Americans came to North Africa, you will see that the Germans were right into the Caucasus. Turkey might have joined the Germans and the whole area could have crumbled. Palestine might have gone."*

Warwick recognized that initially there was a lot of sentiment in the United States against an involvement in the second great European war.

"The British worried about US commitment but it was entirely natural," he explained. *"Apart from the fact that there were many pro German organizations funded by Hitler in the US, the fact was (that) many Americans had emigrated from Europe to escape from the terrible tribal wars that continually ravaged the old continent - the wars and economic poverty.*

"Then they join in the 'war to end all wars' (1914-1918) and millions were slaughtered. There was the lunatic Admiral Foch shouting, 'Attack, Attack, Attack' and a whole generation of young men, including a lot of Americans, bled to death. Then, fuck me , twenty years later it starts up all over again". It was not the most attractive prospect. However, no sooner had the war begun than the American Eagle squadron arrived - a group of very distinguished fliers who formed their own squadron.

Roosevelt provided support, often covertly, in many other ways. American "Liberty ships" provided vital food and other supplies and the British navy sailed very close to American territorial waters even when the US was officially neutral.

When, in the early stages of the war, Warwick sailed out in the convoy to reinforce the North African campaign, his ship went so close to the US shoreline that one of his comrades told him there was *"no need to worry. If the Germans torpedoed the ship, the survivors could swim to America."*

"The British desperately needed their strong, reliable ally", said Warwick. *"The only allies the British had at the time were the remnants of the defeated French, the Poles and the Czechs"*, whom Warwick regarded as *"a troublesome fucking bunch."*

American volunteers joined the British Royal Air Force, before America's entry into the war in December 1941. They formed three fighter squadrons and drew the lifelong admiration and gratitude of many among the Allies, including Warwick.

TRITE PHRASES

In the US, in 1944, Americans were beginning to understand the contribution Warwick had made to the war effort. Under the headline "Monty's Fighting Editor" the May 1st issue of *Time* magazine reported, *"Probably the only editor in uniform who has attacked his own Government again and again and got away with it is Warwick M.J. Charlton, editor of the British Eighth Army News ..."*

Eighth Army News the testy, griping pal-print of the "desert rats" who followed Monty from Egypt to Italy, was born in September 1941, during the siege of Tobruk. When General Montgomery arrived in Egypt to take over the Eighth he quickly recognized the battle weariness of his men, found it important that the troops know what was going on in the world and the need to have a place to air their problems.

To tall, slim, 26 year old Captain Charlton, one-time London Daily Sketch man, Monty gave free rein and backed him up when the war office was howling for suppression of the paper, and even Winston Churchill was making known his disapproval.

Until the capture of Tripoli, Charlton got out his News on captured Italian mobile presses (once he used Italian prisoners' confiscated maps for paper). He dressed up his sheet with German propaganda pictures. Monty himself, at times, delivered bundles of (Eighth Army) News in his command car.

Editor Charlton prodded soldiers to write him letters about the slow mail service, editorialized on it, and it finally stirred the House of Commons to action. There was a campaign on the low pay of British combat troops - and Parliament moved again. Charlton (and the soldiers' letters) beefed about the India tobacco V-cigarettes which even the Italians rejected. Thenceforth only British or American smokes were sent overseas.

Charlton turned his typewriter against British entertainers who visited the troops for only three weeks at a time. His special target was Britain's middle aged comic music hall darling, Gracie Fields. Whitehall's brass hats rushed to defend her, demanded that the News be suppressed, declared that Winston Churchill felt it unfair that Gracie should have been singled out. Monty was told that certain other articles had not met with Churchill's approval.

As the Eighth advanced, Charlton established other papers for rear areas (also printed in Italian for the natives): The Crusader, Tripoli Times, Syracuse News. In these and the Eighth's News he jumped from the military to the political field. He roasted the US for not imprisoning more fascists in Italy, criticized the unchecked Italian profiteering, the kid-glove treatment of King Victor Emmanuel. Last October (1943) Charlton's News attacked Mihailovich's conduct in Yugoslavia. Again Parliament seethed, but later came around to switching sympathies and supplies to communist Marshal Tito.

That cost Charlton most of his press freedom - by policy censorship imposed from England. Through all this Monty defended Charlton, and gave only one censorship order: that there be no criticism of US Lieutenant General George S. Patton, Jr. in the soldier slapping incident. . . . . . *Time* concluded by recording another example of Warwick's inability to tell less than the whole truth no matter what the cost. He could have offered the *Time* reporter a few generous quotes about Monty, the boss whom he admired enormously. Instead, when the leader of the British Army perused his press cuttings for the first week in May 1944 he read the following criticism of his literary skills....

"Even the News' protector has not escaped its editor's barbs," said *Time*. *"Captain Charlton wrote Monty's first Order of the Day,*

thereafter the General wrote his own but Charlton edited some of them. Said the Captain (Charlton) of the General (Montgomery), 'He kept using the same old trite phrases.' "

Others recognized the contribution *Eighth Army News* was making to post war planning as well as current problems like army mail delays, cigarette quality and army thefts. Writing in *Parade* in March 1944 R.J.Gilmore noted that the paper which was started in a tent in the desert received 600 letters a week from soldiers on the subject.

"It is iconoclastic, irreverent of things the army regards as sacred. Tradition leaves it cold. Although it was started as a kind of desert Daily Mirror, Eighth Army News has always carried serious well-informed articles, some of its best contributors being anonymous officers on Montgomery's staff."

In the end not even Montgomery and his trite phrases could preserve his loyal young captain's insubordinate skin. In one published attack on Britain's revered war leader, Warwick had described Winston Churchill as *"a good servant but a bad master."*

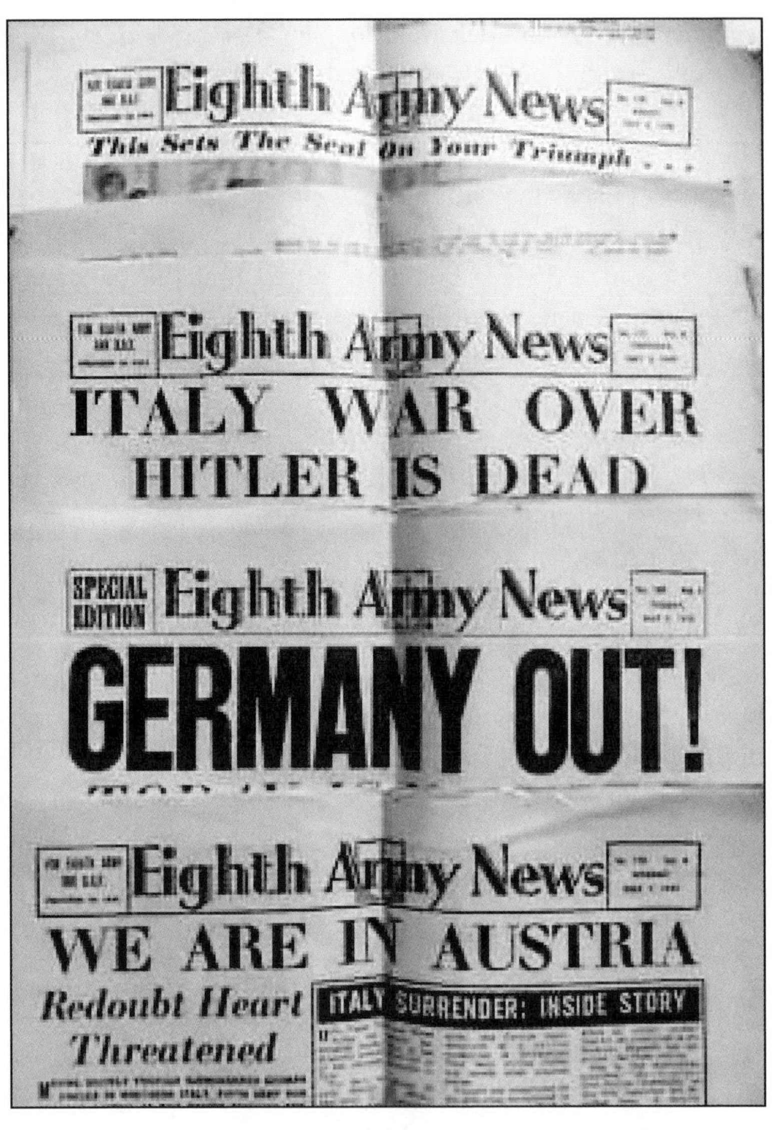

Eighth Army News

This Sets The Seal On Your Triumph . . .

Eighth Army News

ITALY WAR OVER

HITLER IS DEAD

SPECIAL EDITION

Eighth Army News

GERMANY OUT!

Eighth Army News

WE ARE IN AUSTRIA

Redoubt Heart Threatened

ITALY SURRENDER: INSIDE STORY

The ***Eighth Army News*** continued long after Warwick was dispatched to serve out the war in Asia. The paper remained a voice for the soldiers in the battlefield but Warwick's page one banner "THE FREE PRESS FOR A FREE PEOPLE" was dropped.

CHESS GAME

Warwick had become a pawn in a political chess game between Monty and Churchill. Churchill became very concerned about Monty's growing popularity with both his troops and at home and realized he was assembling the means to make a serious political impact after the war. He had a loyal talented staff and his own news media that was building the morale of the troops by enhancing the image of their General. Monty had demonstrated his understanding of political symbolism by agreeing to swap the traditional peaked General's cap for a regular soldier's beret.

Keating's photographs and Warwick's words had given their thin faced, physically unimpressive leader a new aura: the troops came to recognize General Montgomery as a winner, without sacrificing one unnecessary life and without imposing any unnecessary censorship. On the contrary his benign neglect of his wartime ability to censor anything Warwick or his colleagues wrote signaled to the troops that here was a new democrat who really was connected to the common man.

Warwick wrote in *Eighth Army News* that his troops became like those of the revolutionary Oliver Cromwell. *"They knew what they liked, and liked what they knew."* At one point several senior officers at Monty's headquarters began to speculate on ways they could help Monty attain political power in a post war Britain.

The War Office in London responded by proposing that a number of Monty's officers be moved to different postings and Warwick took direct action. He published confidential secret memos of the plan to re-post Monty's top aides, to the acute embarrassment of the War Office. This earned Warwick a court-martial which, in war time, could lead to a death sentence. He was acquitted but his time as Monty's mouthpiece was running out.

Warwick did not help his cause by paying scant attention to army procedures. He was authorized to return to Cairo at one point to produce a dummy (a single mock up) for a new magazine he had dreamt up to be called *"The Crusader."* He flew back to the 8th Army headquarters with not one but 20,000 copies of the new magazine.

As the campaign moved through Malta to Sicily and on to mainland Italy, Warwick produced yet another dummy for a new paper to support the troops that were to invade northern Europe at Normandy. The paper Warwick had designed for the European campaign was eventually produced by less contentious journalists and more than sixty years later it is still running as the vigorous mouthpiece of the British Army. The weekly paper is called *Soldier.*

In Italy Warwick took his democratic beliefs to an extreme that few people could contemplate in peacetime, let alone war. He started Italian language papers for the captured Italian soldiers and set them up with offices, presses and their own staff. *"Write and publish what you want,"* he told them. After a week he had the first issue translated into English and discovered that the paper contained innocuous stuff which had nothing but kind words for the new occupying forces.

Warwick was furious and had the Italian journalists hauled in front of him for a severe dressing down. *"You are wasting paper, print and presses,"* he lectured them. *"What are we doing wrong? As an invading army we cannot be without fault and it is your duty to find it and spell it out. How else can we fix things?"* Understandably, perhaps, the writers and editors had become accustomed to the fascist ways of Italian dictator Benito Mussolini and found it hard to cope with the fresh breeze of democracy blowing in from the African coast.

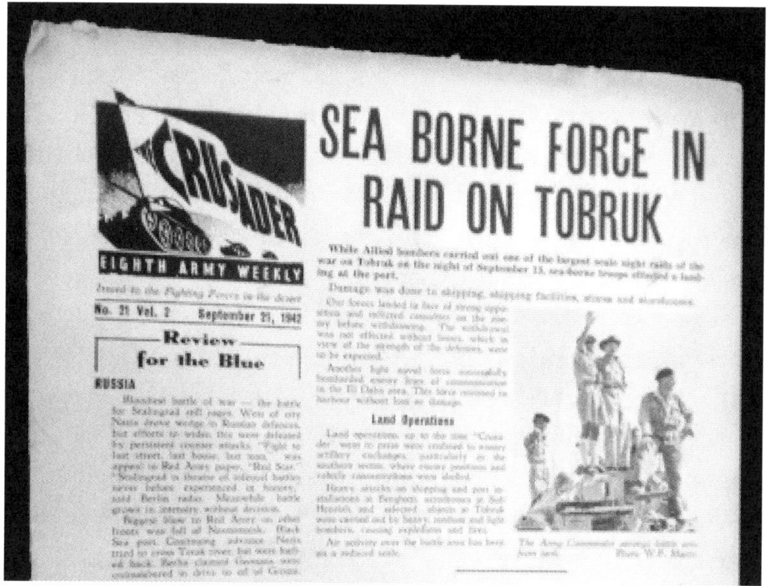

THE CRUSADER

EIGHTH ARMY WEEKLY

Issued to the Fighting Forces in the desert

No. 21 Vol. 2 September 21, 1942

Review for the Blue

RUSSIA

SEA BORNE FORCE IN RAID ON TOBRUK

While Allied bombers carried out one of the largest scale night raids of the war on Tobruk on the night of September 13, sea-borne troops attempted a landing at the port.

Damage was done to shipping, shipping facilities, stores and warehouses.

Land Operations

The Crusader: one of a rash of papers Warwick produced for the desert troops. He was severely reprimanded when he returned to the front line with 20,000 copies of the first edition. He had been given permission to produce just one sample.

After the invasion of Italy, Sir Freddie de Guingand, Monty's chief of staff, requested Warwick's transfer with the General as he prepared to move to the new European war front. The request was denied by Whitehall.

Charlton was relieved of his editorships and transferred to South East Asia where he served the rest of the war on the staff of General Louis Mountbatten, the commander of Britain's forces in Asia.

HOLLYWOOD WAR

If Warwick were to be transferred he could not imagine being banished to a more pleasant environment. The handsome young Mounbatten - a cousin of the Royal Family - was commanding the British forces in South East Asia like an Emperor. Warwick got a taste of a royal privileged life. Indian servants were everywhere and one stood behind each table at dinner to keep wine and beer glasses filled, remove one course and promptly replace it with the next. *"It was the Hollywood version of war,"* recalled Warwick.

Warwick met and worked with a brilliant young journalist, Frank Owen, who would later play a role in the *Mayflower II* story. They edited army newspapers together in Calcutta and Singapore including a picture news-weekly called *Phoenix*. Warwick had plenty of opportunity to pursue his hedonistic tastes as well as moral causes in Asia.

Aware that the troops were making frequent use of local brothels he brought the subject out into the open and wrote a review of them, much as a modern day film or theater critic would inform his readers on the quality of entertainment available. His reports also reviewed the health standards of each establishment.

For those soldiers with jaded sexual appetites he discussed the sexual bible of India, *The Karma Sutra,* in columns normally reserved for news of the battle and the football scores in England. However, his excursion into print with the formerly taboo subject of sex had a serious point.

There was a new wonder cure called penicillin available to soldiers and many believed it would cure everything including syphilis. At any one time up to 250,000 men were receiving antibiotics or reporting sick which was having a serious adverse effect on military efficiency and cost.

Race relations also became an issue when a local five star hotel was less than welcoming to a visiting band of black musicians. The hotel was strongly condemned in one of Warwick's leader columns.

"The colored Ghurkas of Nepal have won more Victoria Cross awards than any other regiment in the British Army. India supplies a quarter of the British Army troops. What is your problem?" Warwick thundered. The musicians were promptly moved to the hotel's luxury suites.

Warwick had a simple view of race relations. People who fought side by side should live side by side.

BRADFORD'S RECORD

Warwick was so bored he would have read lavatory paper. It was 1947 and he was on board an American ship returning to England after the end of the war. The American ship was different from the British ships on which he had sailed previously. The officers' quarters were austere; there were no books and even worse, there was no booze.

At the first opportunity he went down to the crew's quarters because he thought they might have some illicit alcohol. He found what he was looking for - a limited supply of Scotch plus an odd collection of books including *Readers Digest* and some Edgar Wallace thrillers. He had very little interest in fiction and picked up Bradford's *Journal of Plimoth Plantation.* He had never heard of him. It didn't say a lot about the voyage of the first settlers across the Atlantic. There was no reference to the ship by name, just a note that it would carry "180 tons of burden".

Warwick found much of the journal heavy reading but he was struck by the terrible trials they endured including, *"That dreadful business of arrival at the wrong place"* and the first winter in which half of the settlers died. What really impressed him however was the compact the original settlers made to establish the way the new settlement would be governed.

"What was so interesting was that America began with an idea that the people would govern themselves with power flowing upwards to their elected elders." Warwick recognized this democratic idea to be totally foreign to the world of the 1600s when all rule flowed from the top down. Now, more than 300 years later in 1947, he felt that everyone was on a journey towards a new level of democracy. The British men and women who fought in the war

had not voted for five years. In fact, most had never voted and, at the end of the war, they astonished the world. They voted to dismiss Churchill in favor of a new England, a new Jerusalem. Around the world old dictatorships were toppled, old monarchies thrown out and the United Nations was formed. Warwick felt that, *"we were still on the journey that the Pilgrims began over 300 years earlier."*

"The Pilgrims were not Puritans. They were people seeking a new form of government." In the 1600s the idea that people should be governed by officials that they elected was not accepted anywhere in the world. Every Kingdom was theocratic and the influence of the church was absolute.

Warwick was also appalled to read Bradford describe the way in which the first settlers were ill-equipped to deal with their new environment. *"They weren't fishermen, they weren't farmers, they were simple middle and working class people. They couldn't hunt and even the fish hooks they used were too big to catch fish. Half of them died in that horrific first winter."*

Warwick was intrigued to find that Bradford's record revealed that not all the first settlers could resist temptations of the flesh. Masters became too fond of their servants. The colony solved the problem by banishing adulterers to Virginia, an area of the new colonies still firmly under the thumb of the English King.

The combination of high ideals and personal faults of these Pilgrims fascinated the Englishman. He felt total sympathy with these people. He was, he believed, a lot like them, and the issues that worried them in the 1600s disturbed him in the twentieth century. There was still a hereditary monarchy and titles in England which he thought was a nonsense, especially since a civil war had been fought to get rid of them centuries ago, soon after the Pilgrims left England.

He found it bizarre that here he was, sailing home from the Second World War in the twentieth century, in which millions had died, to a Britain where there was still a monarchy with a King and Queen, still Lords, Ladies, Knights and Dames and a church and state that remained intertwined.

Warwick broadcasting during war time. He would soon be broadcasting for the BBC in peacetime.

PEACETIME BATTLEGROUND

Although the post-war period induced a sense of a let-down in much of the population, Warwick did his best to continue as if the battle still raged. He joined the BBC as a scriptwriter where he became friends with the poets Dylan Thomas and Louis MacNeice, among others. They were a hard-drinking, undisciplined assortment but their undoubted talents were gently nurtured by Laurence Gillingham, the Director of Features at the BBC. Gillingham was trying to broaden the appeal of radio beyond the cut-glass crystal accents of Oxford and Cambridge educated elitists.

Gillingham valued Warwick because he would ask questions that nobody else asked. He would dig deep. *"He would look under an Aspidistra just in case there was something hidden,"* said Gillingham. Warwick produced an idea for a weekly radio series called "Meet the People". The half hour program would visit a new type of peacetime battleground, where the former servicemen were now fighting to re-build the country. He went to shipyards, steel mills, factories and offices and interviewed ordinary people. In post war Britain where the privileged classes tried to continue life as before, this was a most unusual departure from normal radio programming.

The poets and writers with whom Warwick drank between assignments, were always short of funds to feed their thirsts. Their immediate boss was Audrey Jones, a middle aged lady with a "blue stocking" academic background. Warwick was delegated the task of asking for an all around raise. As the most presentable member of the group, the writers decided that Warwick could best advance their case by becoming her lover. He accepted the assignment with enthusiasm .

Warwick was constantly looking for new challenges and, in 1949, he collaborated with John Audley and Peter Haddon to write two plays,*"Stately Homes"* and *"Tomorrow is a Lovely Day."* The second play, about a man who could see into the future, played to packed houses as it toured the provinces and it arrived in London to positive reviews. Warwick obtained additional publicity by informing the media that one of the actors had to retire after breaking his arm while rehearsing a fight scene in the play. However, the extra press coverage was lost in a thick London fog. Coal was still the fuel of choice in post-war London and the smoke from several million fires created a toxic mixture in the air, known as smog. It brought the capital city to a standstill and the play's run was ended after a mere three weeks.

At around this time Warwick was involved in a real fight. His mother, Birdie, was at least partly responsible for landing Warwick in court on a serious charge of causing "grievous bodily harm". A guilty verdict would bring a sentence of several years imprisonment.

The trouble arose on a visit to his mother in Hove for the Easter Holidays. An old army buddy, Archie Calhoun, and a friend, were invited along for the long weekend. Archie was one of Montgomery's aides, an educated man who was a professor of Italian studies. The Charlton house was overflowing with guests so accommodation was booked for Archie and his friend at a local hotel. Their arrival at the hotel caused a stir in the lobby. Suddenly no rooms were available in the half empty place. An argument ensued and the embarrassed manager finally volunteered the information that it was not possible to accommodate Mrs. Charlton's guest since one of the party, Archie Calhoun's friend, was black.

Warwick retreated to the street to confer with his mother. She berated both Warwick and her husband, Nigel, who was a former officer in the Scot's Guards. With her instinct for the way to inflame both men, she accused her husband of behaving dishonorably to his regiment and her offspring of being *"no son of mine"*.

The two men quickly re-entered the hotel lobby and began a fight with four waiters who were standing ready to eject them. Some of the waiters were badly hurt and Warwick was dragged before Brighton magistrates on a charge of causing grievous bodily harm.

The Brighton *Evening Argus* reported with some surprise that the charges were dismissed. Warwick had persuaded Peter Haddon, his playwriting collaborator, who was well connected locally, to have a word with the chief magistrate. Warwick's war service and the evidence that he and his step father had been outnumbered were seen as sufficient reason to overlook the fact that a man's skull had almost been fractured.

Warwick was proud of his mother's reactions at the time of the incident but terrified that she would turn up in court. She was quite capable, he knew, of telling the court that the hotel management deserved 40 lashes on top of the punishment that the staff had already received at the hands of her husband and son.

Not long after Warwick's brush with the law, he turned from accused to accuser when he solved a murder that had shocked and intrigued people in both England and France.

An English aristocrat and his wife and daughter were murdered in France on a camping holiday. The murder appeared motiveless and it baffled the French police for weeks.

Warwick was sent to cover the story by *Picture Post,* the best-selling weekly magazine at the time, and he tracked down the murderer, an old reclusive farmer. The police were hesitant to act but Warwick, an avid reader of French history knew enough about French law to know that it was possible for an individual to take out a warrant for an arrest. He did so and the accused was turned over to the police.

Soon after, the farmer confessed and was convicted of the crime.

SWEET TOOTH

In the late 1940s Warwick was hired to do political battle with his left-wing friends in the Labour Government. The issue was nationalization and the subject was sugar.

It was during a period when the post-war Labour Government was systematically taking control of key industries including railroads, coal and steel.

The sugar industry was on Labour's shopping list when Warwick was contacted by Ian Lyle - another old Eighth Army buddy. Ian Lyle was part of the family that owned Tate and Lyle, Britain's biggest sugar manufacturer. Warwick worked with an artist to dream up Mr. Cube, a cartoon character whose face and body was a sugar cube that sported arms and legs.

Mr. Cube appeared on every packet of sugar sold by Tate and Lyle. In those days most households had a packet of sugar constantly on the table to sweeten the milky tea that was the beverage of choice in post war Britain. With the sweet charm of a cartoon character, Mr. Cube gave one reason after another why sugar should stay out of the suffocating embrace of government control. Warwick even persuaded Fred Gullet, the editor of the Communist *Daily Worker,* to join the campaign. The paper ran a series of pin-up pictures in a competition *"To find the sweetest girl."*

The campaign worked and when he was accused of betraying his left-wing principles for a consulting fee he argued that he had never been in favor of dogmatic nationalization of all industries. *"I didn't regard sugar as a commanding height of the economy. No-one was oppressed,"* he said, before adding rather sheepishly *" Maybe I had a sweet tooth."*

For most of Britain, though, the sweet taste of victory had been replaced by a sense of let-down. There was Marshall Aid - the American backed plan to re-build Europe, including Britain. However, Britain had to accept a decline in its power and influence because in the post war world, it could no longer impose direct rule on the countries that made up the British Empire.

Warwick, like many others, found it a very austere time. The great sense of adventure was gone. In the army he had learned how little the average man had - poor housing, outside lavatories, a shortage of jobs. The British entered the war with three and half million unemployed and Warwick, like many others, thought that conditions would improve dramatically as the newly elected Labour government embarked on a period of great social changes. However, even radical new government policies were slow in filtering through to the man in the street and shortages persisted.

"There was an increasing sense of loss," Warwick recalled. *"The British had lost an empire and had not found a cause. All over the world great peace had been achieved and what were the British doing? Building houses. Where was the nourishment for their spirit?"*

CONNOR'S ROCKET

The news in 1953 that a New Zealander, Edmund Hillary, had conquered Everest, the highest mountain in the world, started Warwick thinking about developing his own grand adventure. Then he read a report of some Scandinavians who reconstructed an ancient Viking boat. This lit a spark for Warwick who suddenly remembered Bradford's Journal.

He pondered ways in which the British spirit and enthusiasm for adventure could be re-kindled by re-enacting the first pilgrim journey.

From time to time Warwick dusted off the idea of the rebuilding of the *Mayflower* and tried it on whomever he was with at the time. The more he read about the first Pilgrim settlers, the more he liked them, not for perfecting the voyage to the New World, but for their imperfections. Thank God, thought Warwick, that even men who changed the course of history with the power of their ideas were still subject to normal human frailties.

He discovered that in 1642, there was an outbreak of unnatural vice of all kinds at the *Plantation*. The residents became deeply concerned about the number of illicit unions and adulteries taking place as well as examples of pederasty and bestiality. One lurid case was that of Thomas Granger, aged about seventeen, who was indicted on the charge of bestiality involving a mare, a cow, two goats, five sheep, two calves and a turkey. What wonderful catholic taste for a Pilgrim, thought Warwick. The *Mayflower* idea was coming alive for him. He had to find a way to bring it alive for others.

As the idea of building the new *Mayflower* grew in Warwick's mind it never occurred to him that he would give up everything and take charge of the job himself. He had a good position as a freelance reporter on the *Daily Express.* He thought it would make a good newspaper promotion. Someone else would build it and he would write about it. Apart from anything else he was living from payday to payday and he knew nothing about boats, ships or sailing.

The United States was now the number one power in the world and Warwick kept thinking about the way this new country began its rise to world super power. It all began with English men and women. An Englishman, Tom Paine, wrote "*Common Sense*". Jefferson and the writers of the American constitution were all Englishmen. It was a revolution against the English crown. They just wanted no taxation without representation: Warwick became desperate to persuade someone to help him dramatize the early stirrings of democracy. He turned to the great newspaper barons of the day. They were people with imagination, money and he knew many of them very well.

Warwick first discussed his idea with Lord Beaverbrook, the owner of the *Daily Express. "I thought it would benefit the paper - we could involve the readers. Beaverbrook thought it was a marvelous idea as we discussed it over lunch. Then he discussed it with his accountants. They thought he had had too much to drink at lunch."*

Warwick went to another powerful newspaper owner, Sir Edward Hulton the owner of *Picture Post.* To him Warwick sold the idea of a big picture story. Sir Edward's initial reaction was also enthusiastic. He could see the potential to increase circulation of his picture news magazines some of which were beginning to lose circulation in the face of increasing competition from television. Hulton's wife put a stop to the "crazy" idea.

Warwick found that at lunch-time he could talk the "press barons" into the idea but then they found all sorts of reasons for not going ahead. He tried the British American Pilgrims Society and the English Speaking Union. They thought he was at best eccentric and possibly mad, and would have nothing to do with either Charlton or his idea.

Warwick also spoke to an old wartime colleague, Hugh Cudlipp who had become the editor of the *Daily Mirror*. At the time the *Mirror* was not only Britain's biggest selling daily newspaper but had the largest circulation of any newspaper in the world - over 5 million copies a day. Cudlipp was intrigued but, like the other powerful men Warwick had approached, he found a new way to say *"no."*

However, the Mirror's most famous columnist, Bill Connor, ran a couple of paragraphs in the paper in which he mentioned Warwick's *Mayflower* concept. It was a great plan, declared Connor.

Now Warwick felt he really had to do it. *"Bill Connor's piece put a rocket up my arse"* he told a friend. He developed a reflex of talking about the *Mayflower "to anybody who had two pennies to rub together."*

Bill Connor (Cassandra of the Daily Mirror) (Left), Britain's most influential columnist. Praise for Warwick's idea of a gift to the American people fuelled interest in building *Mayflower II.*

MUSICAL START

One of the people to whom he spoke was a young socialist called Dominic Elwes, the son of a famous painter. He seemed an unlikely prospect but Elwes introduced Warwick to a property tycoon, Felix Fenston, who had lost his leg during the war falling off a bike. He was invalided out of the war early on and had a simple idea - that the war would someday end. He then made a fortune buying unwanted bomb sites and waiting for the post war building boom. Having made his money, Fenston re-invented himself as an aristocrat, and he became fond of sailing.

Felix Fenston

Warwick's first backer who, for his generosity, was rewarded with a company title that would cause problems in America.

Fenston asked Warwick how much money he needed. Warwick was caught off guard by his directness but said he thought it would cost about £100,000 to do the job.

That was not the figure Fenston was looking for. *"If this project is going to be a success it has to have the support of a lot of people,"* he lectured. *" Your difficulty is making a start. So when I say 'how much' I mean how much to get it under way?"* Warwick pulled out another round figure for the startup costs.

"£3,000 ", Warwick declared confidently, pulling the estimate out of thin air.

The next time Warwick called at Fenston's house a few days later he was treated to the sight of a wealthy man enjoying the power of patronage. Fenston was seated at the piano playing Bach's two part inventions. He spoke while he played: *"You know Warwick, I see a lot of people, all of them with different propositions. In the time it takes them to walk from the door to that desk I think I can tell if they are genuine or not."* Felix stopped playing and rested his hands on the top of the piano. *"You will find a cheque for five hundred pounds on that table. Its not much but it's a start."*

A week later Warwick was introduced to the American Ambassador, Winthrop Aldrich, at a meeting in the House of Commons, Britain's Parliament. *"We are going to build the Mayflower,"* Warwick told the Ambassador confidently with Fenston's small cheque still in his pocket. The money was to be raised by a public appeal. The Ambassador was impressed, interested and offered to help in any way he could.

Winthrop Williams Aldrich
(1884-1974)

The American Ambassador to Britain, Winthrop Aldrich, takes a break from the confusing politics of the English *Mayflower* Project and the high drama of the Egyptian Suez Crisis to entertain one of his fellow Americans, Marilyn Monroe.

Soon after the meeting Warwick received a call to go to the American Embassy as a matter of urgency. There was a con-man in London, the Ambassador's deputy explained. He had just received a visit from a distraught American lady who had been relieved of $1,000 by a man who claimed to be building a ship called *Mayflower II*.

Warwick assured the anxious Embassy official neither he nor anyone associated with him was involved, but he could see the potential of this news to damage his embryo of an idea if it reached the press. He would be forced to abort his plans. Warwick could do nothing but wait and hope that no news about the incident would surface.

ACCURATE INKWELLS

Warwick and his partner **John Lowe** turned to an expert at Greenwich Maritime Museum for help in their quest to turn a model of *Mayflower* into a full scale sailing ship, capable of crossing the Atlantic Ocean.

Dr. R.C. Anderson was vaguely amused when Warwick turned up at the British Maritime museum at Greenwich in South London and declared that he intended to build a replica of the *Mayflower* and sail it to America. Anderson was president of the Society for Nautical Research and had a reputation throughout the marine academic world as an expert in ships of the *Mayflower* period. They had become his lifetime study, but he never expected that anyone would want to bring his academic world to life in such a dramatic way.

He explained that no one could be certain of the design of either the *Mayflower* or the other ships of the 1600s that followed her to North America carrying settlers. Until the eighteenth century there were no ships' architects and ship builders had not been required to register their plans. Designs were handed down by word of mouth. To add to the confusion the name *"Mayflower"* was commonly used for ships of that period - there were 19 *"Mayflowers"* in the shipping registers of the time and it was not possible to deduce which *"Mayflower"* had actually made the trip.

Dr. Anderson's research confirmed that ship designs of that period were fairly standard. It was therefore possible, given the fact that *Mayflower's* weight and size were mentioned in *Bradford's Journal* to deduce a pretty accurate picture of her design.

Dr. Anderson had done exactly that when he made a meticulously detailed scale model of *Mayflower* in 1922. He presented it to Plymouth, Massachusetts' Pilgrim Hall Museum. Warwick's enthusiasm was fired when Anderson showed him a film about the *Mayflower* voyage starring Spencer Tracy. The film makers had produced an impressive model for use in the film which was based on information supplied by Anderson.

"What's good enough for Hollywood ought to be good enough for you," Dr. Anderson joked. *"Not quite,"* said Warwick. *"I want Mayflower II, including the inkwells in the Captain's cabin, to be accurate down to the last detail."*

GARGOYLE FANTASIES

The educated mixture of aristocrats, artists and writers at the Gargoyle Club were amused at Warwick's plans to re-build *Mayflower*. Although they thought it was a splendid flight of fancy, none of the wealthy patrons leapt forward to contribute to the fund.

They did buy Warwick drinks though and asked him to explain how he was going to build a seventeenth century sailing ship. They were too civilized a group to mention that he did not appear to have any money and were too captivated by Warwick's enthusiasm to point out it would be helpful if he knew something about ship building, sailing and the sea.

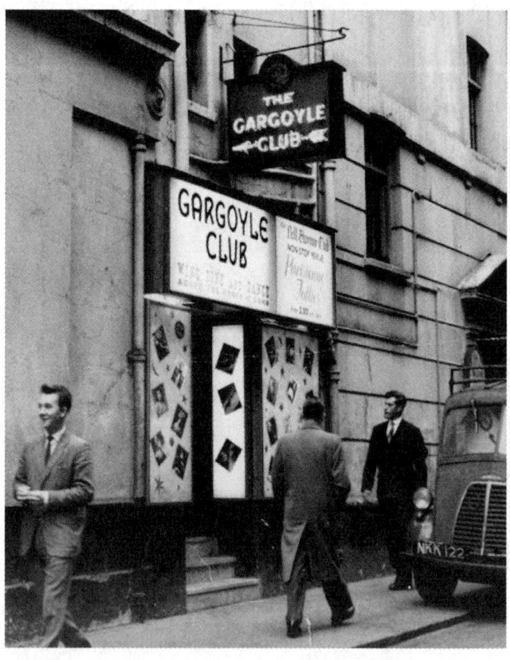

The Gargoyle Club

One of Warwick Charlton's first clients for his new Public Relations company.

A place where he would mix and mingle with the famous and infamous as his career progressed.

The elegant drinking club in London's fashionable West End was founded by the great portrait artist Augustus John and the writers Somerset Maugham and Noel Coward. In the 1950's it was owned by an English aristocrat, the Honorable David Pax Tennant. Warwick, like many members, was impressed by Tennant's beautiful wife Virginia, who later became the Duchess of Bath. She loved to read aloud to selected members from books including "*Paradise Lost*". Warwick remembered that he and other inebriated members were encouraged during late night and early morning readings to flirt with her while she read and her husband pretended not to notice. Warwick could think of few more interesting and amusing places to fantasize with his friends about his dream of building a 17th century sailing ship.

Warwick also drank there for a practical reason. The Gargoyle Club was one of his first clients in a new public relations business he set up in partnership with a friend called John Lowe.

John Lowe

The Establishment expressed concerns about Warwick's partner, John Lowe.

Were their concerns real or an attempt to disrupt the *Mayflower* project?

The fledgling business was operated out of cramped, bare offices in Coleman Street, in the old Wool Exchange building in the City of London. Anything less like a modern public relations office was difficult to imagine. There was no reception area with comfortable chairs, no smart magazines for clients to read, there was no artistic wall paper or designer furniture, no obscure eye-catching art on the wall. There was just enough space to accommodate four or five desks and a couple of filing cabinets. It had all the artistic appeal of a police interview room.

But it was what Warwick wanted. It was an address in the City of London close to the business world that was foreign to him but still a short taxi cab ride from the newspaper world of Fleet Street, where he still earned the bulk of his income from freelance writings. The rent was also a modest £7 a week which was all the two partners could afford.

They had only four clients. Apart from the Gargoyle Club, where there was an overwhelming temptation to drink the fees as they were earned, the early income for the new business came from a strange bunch of clients - the Rubber Investment Company, Capricorn Africa and The International Commission of Jurists. The Rubber Company needed to promote their products and their shares, Capricorn Africa was a lobby group set up to protect British business interests in the African colonies and the International Commission of Jurists were seeking worldwide acceptance of their existence.

Warwick had high hopes for the new partnership with John Lowe. The two men were very different and Warwick saw this as an important advantage. The 34 year old Cambridge educated Lowe was soft spoken and had the demeanor of a gentle off duty guardsman; correct, reliable, a member of the establishment who knew his place. Warwick noted that he did not disturb any room he entered. He had many friends in the establishment including members of the ruling Conservative party.

Warwick's friends were mostly on the left of the Labour party and they included poets, painters, writers and anybody he met who was, at the least, unusual. Warwick, unlike John Lowe, would burst down doors, drunk or sober, spouting his latest ideas to anyone who would listen, including the janitor.

John Lowe would preface his words with quaint terms of endearment *"Dear boy, we should look into this....or Dear soul, you really ought to consider that..."* While John eased his ideas deferentially to the listener, Warwick sold each new concept as though it would change your entire life.

Warwick was ready for the challenge. As a reporter, he found the Fleet Street game tiresome after his wartime experience and believed he could help Britain's emerging businesses improve their images, their marketing and their sales. But most of Warwick's friends were men of ideas, often penniless, living until they sold the next story or the next painting. His only wealthy friends were press tycoons like Beaverbrook but they were a breed apart; self - promoters who needed no help from Warwick.

John Lowe on the other hand, had the ear of Conservative Party leaders where he was a part-time researcher. The captains of Industry would be impressed by John Lowe's political connections. John would attract the clients: Warwick would serve them a platter of glittering promotional ideas.

It seemed to Warwick a perfect partnership in which both men could make a comfortable living. This new *Mayflower* idea would be fitted in somehow, just like another client.

NERVOUS GIGGLES

Dr. Anderson of the Greenwich Maritime Museum was one of the few people to take Warwick's *Mayflower* plan seriously from the beginning. Perhaps it was Warwick's detailed knowledge of early American history or his new address in the heart of London's financial district. Whatever the reason, he gave Warwick the benefit of a lifetime spent studying marine history. He seemed faintly amused that this man of the world was so anxious to bring his unworldly academic endeavors to life.

The minute Anderson opened his copy of the magazine *Neptune* and read of plans of a group of Americans in Plymouth, Massachusetts to build a replica of *Mayflower* he called Warwick's office. Anderson knew the people at Plymouth quite well. They had been writing to him for years. He gave Warwick a phone number and the name of Arthur Pyle, a school teacher. Apparently this Mr. Pyle was coordinating the efforts of the Americans, who also hoped to find a way to build the ship.

Warwick dialed the number and was mildly shocked when Arthur Pyle answered the phone. In those days trans-Atlantic cable carried few lines and it was normal, even for journalists, to write or send telegrams to the United States. Pyle confirmed that the *Neptune* report was accurate and invited Warwick to come over to Plymouth immediately to discuss his plans.

Warwick decided John Lowe should be the one to go to America. He had an instinct that his 6ft. 5in. tall, ultra British partner with the understated gentle manner and conservative, but elegant, taste in clothes would make a better first impression. He was academic and intellectual and wouldn't run off at the mouth and intimidate the Americans, who sounded, to Warwick, like a scholarly lot.

John Lowe was very reluctant. This was Warwick's idea not his. They debated back and forth and the two secretaries in their Coleman Street office joined in the discussion. Eventually Warwick was worried that he might not get his way so he threw himself to the floor and announced that he would lie there prostrate until John agreed to go.

The office staff broke into nervous giggles and John was too embarrassed and reasonable to do anything but agree to Warwick's demands. Warwick's action in using bizarre behaviour to get his way was strangely reminiscent of his father Randal's decision many years previously to throw his 6ft 5in elegant frame to the floor in order to persuade a newspaper owner to permit him to go on a hairbrained search for funds to keep the paper open.

INDIAN ARROWS

John Lowe's ticket cost £119 but the two men took advantage of a hire-purchase programme offered by British Overseas Airways Corporation designed to encourage transatlantic travel. Warwick took a taxi to Lock's, the famous hat makers, for the finishing sartorial touch for John Lowe's outfit for the trip; a British bowler.

Henry Hornblower II

Was he a timorous man, as Warwick believed, or a master of business tactics with the patience to persist and get everything he wanted?

Harry Hornblower could not quite believe his ears when Arthur Pyle, the Secretary of *Plimoth Plantation,* told him that some Englishman had telephoned to say they were building a replica of the *Mayflower*.

He could not quite believe his eyes when the 6 foot 5 inch John Lowe turned up in Boston wearing his bowler hat and formal pinstriped dark grey suit. John Lowe was accompanied by two men - Mordant Smith, who claimed to be a public relations expert and Dominic Elwes, the young man who had given Warwick the introduction to Felix Fenston.

Hornblower wasn't sure he knew what public relations had to do with American history and he couldn't understand why this motley crew could be interested in solving his problem.

Hornblower had been trying hard to find a way to build a replica of the *Mayflower* for eight years. That was when, with his father's financial support, he had set up *Plimoth Plantation.* In November of 1947 he had started writing to British shipbuilders but had made little progress.

He had obtained a quotation for $800,000 which he dismissed as outrageous and at one point had invited quotes from American shipbuilders in a fruitless effort to get a lower price.

Hornblower did have a small model for the *Mayflower* that was on permanent display in the Plymouth Memorial Museum. It had been presented to the city in 1922 by a world expert on sailing ships, Mr. R. C. Anderson of Greenwich Maritime Museum in London - the same man that had been giving Warwick his lessons in 17th century shipbuilding.

John Lowe phoned from America with his first impressions. *"You are not going to believe this dear boy but I was met by a guy called Harry Hornblower."* John Lowe reported that Hornblower was leading a group of well-to-do Bostonians who were interested in building something called a water line model of the *Mayflower.*

Hornblower came from a family of blue-chip Boston stockbrokers but his real interest was archaeological research into Indian life, John reported. *"Hornblower talked endlessly of Indian arrows. He pounded my head."*

Before John had boarded the plane for America, Warwick had issued a formal announcement through Reuters, the world wide news agency, that his project was to go ahead. One of the many Fleet Street journalists, with whom he had discussed the story, was planning to run a garbled version, he explained, so he had to set the story straight. However, Warwick knew that his story would be sent to the US news agencies and be picked up by the papers in New England. He guessed that the American, whom John Lowe was due to meet, might well take him more seriously after reading about the English plans in the *Boston Globe.*

In fact, both the story and Warwick took flight in England. Bill Connor, Warwick's friend on the *Daily Mirror,* ran this comment in his regular column: *"So the Mayflower will sail again. A replica of the Pilgrim Fathers' ship, meticulously exact in every detail, is to be built in Britain at the cost of £110,000. It will then sail from Plymouth to the United States and be presented to the American people as a gift from the British people."*

"An excellent idea."

The *Mirror* continued, *"A few years ago the Danes had a similar inspiration, and brought a Viking ship across the North Sea to visit us. It was great fun and the goodwill between ourselves and Denmark was helped enormously by the cruise."*

"When people start building decorative boats for each other instead of H-bombs, well, it makes a nice change."

However, senior officials in the British Foreign Office were not at all convinced that building a replica of the *Mayflower* was such a clever idea. Indeed it seemed to some senior government officials like a meaningless gesture. It might have popular appeal but any money spent on the project was thought to be a waste of financial resources. The British Foreign Office certainly wanted to build close ties with the US but they believed the best way to do that was through cultural exchanges between the elites of both countries, supporting ways to work more closely in NATO, the International Monetary Fund and the United Nations.

Existing, well-established organisations like the English Speaking Union and the Pilgrim Society seemed to government officials to be the logical vehicles for any initiatives. Officials in London, Washington DC and Boston were asked to keep a close eye on the progress of the proposed *Mayflower* adventure.

The Foreign office needed to decide whether their hostility to the *Mayflower* project should be declared publicly or efforts to sink the ship should be conducted quietly.

DESPERATE BUILDER

Warwick made his way out to London Airport soon after John Lowe had left for America. He flew to Exeter in Devon, a journey of less than 200 miles. It was a tiny airport with no regular scheduled flights and it would have been a lot less expensive and not much longer to catch one of the fast, efficient trains that left from the center of London but Warwick felt he had to make a very big impression on the man he was going to see. Warwick had never bought a house, a car, anything more valuable than a good wrist watch and he was setting off to meet a ship builder with no more than Fenston's £500 to support his cause. He suddenly felt way out of his depth in his new role of shipping magnate. A grand airport entrance would help his credibility.

Warwick needn't have worried. Stuart Upham was desperate to build *Mayflower II*. He had thought of little else since his wife, a couple of weeks earlier, had rushed up to their bedroom in the early morning with the latest edition of the *London Illustrated News*. He loved that paper and it was his custom to save it until Saturday night to read by the fireside, but Mrs. Upham insisted her husband sit right up in bed and read it immediately at the pages she had opened.

He stared at a two page illustration of *Mayflower* and the story Warwick had given the paper of his intentions. *"I'm going to build this ship,"* Stuart Upham told his wife and he went to the post office as soon as it opened to send a telegram to "Project *Mayflower*" in London.

Neither Stuart nor Warwick spoke much on the drive from the airport but once they reached the small ramshackle tin roofed ship yard in the center of Brixham neither man could contain himself any longer. Stuart almost shouted to Warwick, *"You know we can do it. This is the place to build her."* Warwick had no intention of disagreeing or playing hard to get.

As Stuart Upham took Warwick on a tour of the small yard he explained in his soft west country accent that his firm J.W. & A. Upham Ltd. had been building wooden ships for nearly two hundred years. In recent years they had specialized in a small fishing vessel known as the 1908 Brixham trawler. They were small, easy to handle sailing boats, ideal for working the coastal fishing grounds. Now these work horses of the sea had been replaced by modern trawlers. Stuart Upham recalled, sadly, the days *"When I was a boy and the harbor was dark with their sails. Now to the best of my knowledge, there is not one Brixham trawler working under sail today."*

Stuart Upham at whose ship building yard in Brixham, Devon the *Mayflower II* was built and launched.

Upham's yard had been used by the British Navy during the war to repair and equip over 1,100 ships, and they had built 35 wooden mine sweepers and motor torpedo boats, all over 100 ft. long. Warwick was even more impressed by Stuart Upham's enthusiasm than his considerable experience and he decided, while standing in the yard, that he had no need to visit other shipyards and seek competitive quotes - Stuart Upham would build *Mayflower II.* He also decided that next time he came down to Brixham there would be no need for a grand entrance. He had already formed a bond of friendship with Stuart Upham. Next time he would take the train.

Before Warwick left, the two men ran over the problems they faced. Stuart Upham asked to look at the building plans.

Warwick only had plans for a model that had been used in a film of the *Mayflower* voyage starring Spencer Tracy. Stuart Upham was shocked. *"Well, you will just have to find a way to scale it up,"* the now confident client told his builder. *"What about insurance"*, Stuart Upham asked. Warwick was quick on his feet. "*That will be easy to organize"*, he declared. *"Both you and I are going to sail to America in her. That should give the insurers confidence."*

Stuart Upham had serious concerns about finding enough men with the necessary experience. *"We have a nucleus of them. They are the ones with the craft and they will teach the others."* Warwick left Stuart Upham to ponder the myriad of practical problems of construction and to come up with a price.

DETECTIVE WORK

Meanwhile, in Boston, Henry Hornblower gained confidence in his visitors when he learned that they also had been conferring with Anderson in an effort to finalize a design. However, Hornblower knew it would be extremely difficult simply to give a shipbuilder a model, no matter how well constructed, and say *"build this, only life size."* For this reason, in 1949, he had commissioned a Mr. William Baker to research and develop full scale plans that a builder could use. Baker, was an executive with the Bethlehem Steel Corporation who had made the design of sailing ships a serious lifelong hobby.

Over five years Baker had made considerable progress in what was necessarily a combination of detective work, scholarship and guesswork. He had conferred many times with Anderson and others in England. He knew that the *Mayflower* had been built before naval architects were obliged to lodge plans with the Admiralty. He knew from Bradford's Journal that the *Mayflower* weighed approximately 180 tons and he discovered from historical documents the common design of merchant ships of the time.

Bit by bit a detailed design for the *Mayflower* had taken shape. The hobby became work and Hornblower agreed to pay Baker a few thousand dollars for his time and expenses on visits to England.

Even so, Hornblower did not see how they could possibly raise the money to build a *Mayflower* that would actually sail. He planned to use Baker's research to build a waterline model that would sit in a Plymouth building for visitors to look at. They would have to take account of modern safety regulations. Since there were none relating to the housing of boats, the authorities told Baker and Hornblower to make their design conform to the laws relating to the safety of dance halls.

Now the soft spoken Lowe was proposing a deal. *"Give me your plans and we'll give you the ship. You can have it for a dollar; it will be a gift to the American People. We'll establish a trust fund to be jointly run by the trustees from both the British and American sides. All income will go into the trust to meet the expenses of maintaining the Mayflower. Surplus funds will be used to establish a scholarship fund to foster Anglo-American relations. The joint British American Board will decide how to spend the money."*

Hornblower had no great interest in Anglo-American relations. His interest in history lay in the thin granite soil of New England. He had published papers on the archeology of the area and was building a reputation for *Plimoth Plantation* with scholarly treatises on the Wompanoag and other tribes. However, the *Mayflower* was an important part of the story.

As he always did before agreeing to any transaction, Hornblower talked with his attorney, Lothrop Withington. The English offer was almost too good to be true they agreed, but it was an offer which couldn't be refused. Detailed documents of agreement were produced and signed which clearly set out the responsibilities of each partner.

Walter Haskell, the news editor of the local paper, *The Old Colony Memorial,* was invited to report on the historic agreement. Photographs were taken of everyone involved admiring one of Baker's models and an extensive article on the subject appeared in the following week's paper.

John Lowe telephoned Warwick in London before leaving Plymouth. He was ecstatic. They had written agreements, they had a site to berth the ship when it arrived in America and

Lowe was bringing home plans that would allow a builder to start work on *Mayflower II* - or so he thought.

Hornblower had been far from convinced that his new English partners could succeed where he had failed for the last 8 years. Neither he nor the four other conservative members of the New England establishment who comprised the *Plimoth Plantation* board, could work out why the English were doing it.

They might even be con men. Hornblower decided to move very cautiously. He gave Lowe only general plans for the *Mayflower II* and held back the detailed drawings that would be essential for construction to start.

Hornblower's colleague, Bill Brewster, visited England on business two or three times a year. He was chief executive of a company that made shoe manufacturing equipment. He had clients in Northampton, England and he was a hard-headed businessman. He would find out how much support Lowe, Charlton, and the others had.

Then, after Lowe left for London, Hornblower wrote him a short note to inform him that the plans he had been given were not quite complete.

SOBER MOMENT

Back in the claustrophobic confines of their Coleman Street office, Warwick and John Lowe considered their next move. They now had a builder and a place to berth the ship in America but they still had only £500. They decided that they must launch a public appeal to raise the money.

Respectable members of the establishment from different walks of life and religion must be found to give the appeal national credibility. It was a massive task but they had to make a start somewhere. Warwick sent out a press release announcing the agreement with *Plimoth Plantation.* The release stated that *Mayflower II* would sail to America in October 1956. That was the next year, only 18 months away. Warwick decided he needed a drink.

He had learned to drink hard in the army and he got a doctorate in the subject when he graduated to civilian life. Many of his artistic friends, including Dylan Thomas the poet, Francis Bacon the painter and Frank Owen, the journalist, spent long hours in the pubs and clubs of London's Soho district. Others included most journalists in Fleet Street who were simply heavy drinkers. Many, like Warwick, would write sober but as soon as they had done what was necessary, they got on with the real business of the day, which was boozing. Sometimes he would start drinking at 11 a.m., sometimes at 1 p.m., and sometimes not until early evening, but whenever he started Warwick normally ended up inebriated and often in spectacular style.

It was the culture of the time. Of course, as a journalist, it often helped to loosen up someone if you did the interview in a pub, but that was really just an excuse. Experienced publicans would shudder when Warwick walked in the door and from time to time his behaviour caused him to be banned from several drinking establishments. As the *Mayflower* idea took hold he slowed down a little but was still consuming more than enough to render most men unconscious.

At the Red Lion Pub, just off Fleet Street, he ran into a friend from the *Daily Express* and began talking as usual about his latest *Mayflower* press release. His drinking partner was unimpressed. *"It's never going to happen, Warwick. Why don't you face facts?"* Warwick removed the glass of beer from his lips and slammed it down on the table. He swore not to take another drop until the *Mayflower* set sail.

As they left the pub that night there was at least one other person who thought Warwick might get the ship built. Warwick didn't drink again for several years. *"It just became a habit to stay sober,"* he told an astonished friend a few years later. *"I was amazed how much time there was in each day to do things."*

John Lowe continued to work his contacts in the establishment, and excited the interest of an eminent industrialist, Sir Patrick Hannon, who was an advocate of British trade in general and Anglo-American friendship in particular. Sir Patrick introduced John to leading members of the Conservative party including Harold MacMillian, as well as members of the House of Lords, (Britain's upper house of parliament), and he received polite interest.

Sir Patrick recommended John Lowe to work with the Pilgrim Society and the English Speaking Union, but both John and Warwick viewed these organizations as dining and debating clubs for the elite They were supporters of cultural exchanges but hardly organizations that could get their hands dirty and build a ship.

Warwick received encouragement for his *Mayflower* plans from leading politicians in Massachusetts,
Including this gift of a painting of an early sailing ship. However he struggled to get British politicians behind his project.

NAVAL INTELLIGENCE

Something was missing. Warwick was overlooking a vital piece of the puzzle but he wasn't sure what it was. He went to see his old friend Randolph Churchill, the son of Britain's great war time leader. Many people found Randolph difficult to deal with but Warwick loved the man's candour and forthright views. Of course he went over the top at times, but so did Warwick. *"The man was a damn good journalist whose lifelong tragedy was always to be compared to his father, whom many regarded as the greatest living Englishman."*

Randolph Churchill was true to form. *"You have no credibility,"* he told Warwick bluntly. Of course at the time of the first *Mayflower* nobody gave a second thought to going to sea in a little wooden boat. Everybody went, including women and children. It was part of life. Today the sea is regarded as a place only for well trained, experienced sailors. *"You need some big name naval types on your team".* Churchill offered to introduce Warwick to Ian Fleming.

Work on the ship went faster than the fundraising.

Warwick turned to Randolph Churchill for advice.

Warwick was puzzled. *"I thought he wrote James Bond spy novels."*

"*He is very well connected*", Churchill explained. *"He was in naval intelligence in the war and knows every admiral in the British Navy. As a bonus he is currently dating Lord Rothermere's daughter. You can't get better connected than that."*

Fleming, the man who invented the spy master 007, introduced Warwick to Lord Fraser of North Cape - one of Britain's most distinguished war time admirals. Fraser thought the *Mayflower* was a great idea.

With Randolph Churchill and Ian Fleming opening the doors, Warwick soon added a long list of well-known names to his roster of patrons, including Commodore C. H. Grattidge who captained both the Queen Elizabeth and the Queen Mary - the world's two largest passenger ships at the time. Lord Jowitt, a former Lord Chancellor, agreed to become a patron, as did Sir George Nelson one of Britain's foremost industrialists and Sir William Rootes, C.B.E., the Chairman of the government supported Dollar Export Council.

Sir William Rootes

was responsible for promoting exports to the US as the post-war government desperately sought US dollars. He found the Mayflower project intriguing but worrying.

As each patron consented to be involved, Warwick added their names to his Project *Mayflower* letterhead. Before long the list of patrons ran the length of the letterhead paper and typists had limited space to fit correspondence into the remaining area. Warwick was unconcerned about their difficulty - he was setting the scene for a national appeal to be launched sometime in 1956 - probably the spring.

Warwick knew it would not be easy. The British people were still recovering from the war and there was a government imposed credit squeeze in place. Several deserving fund raising efforts had failed miserably in recent months. In one instance a national appeal for victims of an east coast flooding disaster had raised a paltry £47. Everything had to be just right for Warwick's appeal to work, including the timing.

Warwick asked the accountants in the office next door to his to help him form a 100 pound company called Project *Mayflower* Ltd. He intended to issue two shares, one to himself and the other to John Lowe, his business partner in the infant public relations business. Warwick had little or no idea about company law but he decided that he would be Chairman which meant that John would do things his way.

Later Warwick promised to issue a third one pound share to an old wartime buddy, Frank Owen. He liked Frank. At 23, Frank had become the youngest serving member in the House of Commons. Now he was editor of the national newspaper *The London Daily Mail*. Frank was always dead broke and had no money to put into the *Mayflower* project but he was president of the Anglo-American Association and had taken an interest in Warwick's *Mayflower* obsession from the beginning.

Typically, Warwick never got around to issuing the share certificate to Frank Owen - in his mind that was a minor detail.

What was important were the aims and objectives of his new company. Most businessmen who set up new companies used standard boiler plate wording for their Articles of Association; it was wording that permitted their companies to carry out virtually any business. But Warwick wanted Project *Mayflower* Ltd.'s objectives clearly and narrowly stated:

(A) To raise any sum required, by public or private subscription, in order to build, equip, and maintain a replica of the Mayflower.

(B) To sail the ship across the Atlantic and present her to the people of the United States.

(C) To promote, support and encourage Anglo-American relations in any form whatsoever, and to remind English-speaking peoples of their common heritage.

The Articles of Association decreed that:

" ......nothing herein shall be construed as giving the right to the Company to carry on any of its primary objects for the purpose of profit and that is a fundamental part of the construction of the company."

In other words the main objectives would be carried out as a non-profit making exercise.

MYSTERIOUS TOOLS

Warwick went back to Brixham to see Stuart Upham who had done his homework. Stuart calculated that the ship would cost about £58,500 to build including the cost of all materials. Warwick had accumulated about £3,000. He was £55,500 short.

Both Stuart and Warwick discussed the possibility of persuading suppliers of timber, hemp and sailcloth to donate some materials in return for having their name associated with the *Mayflower.*

Both men agreed that, since donations of materials were possible, a "cost plus" approach rather than a fixed cost price would make the most sense. Upham's yard would charge a fee for their labour and a small mark-up over the use of materials that were supplied through donations. Perhaps this way the price could be reduced somewhat.

Warwick asked how much it would cost to lay the keel. Upham said, *"Three-thousand pounds."* Warwick agreed to send him a cheque for £1,000 the following day. They had no contract but they shook hands. Both men were anxious to start building. Warwick took the train back to London and wondered where the rest of the money would come from.

He soon made further visits to discuss construction with Stuart. There were real problems in obtaining the wood necessary which, in post war England, was still strictly rationed. Warwick realized that Stuart was a keen student of old ship building methods and he was soon infected with the builder's enthusiasm for the history of his craft. Warwick forgot about the cost considerations and determined that the *Mayflower* would be built in an historically accurate manner, using the tools and methods of 17th century England.

"Some of those old methods were slow," Stuart warned. *"Some of the tools no longer exist and haven't been used for centuries. My builders will have to be trained to use them."*

"Let's make them and train your men," said Warwick. Before long the two men were trading shipbuilding terms such as nippers, maul, gauges and adze like a couple of old hands from a bygone century.

Old oak timber that was large enough and bent in the correct shape was difficult to find. A search of the countryside, however, revealed some suitable trees that vanished one night only to reappear in Upham's yard.

Upham especially needed hard seasoned oak for the tree nails he was to use. Old cider oak casks were found which contained the well seasoned wood for which he was looking. The tall masts presented a major problem because no trees in England grew tall enough, but a small quantity of Oregon pine was located which was perfect for the job.

In the months that followed, Stuart Upham scoured the West Country to assemble the materials to go to work.

CREATING HISTORY

In London, Warwick began to put in almost daily appearances at the Wig and Pen Club - an historic drinking and dining club in the heart of London. It became his second office as he courted investors and potential patrons there, dined with potential suppliers of goods, entertained visiting Americans and bought drinks for journalists who dropped by to get the latest on *Mayflower*.

When there was no one to talk to he could be found screaming down one of the open phones in the lobby. It was the perfect venue for Warwick to sell the *Mayflower* story, because the place had the feel and touch of the seventeenth century, the era in which *Mayflower* had sailed. In fact Warwick helped to create the unique atmosphere of the place.

The club was opposite London's Law Courts and at one end of Fleet Street which, at the time, was the home of virtually all the national newspapers and magazines in England. The building itself is several hundred years old and consisted of four floors of tiny oak beamed dining rooms and bars that could be reached only by narrow, uneven stairs. No modern fire marshal would ever approve the place for occupation.

The owners were Joe Coral, a well known London bookmaker and Dick Brennan an old war time buddy of Warwick's. Warwick had introduced the two men to the Wig in 1951 when they were looking for a place to take bets from wealthy punters. Gambling was still illegal in those days and bookmakers and their customers got around the law by using clubs of one sort or another.

The Wig was in a sorry state when Warwick recommended it. *"Don't worry,"* he told his old army friend Dick Brennan. *"The place has history. I'll help you discover it."*

Warwick discovered that the place dated back to the seventeenth century and had been used as a dwelling for the

The Wig and Pen

A place Warwick had helped turn into a dining club steeped in history. It became his meeting place for everything to do with *Mayflower II*.

clergy before becoming a coffee house and a meeting place for jurists, journalists, and authors, including his father, Randal Charlton. The place was redecorated and Warwick helped Dick bring its history to life in a manner that no visitor could ignore.

Copies of newspaper front pages documenting events in recent history crowded the walls. There was a copy of the declaration of the second World War, the news of the Japanese bombing of Pearl Harbor and the infamous headline of the Chicago Tribune declaring incorrectly that Dewey had beaten Harry Truman in the 1948 presidential race.

The rich history of the law courts was depicted in the form of cartoons of famous judges and barristers. By the time Warwick had finished with his decoration of the walls, the place felt like a living museum dedicated to the great men of law and the noble profession of journalism, rather than an eating and drinking club for gamblers to place their bets in comfort.

The building was soaked in history but Warwick may have stretched the truth a little with a claim that it was the only building in the area to survive the Great Fire of London in 1666.

MAYFLOWER MARRIAGE

Nigel Gaydon sat at his desk at the British Embassy in Washington DC and stared down at the name on the memo. It was a request from a friend in the Foreign office for any information on a man called John Lowe.

How much would the Foreign Office like to know? Nigel Gaydon had been John Lowe's commanding officer during the war when both men worked at Bletchley Park, the center of Britain's code breaking efforts against Nazi Germany. Lowe was so difficult to work with, reported Gaydon, that he gave up trying and exiled him to a back room where he ran his own section.

Lowe was a man of great charm, enthusiasm and possessed great powers of persuasion, Gaydon reported, but he was prone to advancing cockeyed schemes that always failed because someone else let him down: though he was an intelligent man, (and had a double first from Cambridge University to prove it) he was, according to Gaydon, so lacking in common sense that he often managed to deceive even himself.

"Lowe is a very complicated personality", Gaydon concluded. After reviewing Gaydon's report, Lord Redding at the Foreign Office expressed the view that *"the standing of the people responsible for this (Mayflower) enterprise (is) still unsatisfactory and obscure"*.

He and other officials at the Foreign Office fretted that the Mayflower project might end in failure, to which they did not object, and embarassment, which they did. They feared harm to the British image abroad.

Warwick received a call at the Wig and Pen Club from Lord Fraser of North Cape, one of his leading *Mayflower* patrons, who wanted to see him as a matter of urgency. Warwick dashed off in a cab to meet him in the House of Lords. There was some concern about John Lowe, Warwick's partner, he was told discreetly. John Lowe appeared to have only male acquaintances. It would be difficult to continue to provide support if the possibility of a scandal existed. In those days homosexuality between consenting adults was still illegal in Britain.

It was the sort of problem that Warwick delighted in solving. He sat John down and told him he needed to get married. Warwick dragged a few names from him of girls he had recently met and found attractive, then he proposed to one of them on John's behalf citing John's chronic shyness as a reason for acting as his substitute.

Within a few months John and Pamela Lowe emerged from St. Bride's Church on Fleet St. just down the road from the Wig and Pen Club. Naturally members of the Press were invited to meet, interview and photograph the lovers who had been brought together by a common affection for the *Mayflower*. It was another good *Mayflower* story and most of those present in the church continued their celebration at the Wig far into the evening.

A few years later, as he analyzed his actions in those days of the *Mayflower* project, Warwick's voice would go quiet when he referred to John Lowe; sentences would trail off into silence and his face would reflect the pain he felt. If only he had listened a little more to John's gentle, sensible voice.

LONELY OAK

There was nothing really to look at in Upham's yard *"just a large stick of wood"* but Warwick dressed the place up for an official keel laying ceremony. They had to begin getting the public's interest. Nothing much had appeared about *Mayflower* for months apart from Bill Connor's piece, a short report in the *Illustrated London News* and the announcement of the partnership with *Plimoth Plantation*.

Warwick's office staff dressed in pilgrim costume get the attention of London policemen and the national press.

Enormous American and English flags hung from the beams above the keel and Warwick assembled the living props he thought necessary to give the occasion some credibility - the American Ambassador, Winthrop Aldrich, was invited as well as local dignitaries and, of course, the local vicar to provide a blessing with his captive audience of choirboys. A marine band provided some stirring nautical tunes as well as the national anthems of Britain and America. The use of church members and the army also meant that the entertainment was essentially free of charge.

Warwick dressed up Upham's shipyard with American and British flags and tracked down a man whose ancestors had sailed on the original *Mayflower* to officiate at the laying of the keel of *Mayflower II*. Lieutenant Commander D.K. Winslow, a retired naval officer is pictured laying a ceremonial hammer onto the 'lonely stick' while invited guests, shipyard workers and a church choir look on.

Warwick knew he needed something special to spark media interest which, at this stage, was still highly skeptical. In the

Surrey countryside, not far from London, he found someone who would bring life and meaning to the 58 ft. long piece of large, naked, oak lying in Upham's yard.

Lieutenant Commander D.K. Winslow was retired from the British Navy and had plenty of time on his hands. He had researched his family history and discovered that two of his ancestors had traveled to America in the *Mayflower*. Warwick invited him to be the principal guest at the keel laying ceremony.

Surrounded by ladies in their best Sunday church clothes, choirboys in cassocks, shipyard workers in their normal coveralls and a few visitors from London and America in city suits, Commander Winslow struck a ceremonial hammer blow on the hard twisted oak that was to become *Mayflower II's* keel.

This piqued the interest of the BBC and a few local papers, including the West Country's largest and most respected paper, *The Western Morning News.* Commander Winslow became Warwick's mouthpiece for the *Mayflower* story. He proudly revealed to the slightly bemused Press that the first *Mayflower* would probably never have made it to America without the ingenuity of his ancestor, Pilgrim Edward Winslow.

Edward, a printer, had taken his press along with him and when the main beam collapsed he jacked it up with his press*, a support that kept the ship intact for the completion of the trip.

The Press was also given a lesson in the craftsmanship that would be required to construct a replica of a seventeenth century ship with almost no straight lines.

** Historians have found no historical evidence that Winslow took a printing press. He may have had a jack screw for use in house building which was used to bolster the main beam.*

The single oak log, that was all there was to see, had been cut from a twisted, 120 year old Devon oak tree. It had taken the carpenters 40 separate turns with the lathe to reduce it to the required shape - 58 ft long, curved at the ends and 14 by 12 inches across with true edges. To do this the carpenters had to go right out to the bark at one point and join two pieces together with a keel scarf.

Bill Baker, the quiet, thoughtful ship's architect, had flown over from America for the ceremony with his wife Ruth. He was a man of very few words but turned to Warwick at one point with slightly strange words of encouragement. *"Warwick, I feel sure that you are the right man to build her."*

William Baker made the research of sailing ships a lifetime hobby.

SUSPICIOUS MINDS

The men paying Baker's expenses back in Plymouth, Massachusetts were not at all sure that Warwick was the right man for the job. Hornblower had asked Baker to talk to as many people as possible between design conferences with Stuart Upham. His assignment was to find out more about Charlton and Lowe. Why, for example, did organizations like the English Speaking Union have no connection with or interest in the project? Baker ultimately stood behind the verbal support he had given Warwick.

He sent a memo to Hornblower which supported Warwick's view that the English Speaking Union were mere wordsmiths who would be totally ineffective as participants in the project.

"Ordinary people were greatly interested", said Baker. He also agreed with Warwick's avowed intention to keep the team controlling the project, small, to avoid getting bogged down. *"You do the same with the governors of Plimoth Plantation,"* Baker reminded his American colleagues. *"Charlton and Lowe may be opportunists but their technical advisors are not the sort that could afford to be associated with a shady deal."* Hornblower was reassured but decided to keep close tabs on his new partners.

His colleague and the *Plantation*'s governor, Bill Brewster, also visited Upham's yard when he came to England to deal with his shoe manufacturing business. He got on well with Stuart Upham but didn't know what to make of either Warwick or John Lowe. He couldn't work out what really motivated them. He had heard their story that the ship was to be a gift to the American People - a thank you for the American Land Lease program that helped rebuild Europe after the war, but he wondered if that was just a public relations story. He was wary of the two smooth-talking charmers from Britain.

Progress was painfully slow at Upham's yard after the celebration of the keel laying in July 1955. Stuart Upham was still assembling the men and materials he needed and as he scoured the country for the right crooked oaks Warwick scoured the country for money. Six months later at the year's end only one rib had been added to the keel. The Project *Mayflower* bank account was just as bare.

Massachusetts Governor Christian A Herter (seated left) listens as Warwick explains his plans to build *Mayflower II*. Looking on are (left to right) Henry Hornblower II, David Longfellow Patten and William Brewster.

TREASURE CHESTS

The concept of corporate sponsorship was virtually unknown at the time but Warwick sought to appeal to industry with a unique idea which a friend and supporter, Kennerly Edwards, had given him. Edwards was a freelance photographer who occasionally worked with Warwick and as he did so he became a part of the *Mayflower* Project.

"Mayflower II should carry 20 treasure chests as cargo, each containing samples of the best British products," Edwards suggested. The chests would be exhibited in America after the journey to promote the best of British goods and would generate desperately needed foreign revenue.

As with everything Warwick did in connection with the *Mayflower II,* these chests had to be as historically accurate as possible. A world renowned furniture maker called Neil Morris of Glasgow, offered to carve 17th century replicas and donate them to the project. Warwick decided arbitrarily to charge industry £460 for each chest - which was the exact amount by which Stuart Upham's bill was rising each week. A list of British exporters was obtained from the Dollar Export Council and over 1,000 British firms were invited to clamber aboard. The response was less than overwhelming: only three positive replies were received.

Two of the early sponsors were International Paints and an Anglo-American company, Colgate Palmolive. Warwick determined that he would find a way to repay their faith as soon as possible. As the thin light of the British autumn gave way to the dark, dank days of winter, Warwick believed that it was critical to launch a national public appeal for funds. In the months since the keel laying he had accumulated an impressive list of public figures who were prepared to back the appeal. Now it was time to use their support .

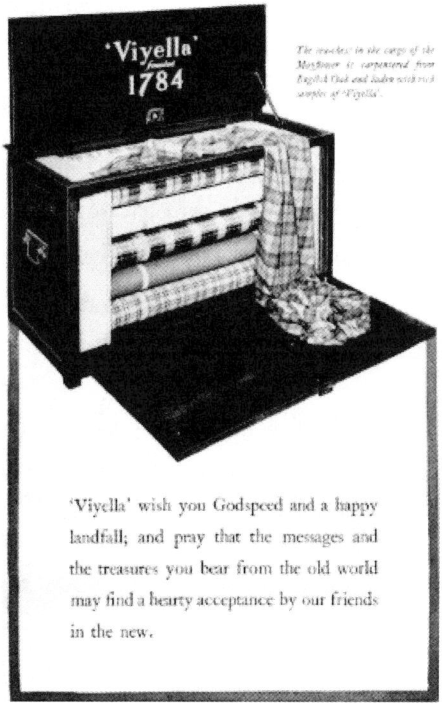

Leading British businesses were invited to buy **Treasure Chests** that would be on the *Mayflower II.* On arrival, the chests would be exhibited across the US.

"The first stage is over", Warwick announced in mid November's public statement of progress. *"To deal with the second stage of a public appeal, preparations have been made to put into effect a more elaborate constitution for the Mayflower Project. The complex legal work involved in this task is now practically complete. A Board of Trustees is being formed from leading public personalities and details of the expanded constitution, together with the appeal for the remaining sum, will be published in the near future."*

Warwick was not sure he believed in the wisdom of his own public pronouncement. As far as he was concerned, he and John Lowe would still run things and the patrons would allow their names to be used in the cause. He knew no other way to operate.

In the army and on Fleet Street he had always done his job without interference, often with the protective support of a general or press baron who guarded his creative talents from the suffocating caution of committees, censorship and red tape. He wasn't about to change now.

Page 10 MAYFLOWER MAIL

"Goodwill created by the project should benefit the sale of all British goods in the United States" —London Chamber of Commerce Journal

Industry Supports Treasure Chests Scheme

Sir William Rootes, Chairman of the Dollar Exports Council.

WE STILL HAVE THE SPIRIT OF MERCHANT ADVENTURERS

REMINDER OF OUR TRUE QUALITIES

"I visited an old shipyard down in South Devon, at Brixham. There on the stocks a small wooden ship is taking shape. You will no doubt have heard of her, for she bears a famous name—the MAYFLOWER. She is to be a replica in every respect of that Mayflower which took the Pilgrim Fathers on their hazardous journey 300 odd years ago. This one too will sail across the Atlantic and be berthed, like her predecessor, at Plymouth in Massachussets Bay, and there will remain as a gift from the people of England and as a symbol of our common heritage and our common love of freedom and justice, and of all those things which money cannot buy. It was for them that that gallant band of 100 odd souls set sail in 1620, and perhaps when this new, old Mayflower sails again she will serve to remind us and others of the true qualities of this island race, which surely still endure. We have, too, always to be looking beyond the horizon, and for us life should always be a great adventure."

—(Colonel Alan Wilkinson, President of the Institute of Practitioners in Advertising).

Reprinted from the Chamber of Commerce Journal, the official organ of the London Chamber of Commerce.

Warwick persuaded London's Chamber of Commerce to support the effort to attract businesses to sponsor *Mayflower II* but members of the British government were not convinced.

CAPTAIN'S CREDENTIALS

The continued promotion of *Mayflower II* brought a steady build-up in the mail that arrived daily at Warwick's London office. Hardly any contained money. By the end of the year several thousand people of both sexes, aged from eight to eighty-two had written to apply to sail as members of the crew. Warwick found it absolutely impossible to say no to any of them. *"The captain will make the final decision"*, was his standard evasive response, even to an old man who wanted to go on the voyage to see if it would help his arthritis.

Alan Villiers

Warwick declared that Alan Villiers brought the scent of sea air into the room when he came to Warwick's London office to ask for a place on the crew.

As the ship's captain he brought a competitive edge with which Warwick would struggle.

Warwick's secretary, Miss Jeans, took him to task for his dishonesty with some of the most obviously unsuitable candidates, but he could not change. He spent every waking hour promoting *Mayflower* - how could he disappoint someone he had enthused? He had to find a captain fast and when Alan Villiers walked into his Coleman Street office, Warwick instinctively knew he had found his man.

He had glanced briefly at his background which seemed pretty good but it was the manner of the man that made Warwick sit up and pay attention. *"Although he wore civilian dress and a thick overcoat, he seemed to bring the sea into the office with him. And he sounded like the brusque, larger than life, Charles Laughton, the actor who played the Captain in the film, 'Mutiny on the Bounty'."*

Villiers volunteered the fact that he had taken the liberty of speaking to *National Geographic Magazine* and the magazine's editors had agreed to run an extended story on the *Mayflower* voyage, if he were selected as a crew member.

"What an endorsement," thought Warwick... *"One of the world's most respected journals."* He immediately offered Villiers the captain's job. The two men spent the rest of their first meeting discussing the design of the ship, the way she would sail, the route they would take and the type of crew they would need. Warwick was energized by the conversation. He was heading for America with sails billowing in the wind.

After Villiers left, Warwick was still congratulating himself on finding someone who could guarantee an article in *National Geographic Magazine.* He decided to re-read the man's background more carefully to learn a little more about his new captain.

Captain Villiers probably had more experience on large sailing ships than anyone else alive. He had left his home in Australia at 15 and signed on with an ancient Scottish ship supplying timber to New Zealand.

Over the next 25 years he gained experience on every type of sailing ship. He had even put to sea in the wooden deep sea dhows that sailed the Arabian gulf, the Indian ocean and the coast of Africa. Before the war he had obtained his own sailing vessel, a Danish training ship, which he renamed *Joseph Conrad* and sailed around the world.

In the war, Villiers commanded a squadron of landing-craft during the allied invasions of Sicily, Italy and Normandy and was awarded the Distinguished Service Cross. In addition to being a man of action, he was also a Trustee of the National Maritime Museum and a member of the Council of the Society for Nautical Research.

Warwick sat back in his chair as he considered the magnificent qualifications of his newly appointed captain.

"My God", he thought. *"What a bonus on top of a guaranteed story in National Geographic"*.

As the new captain began to wade his way through the mountain of applications for a place on the crew, Warwick found he had other captains to deal with, at least one of whom seemed more like a pirate than a friendly face.

MR PRESIDENT

When Warwick assembled his distinguished patrons for the public appeal he pondered a title for Felix Fenston. Warwick had found him very difficult to contact after he had given the first seed money and he didn't expect Felix to play an active role in the enterprise, but the man deserved recognition. He had offered his elegant home for meetings of the patrons. "President" seemed to fit.

The name meant nothing in English company law where the chief operating officer of the company is known as the general manager or managing director. The title "President" was occasionally given to someone past retirement who had once given important service, a sort of business version of the academic honor of professor emeritus.

To Henry Hornblower the title of "President" was anything but academic. His country's chief executive was respectfully referred to as Mr. President. In the American business world the chief executive officer was often also titled president and Hornblower himself was the president of *Plimoth Plantation*. Hornblower decided to get close to this man called Felix Fenston, the person he now figured to be really in charge of the English operation.

Fenston had little time for talk about a non-profit making venture. He had a large real estate operation to worry about when he was not overseas big game hunting in Africa or deep sea fishing in the West Indies. He told Hornblower to keep in touch with his attorney, Sir George Bull. The beknighted lawyer would have plenty of time to liaise with Hornblower and to impose some discipline on Warwick Charlton. Bull saw the need for a new set of rules for Project *Mayflower*. Warwick would be expected to take orders from a committee who would approve policy decisions and all significant spending requests.

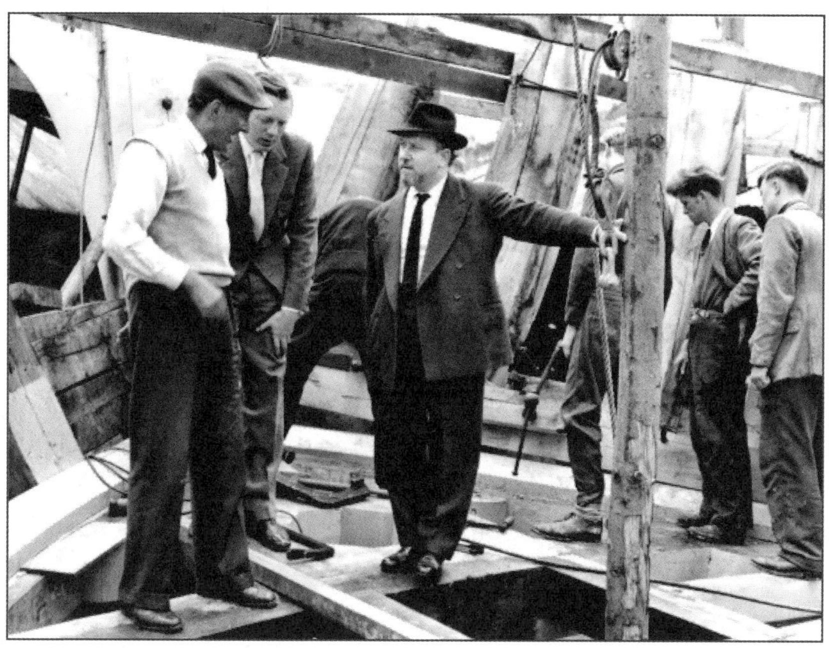

Stuart Upham, Warwick Charlton and "President" Fenston

While Hornblower and Sir George Bull conferred behind Warwick's back, Warwick worked feverishly to keep the project in the papers. Publicity would breathe life into the ship. Although by Christmas 1955 only three firms committed to pay £460 for the privilege of placing their own Treasure Chest aboard *Mayflower II,* several companies had offered gifts in kind; rope, timber, instruments, food for the voyage. Every gift drew a press release from Warwick. He was building momentum for the project.

Then *Life* Magazine offered to buy the rights to the voyage. They were still far from certain that the ship would be built, let alone sail, but, as an insurance, they offered to pay £1,000 up front for the exclusive rights to photograph the voyage.

Warwick, desperate for both cash and credibility, accepted on condition that they keep the amount confidential. He immediately issued a statement in which he denied receiving £100,000 from *Life*. Warwick would come to regret taking the money from *Life* magazine.

Other stories were more genuine. Warwick believed that there had to be some special people on *Mayflower II* in addition to the experienced crew that the captain would assemble. He wanted the passenger list to include at least one direct descendent of the people who sailed in the 1620 ship. He offered a place to John Winslow, the son of the retired naval officer who officiated at the keel laying ceremony.

It was also important to Warwick that the youth of both Britain and America be represented. He invited the Boys Clubs of both countries to select a candidate in nationwide competitions. The competitions would generate interest over many months.

Good Luck to
the 'Mayflower,' 1957
May good luck attend the Mayflower on her long voyage to America! Unlike her namesake, she has the advantage of many modern scientific discoveries to make her journey safer and more comfortable. And — another sign that this is the 20th century — she has many well-known Heinz varieties on board.
Crossing oceans is no new experience for Heinz, for distance does not matter when it's a question of securing the very best ingredients for the 57 varieties. When you buy Heinz, you know you're buying the best. That familiar Heinz label is in itself an assurance of unfailing goodness and quality wherever you see it.
HEINZ 57

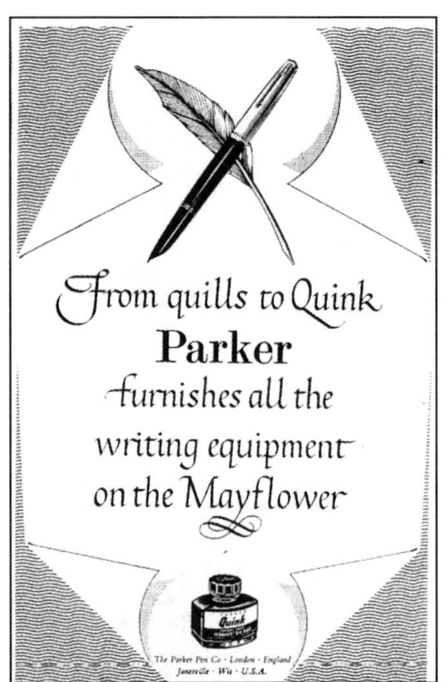

From quills to Quink
Parker
furnishes all the
writing equipment
on the Mayflower
Quink
The Parker Pen Co · London · England
Janesville · Wis · U.S.A.

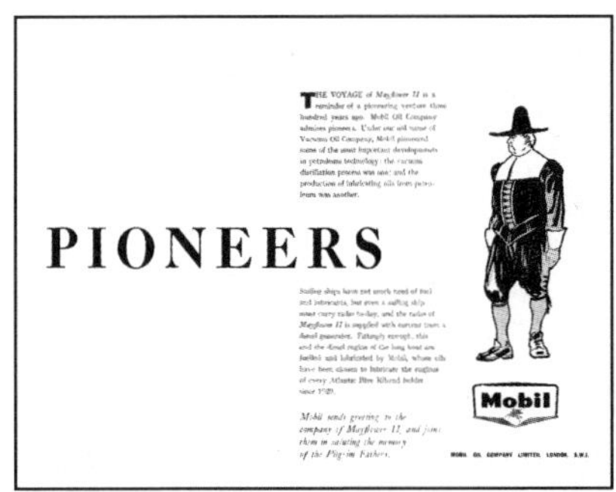

Desert boots on stormy ocean
"Bon voyage, Mayflower!"
Clarks OF ENGLAND

Advertisements for soup, oil, shoes, pens and dozens of other British products appeared in *Mayflower Mail*. Often the ads were free, a reward for supplying material to build the ship or provisions for the voyage.

DIRTY COMMERCIALISM

SHIP'S SOUVENIR PAPER

Mayflower Mail

SHIP'S SOUVENIR PAPER

JANUARY 1956. JOURNAL OF THE MAYFLOWER PROJECT ONE SHILLING

THE MEANING OF MAYFLOWER

Throughout the world, Mayflower's rebuilding makes headline news. From London and New York, from Hong Kong and Rio de Janeiro, imaginations have been fired by this gesture. Only a short time ago it was merely an idea, to create a living symbol of Anglo-American unity.

Today, the old Devon shipyard rings with the toil of craftsmen on the rapidly growing hull. British commerce and industry have already provided a great part of the materials and equipment for the vessel and her complement.

Harbours and cities of these islands, through their civic authorities under the Presidency of the Lord Mayor of London, are helping in the task.

The historic site in America's Plymouth, where the Pilgrim Fathers landed to found a nation, has already been given for the berthing of Mayflower after her voyage.

What is the secret of such progress? How did this goodwill offering of a few people so rapidly grow to one of the century's most striking international gestures?

The sailing of Mayflower recalls one of the heroic journeys of history, when another small group, in search of freedom to worship and to order their own lives, faced perils beyond our imagining.

Their courage was crowned with ultimate triumph, and the ship that shared their enterprise has become the symbol of a common blood and common heritage.

This Project is a striking complement to the work of explaining the vital significance of Anglo-American unity in the structure of the free world.

By its intrinsic interest, it is already bringing this lesson to the minds of many who would otherwise have been untouched by precept or exhortation. It is a deed to vivify words.

The surplus revenues of the Project are to be devoted to maintaining Mayflower in perpetuity as part of America's Pilgrim shrine, and to establishing a Trust Fund for Anglo-American exchange scholarships.

The ship will thus be a lasting monument, served by living emissaries in the task of commemorating the shared heritage of the English-speaking peoples.

She crystallises the vicissitudes of international affairs in a little vessel and her handful of crew. She is adventurous in an age of security and the humble affirmation of human endeavour amidst a world of mechanical marvels.

"Thus out of small beginnings greater things have been produced by His hand that made all things of nothing, and gives being to all things that are: and as one small candle may light a thousand; so the light here kindled hath shone unto many. . . ."

Drawing by Emmwood

LITTLE SHIP WILL SAIL THIS YEAR

PROJECT EXCITES WORLD INTEREST

Mayflower, the replica of the ship in which the Pilgrim Fathers sailed to America in 1620, will be under sail in the summer of this year. This was confirmed by the "Mayflower Mail" reporter who visited Upham's shipyard, Brixham, Devon, this week.

Progress on building since the keel was laid five months ago has surpassed the expectations of Mr. W. A. Baker, the naval architect, who stated on a recent visit to the shipyard: "I am very happy indeed at the way the ship is taking shape and at the speed of work. Your Devon shipwrights are proving they not only know the job, but how to get on with it."

Mr. Stuart Upham, the shipbuilder, said: "The working designs which we are using are superb. We are constantly reminded of this as we progress from drawings, to the lines on the mould-loft floor, to the pattern shapes, to the cutting of the timber and the final assembly in the shipyard. The precision of Mr. Baker's drawings gives us confidence that the present rate of building will be maintained."

The complex work on the rigging has been carried out in its entirety by Upham's shipyard. This was done in the first place on a five-foot scale sailing model which is being featured at the National Boat Show.

The exact date of Mayflower's departure for the United States will be announced after she has completed her trials in Torbay Harbour.

A SYMBOL OF FREEDOM

The building of the replica of Mayflower is exciting worldwide interest. Television, radio and newsreels are recording her progress. There is to be a book of the voyage and a film of the voyage. Newspapers as far afield as China, South America, Portugal, Australia, Chili and, of course, America, are all carrying progress reports on the ship.

Manned by a crew of 21, the same number as on the first Mayflower, who will be selected from volunteers, and carrying 30 passengers, some of whom will be direct descendants of the original voyagers, Mayflower II will set sail from London in 1956.

In the first light of a bleak December dawn 335 years ago, the Pilgrim Fathers gazed at the blurred horizon and wondered how the New World would receive them.

There will be no such doubt in the minds of the 1956 "pilgrims." America awaits with anticipation the coming of the vessel whose historic name has echoed down the ages, as much a symbol of freedom as the Statue of Liberty.

"A FINE STICK"

Extensive research has been necessary to re-create the famous vessel.

"One big problem," said Mr. Stuart Upham, a member of the Brixham firm where Mayflower II is steadily taking shape, "was timber. We have had a great difficulty in finding the oak, the pine and other timber necessary to meet specifications for the hazardous Atlantic crossing." More than half the timber required is now in the shipyard. Foreman George Phillips, with the pride of a master craftsman, describes the keel as "a fine stick."

Emmwood, one of Britain's most famous cartoonists, gave Warwick this illustration for a souvenir edition of *Mayflower Mail.* It depicts three famous Englishmen - Sir Walter Raleigh, Admiral Lord Nelson and Sir Winston Churchill waving *Mayflower II* away towards the Statue of Liberty on the other side of the Atlantic Ocean.

As 1956 dawned, the Project *Mayflower* bank account was virtually bare and the four public relations clients of Warwick and John were feeling increasingly forgotten. They were certainly not inclined to continue paying fees to their inattentive public relations men who were working feverishly to produce a new newspaper called *Mayflower Mail.*

A printer was persuaded to accept delayed payment, and 25,000 copies were produced for a major boat show sponsored by the *Daily Mail* at London's Olympia exhibition hall.

"Little Ship Will Sail This Year" the front page headline announced confidently. *"Project Excites World Interest."* Half the front page contained a cartoon, produced free of charge, by Emmwood, a friend who worked on the *Daily Mail.* The cartoon depicted Sir Francis Drake, Admiral Nelson and Sir Winston Churchill all waving the *Mayflower II* good luck as she began her voyage to America.

Warwick spent precious pounds on an exhibition booth at the Daily Mail boat show. A model of *Mayflower* was displayed and the Coleman Street office staff dressed up in Pilgrim costumes and handed out copies of *Mayflower Mail.* If interest flagged, Warwick rushed up to the main announcement booth and asked the announcer to request someone - John Smith, John Doe - he made up a name - to go to the *Mayflower* booth on Aisle 20, Number 237 for an urgent message.

In that first edition of *Mayflower Mail,* Warwick repaid any business that offered so much as a nail with generous mentions and inexpensive advertising space. They included the food giant Heinz, the massive construction company Taylor Woodrow, International Paints, Plymouth Gin and Maxwell House Coffee. Between them these big name companies had actually committed less than £2,000 in cash so far, but their names and their advertisements re-enforced the ultra confident tone of the editorial.

Soon after the boat show, a tall burly American with a gentle manner and an English sounding name, walked into Warwick's Coleman Street office and with typical American forthrightness asked how he could help. John Sloan Smith had picked up the publicity that Warwick was generating across America, and had immediately fallen in love with the idea. He contacted the American Embassy in London to confirm that the newspaper reports of this plan to re-build the *Mayflower* were for real, then boarded a plane for London to see for himself.

Mr. Sloan Smith was president of the *Aero Mayflower Transit Company* of Indianapolis, Indiana, a nationwide network of franchises that moved both commercial and domestic products all over America.

John Sloan Smith

Mayflower Transit Company CEO, John Sloan Smith, was so impressed with Warwick's oratory that he sent him out to speak to the same audience twice on the same day.

Not surprisingly, Warwick and John hit it off right away and the following day they took the train down to Brixham to visit Upham's yard. There was still virtually nothing to see - just this big stick laid out on the floor, but after several hours in each other's company, discussing the history of America and the history of shipbuilding, John Sloan Smith was even more anxious to get an answer to his first question: How could he help? It was surprisingly difficult for Warwick to answer. He desperately wanted to raise the funds from British sources without a penny of American support. To take American money would be to dilute the intended message of the second *Mayflower* sailing.

Mayflower Transit trucks took the Treasure Chests that arrived on the *Mayflower II* to be exhibited across America. One chest contained a gift of animal feed destined for President Eisenhower's Virginia ranch.

A cash contribution was out of the question at this point but Warwick figured that there was nothing to stop the trucking company becoming involved once the ship had arrived in America.

Both men agreed that the *Mayflower* Transit company would deliver the Treasure Chests of British goods to the various stores across America, where exhibitions were planned. Sloan Smith said they would find other ways to help. He would keep in touch with the progress of construction and come over again himself or send his people.

Warwick was elated to have found someone with such enthusiasm and he contacted Henry Hornblower to let him know of the important new supporter that had appeared at the office. Hornblower was not overjoyed. It smacked of dirty commercialism to him. He wasn't sure how this mid-western trucking company could do much good for *Plimoth Plantation* and the *Mayflower II.*

Warwick found Hornblower's reaction hard to understand. Here was an American displaying the reserve and commercial caution for which the English were normally criticized. It didn't make sense to him.

PENNILESS PUBLICIST

Commodore Grattidge, OBE, the former Captain of the world's largest ocean-going liner, the Queen Elizabeth, was used to commanding any ship with which he was associated. The *Mayflower* was no exception. Unlike some of the other patrons, Captain Grattidge was not content merely to allow his name to decorate Warwick's letter paper. He saw the growing interest in the project and he pushed hard for the patrons, like himself, to have overall control of the project.

Brixham craftsman work inside *Mayflower II*. Meanwhile Warwick's patrons are more interested in examining the financial records of Project *Mayflower*.

Grattidge needed more information to advance his case and in early 1956 he contacted Warwick's auditors, Price Waterhouse, for a full report on Project *Mayflower* Ltd. It made sorry reading.

Warwick had set up Project *Mayflower* Ltd. in April 1955 but he had been so unconcerned with company formalities that almost a year later he had still not bothered to issue any shares. There was all of £3 in the company bank account on January 20th, 1956, hardly enough to buy lunch for one person in the Wig and Pen Club. The accounts revealed that Warwick and John Lowe had raised a mere £5,967 to date which had been used to meet *Mayflower* expenses but they had already accumulated an additional £10,423 of unpaid bills. The company appeared to be insolvent.

In spite of a great deal of publicity on both sides of the Atlantic, only £2,358 had been received in donations in addition to Fenston's £500. British Industry had so far committed the paltry sum of £1,380 and the balance of the income to date had come from selling publicity rights and from sales of *Mayflower Mail*. The shipyard bill alone was expected to be £58,750 and other costs could double the figure required.

Although the financial picture could hardly have been worse, the auditors report noted that Warwick had some very creative ideas for a public appeal that would raise the bulk of the money required. Among other things, beautifully bound red leather books were to be distributed to major cities so that each donor, no matter how small, could record their contribution. The books would travel with the ship. In addition, the auditors noted that Warwick appeared to be increasingly successful in persuading businesses to donate materials such as rope and canvas for *Mayflower*'s construction.

Warwick was furious that Price Waterhouse had given Grattidge confidential information on the finances of Project *Mayflower* Ltd. and fired off an angry letter threatening to sue them. They had almost certainly been overcome by the commanding tones of Captain Grattidge's instructions and had no right to release any information without Warwick's approval, but it was too late. His establishment patrons would all now know what a fragile financial ship in which they were sailing.

Warwick didn't know it but on March 6th a full copy of the report arrived on Hornblower's desk in Plymouth, Massachusetts. It had come to them via Fenston's attorney, Sir George Bull, who was working closely with Captain Grattidge, who made sure the Foreign Office was also informed .

Hornblower was shocked. The public relations man who had confidently promised to build the *Mayflower II* and give it to them before the end of the year had an empty company bank account and debts of over £10,000. The relatively wealthy governors of *Plimoth Plantation* had tried and failed to build *Mayflower* for the last nine years. How on earth could these penniless publicists succeed?

Officials at the Foreign Office mulled over their options. If the project were to go ahead they believed the only way forward was for it to be taken over and managed through the appropriate channels, which they deemed to be the offices of the English-Speaking Union, where the Queen was the patron and Winston Churchill, the current Prime Minister, was a vice president, as was the former prime minister Clement Atlee.

Although the British Foreign Office was reluctant to denounce the efforts of Charlton and Lowe publicly, they decided to continue to exert quiet hostility towards the *Mayflower* project.

Officials at the English-Speaking Union were advised to stay clear and the concerns in Whitehall were passed on to the British consul-general in Boston, who in turn informed Plimouth Plantation that the finances of Project Mayflower were shaky and the reputations of its organizers none too savory. Lord Jowitt, a vice president of the Pilgrim Society, was advised not to allow his name to be used in connection with the project.

Lord Jowitt

Warned by the Establishment not to get involved with the Mayflower Project.

The knives are out as the UK government tries to undermine the project.

RIPE PLUMS

A worried Hornblower called Warwick to tell him he had decided to send one of his colleagues, Mr. Herbert Boynton, to check on progress.

Warwick, confident in adversity, put Hornblower firmly in his place with a strangely formal letter written on March 5th 1956 that contrived to be both threatening and conciliatory. Throughout the letter Warwick dropped names like ripe plums designed to satisfy his reader's hunger for reassurance. Good contacts were a vital form of currency to Warwick and he was certainly amassing plenty of them:

"I am waiting to hear from Mr. Boynton, in the meantime I have been spending quite some time down at the shipyard where progress is very good indeed.

"Sir William Rootes phoned the other day and told us he was very impressed with what you are doing at Plymouth. I was pleased at this because there had been some talk this end about Plimoth Plantation not being big enough to tackle the job. This cut no ice whatsoever with us, in fact I do not think it appropriate that large organizations should become barnacles on the side of Mayflower.

"Simplicity is, in my view, the keynote to our activities on both sides of the Atlantic. If the building of this ship to further Anglo-American relations and in memory of the people who sailed on her, is turned into a pompous shindig, and there has been a danger of that, then we would certainly not be true to the memory of the Pilgrim Fathers.

"NBC asked me to do a broadcast the other day after I had spoken at a Plymouth Civic Reception, and I did make this point both in my

speech and at the broadcast, that we wanted to keep this as far as possible free from pomp and ceremony.

"With regard to Mr. Boynton, I am looking forward to meeting him. I do hope he has time to make a visit to the shipyard. The ship is beginning to speak for herself and is truly an impressive sight. With regard to financial support at this end we have decided that there is no need to make a public appeal. I am very glad to be able to report this, because it does show how the idea of Mayflower has caught on. There is never a day that goes past without some gift to Mayflower; the other day the town of Brixham presented a beautiful 17th century bell.

"Lloyds of London also offered us a bell, but I had to tell them that Brixham had made the offer first, so we are accepting a log book from Lloyds. Even the brushes to put on the paint have been presented. At the same time I am getting money at a very satisfactory rate."

The truth, of course, as even Hornblower now knew, was a little different. Industry was very slow in responding with support and Warwick was falling behind on his payments to Stuart Upham, the builder. He was certainly in no position to abandon the idea of a public appeal.

It was in the same letter that Warwick sounded a belief that he was to maintain throughout the project; that the building and sailing of the second *Mayflower* should reflect the simple values and objectives of those that had sailed on the first vessel.

He had already decided he wanted an ordinary person to launch it at the traditional launch ceremony rather than some admiral or member of the Royal family or other establishment figure. These were the people from whom the Pilgrims had been trying to get away.

The captains of the sea and industry, lead by Grattidge, continued to make it clear that they would prefer Warwick and John Lowe to become crew members rather than leaders of the *Mayflower II* project. Drafts of a new constitution which would give the patrons some official legal say went back and forth between attorneys.

They argued that Project *Mayflower* Ltd. was a company wholly owned by Warwick and John. There was no guarantee that this company would be given charitable status which was essential to avoid income tax. It therefore made sense to establish a new legal entity, which would definitely qualify for charitable status.

Warwick or John agreed with the argument for a new constitution but neither had any thoughts of handing over the day-to-day management of the project to a committee of patrons.

At one point the debate over the proposed constitution became mildly farcical. In February 1956, a meeting was held in the absence of both Warwick and John to discuss Project *Mayflower* Ltd. at which the VIPs present included the American Ambassador, a representative of the English Speaking Union, Mr. Boynton representing a governor of *Plimoth Plantation* and a senior Foreign Office official.

The meeting had been quietly arranged by Fenston's attorney, Sir George Bull. Few of those present had the slightest idea what was going on and the American Ambassador subsequently telephoned Warwick to say he had difficulty in understanding the purpose of the meeting.

The patrons were becoming more trouble than they were worth. Warwick was increasingly being told that a public appeal had little chance of success. He needed too much money. The British people and British industry was still more or less on their financial knees. *"Think about what you are asking for"*, a Fleet Street friend advised - *"You want people to cough up for a gift to the richest nation on earth; a nation whose Secretary of State, John Foster Dulles, had described Great Britain as great has-beens."*

Warwick decided to delay the public appeal till the autumn. By then, he reasoned, most of the money might be raised from industry. It might then be relatively easy to get the final cash to finish the job from a public appeal.

However, Captain Grattidge remained determined to take charge and by the end of March 1956 the voices of the patrons were becoming louder and angrier. In April 1956, Lord Rootes, the chairman of the Dollar Export Council tried to smooth over the differences between some of the patrons and Warwick. This was a most important undertaking, he reminded a meeting of the participants. Let's forget past differences and make a new start.

It was agreed that a further meeting would be held at the Hill Street home of Felix Fenston. The meeting's objective would be to try and hammer out a new constitution acceptable to all. Warwick had other agreements on his mind.

Henry Hornblower II, the Chairman of *Plimoth Plantation* was due over in the last week of April. He couldn't have Harry talking to discontented patrons. Who knows, he might get nervous and withhold his support for a while. If he did that, his fundraising ventures might flounder. Meanwhile Stuart Upham's bill was growing. Warwick dashed off an instruction to his attorneys, Messrs. Alle and Overy.

"I am most anxious, with the least possible delay, to have an agreement drawn up between Project Mayflower Ltd. and Plimoth Plantation Inc."

Warwick listed the points to be included which ended with the instruction that *"there should be definite agreement with regard to the terms of the trust fund which . . is to be created for the purpose of handling funds resulting either from surplus income . . in the construction and exhibition of the ship en route to Plymouth or raised by the exhibition of the ship, after it is handed over to Plimoth Plantation.*

Warwick was not budging an inch from his aims and objectives.

WEEKLY PRAYERS

Harry Hornblower II sat at a corner table downstairs under the ancient oak beams that propped up the Wig and Pen club. Hornblower perused the menu. Warwick didn't need to look. He always ordered the same thing - steak and kidney pie. He could not bear to waste time considering food, when there was important business to discuss.

Hornblower was fascinated by the history of the Wig that was summarized on the back of the menu and was still reading it when the restaurant owner, Dick Brennan, stopped at their table to welcome Hornblower aboard. Hornblower, like everyone else, took an immediate liking to Brennan's cockney good humor. *"Try the oxtail soup and roast leg of lamb,"* he advised the American visitor. *"Then you can tell Warwick what it's like. He still doesn't know after all these years."*

Warwick finally got a chance to explain the things he was doing to get *Mayflower II* built. The chain smoking, restless Englishman seemed to have some rather unusual ideas. Not all of Warwick's food went in his mouth as he concentrated on explaining his plans. Warwick was a great admirer of the methods of the Communist party, he announced, and he was employing their propaganda methods in the cause of *Mayflower II*. In Britain, the tiny Communist party drew attention to itself by infiltrating other larger organizations and getting them to spread the word.

Now Warwick was infiltrating dozens of organizations to spread the word about *Mayflower II*. He had made a start last year by persuading the Boys Clubs of Britain and America to run year long competitions to select a British and American boy to represent the youth of each country. The newsletters and staff of the Boys clubs were spreading the word.

Religious organizations were targeted next. Warwick invited churches and other spiritual groups to hold services at Upham's shipyard every weekend. One week the keel would receive a blessing from a Methodist priest, the next a rabbi would bless the project, followed by the Salvation Army with their rousing songs and tambourines, and then the solemn tones of the Church of England.

After the weekly prayers of support, Warwick issued a press release to the appropriate religious newspapers. During one bleak period when a couple of weeks passed without mention of *Mayflower II* in the press, Warwick persuaded a Fleet Street photographer to take a beautiful young woman down to the boat yard. She posed for pin up pictures in front of the wooden skeleton that was to become *Mayflower II*. The pictures were sold to the Mirror Group.

Meanwhile, Warwick asked a local vicar to preach a sermon denouncing the exploitation of *Mayflower II* in such a tawdry way, in return for a contribution to his church.

Although the vicar was initially reluctant to become part of an obvious publicity stunt, Warwick won him over with his knowledge of religious fundraising ethics. He quoted General Booth, the famous leader of the Salvation Army, who accepted some money from doubtful sources. *"It doesn't matter if it's bad money. We will make it good,"* Booth told one of his doubtful followers. The sermon made news, then as Warwick hoped, the media rushed to reprint the pictures that were the cause of so much distress. The vicar received a contribution to a new stained glass window for his trouble.

Warwick was also hard at work spreading the *Mayflower* story throughout the financial and business world. After the Lloyds insurance market donated a ship's log, a lengthy article appeared in the trade journal of the Insurance industry. After some Scottish firms agreed to donate materials the *Mayflower* story appeared north of the border with a Highland twist. Next, the trade press for the food and beverage industry were told the intoxicating and hot news that Plymouth Sloe Gin and Heinz soups would, in their different ways, keep the crew warm during the voyage.

Warwick also told Hornblower that the Queen's Jewelers were being asked to produce *Mayflower II* medallions, and there was a host of other commercial ideas in the works, all of which would generate cash to complete *Mayflower II*. They included *Mayflower* china plates, *Mayflower* ties, *Mayflower* yacht flags, *Mayflower* stamped envelopes and a special *Mayflower* beer. Then of course there were the Treasure Chests which would soon find plenty of customers.

On top of all of this there was *Mayflower Mail,* the paper Warwick had produced for the boat show in January 1956. It had been very well received and he planned three or four more issues. The *Mayflower Mail* had been so full of historical and technical information that it was appealing to school children and sailors, historians and people in commerce. *Mayflower Mail* could generate several thousand pounds, and so, one way or another, the money would be found.

At the end of Warwick's long lunch with Hornblower, Dick Brennan was at the door to say good-bye. *"Has Warwick told you I will be coming to America on board Mayflower II as the cook?"* he asked. Hornblower smiled. First, he had to get some second opinions about the progress of the project. He would have a private meeting with Felix Fenston's attorney, Sir George Bull, and Captain Grattidge to get their views.

Henry Hornblower was unconvinced that publicity alone would help to get the job done. So, too, for different reasons, was Stuart Upham. He complained to Warwick that work was being held up at the yard by an ever increasing stream of visitors who were somehow finding their way to Upham's yard that spring.

"We are spending more time answering questions than getting on with the work," Upham complained. *"You have to do something about it."* Warwick took immediate action but it wasn't at all what Stuart Upham expected.

One of many church services Warwick organized at Upham's Yard as the *Mayflower II* was under construction.

A TAXING MATTER

Warwick applied to the tax authorities for an exemption from an entertainment tax that was imposed by the government of the day on a wide variety of activities where the public was asked to pay an entrance fee. To the amazement of his legal advisers who thought that Project *Mayflower* Ltd would not qualify for relief, the authorities had no concerns about issuing a certificate of tax exemption, and with Upham's agreement turned the yard into a public exhibition.

The first rib of *Mayflower II* is in place. There was not much to see but Warwick found a way to dress up the emerging skeleton of the ship and the public flocked to see the work in progress.

There was still precious little to justify an entrance fee...*"just the ribs of a wooden whale"*, so Warwick commissioned a replica of a Pilgrim hut and blew up a few pictures to help tell the *Mayflower* story. Two staff members, who normally worked in Warwick's London office, were dressed as Pilgrim maids, and for the next several weeks acted as exhibition guides. Boat tours from the nearby holiday town of Torquay brought hundreds of visitors across the bay to Brixham. Sightseers paid 2 shillings each to look at *Mayflower II.*

"It's my boat but it's your yard," Warwick told Stuart Upham. "You can keep all money and put it towards the cost of the boat." Before the end of summer over 250,000 people had contributed over £18,000 to the building costs.

All visitors were asked to sign a book, which they were told would record their visit and their small but important contribution. The book would travel on *Mayflower II.* The names and addresses provided more publicity material. Every day the visitors book was scanned for the unusual, interesting or distant visitor. If a school party came, the local paper from their town was informed. If a mayor, Member of Parliament or other person of note appeared, their local press received a release and a story was sent to America every time an American tourist turned up. The staff were instructed, however, to return all entrance fees to American visitors.

Warwick insisted on this small but symbolic act as a way of explaining that this was to be a British venture. *"The Americans were shocked,"* he said. *"It was the first and probably last time any Americans had money returned to them in Europe."*

Warwick thoroughly enjoyed playing politics with other peoples' lives and most of them were grateful for the interference. Peter Walker, who was to become the longest serving Minister in Prime Minister Margaret Thatcher's cabinet, and later Lord Walker, was to benefit from his association with Warwick, and in return would help *Mayflower II.*

When the two men met, Walker was occupying a desk in the corner of the office next door to Warwick's. The young man,

Mayflower Mail

THE JOURNAL OF ANGLO-AMERICAN RELATIONS

BUILDING EDITION

LAUNCHING IN SEPTEMBER

Warwick celebrates progress in another issue of *Mayflower Mail*. Now he has to worry about insurance.

still in his twenties, was set on a career in politics and was already chairman of the powerful Young Conservatives. To achieve his goal he first had to make his fortune, which he aimed to do in London's class-ridden financial and insurance markets.

He was different from the traditional Tory of those days because he had a working class background, which, Warwick observed, he tried to disguise. *"You must do the opposite"*, he counseled his young Tory friend. *"The party desperately needs to connect with working class people and you can help them do it"*.

To prove his point Warwick planted a story in the London Evening Standard highlighting Peter Walker's humble beginnings. The article hit the mark. The working class politician heard from leading members of the party. *"Good show,"* one top Tory wrote. *"Keep it up old boy. There is room for everyone in our big tent."* Walker also received several donations to his political campaign chest.

Peter Walker repaid the favor by helping Warwick to organize insurance for *Mayflower II.* Among other things he introduced Warwick to a man who was specializing in the American insurance market - George Stewart.

George Stewart really didn't have time to go to Brixham. As he entered the little village on the south Devon coast, he wondered why he had persuaded himself that it was worth a day to drive the 200 tiresome miles from London, down winding roads that were often so narrow, that it was rarely safe either to overtake or drive more than 30 to 40 miles an hour.

Back in London and over in New York, he had 14 companies to look after. As an insurance broker and underwriter at Lloyds he was an expert on insurance, particularly the developing American market. Lloyds brokers were asked to insure all manner of risks and he was rarely surprised by either the size or the type of cover a client required. He was intrigued, however, by the request he had received through a friend, Peter Walker, to insure the hull of a seventeenth century sailing ship replica, *Mayflower II,* for £80,000. His interest was raised a notch higher when Peter Walker told him that the client insisted that the insurance document was to be produced in the form and wording of the year 1620.

It had taken some research and the underwriters could find only three remaining copies of policies of the period. However, they were able to use them to produce a policy written in the English of the day.

In order to sign the policy manually - as was the way in 1620 but no longer the procedure - the underwriters had to obtain special permission to sign their names in ink. The finished insurance document, written in ink, on parchment and sealed with wax was so attractive that Stewart promptly ordered 5,000 copies to give away to his American insurance clients as souvenirs.

The insurance certificate began *"In the name of God amen be it known unto all men by these presents that Project Mayflower do cause themselves and every one of them to be assured..."* Before issuing the policy, Stewart decided to ignore the demands of his 14 twentieth century companies for a day or two, while he traveled back in time to Upham's yard to inspect the ship that was the subject of this special insurance treatment.

to the assureds the executors administrators and assignes for the true performance of the premises Confessing ourselves fully satisfied contented and paid of and for the consideration due to us for this assurance by these presents at the hands of

Project Mayflower

after the rate of **one per cente** And in testimonye of the truth wee the assurers have hereunto severally subscribed our names and somes of moneye assured geven in the office of assurance in London the first day of June 1956.

£80,000 on Hull, Tackle, Apparel, Sails and/or any other Gear and/or Equipment

£5000 A.B. Stewart £2500 A.L. Marsh

[illegible]

The Insurance Document

The Lloyd's insurance document which covered *Mayflower II* against the hazards of the ocean was signed, at Warwick's request, by all the underwriters together with the amount of risk accepted by each insurer.

He was astonished to find so many others had managed to find their way, off the beaten track, to Brixham. He felt an atmosphere of cathedral reverence in the shipyard and genuine interest among the shipbuilders and visitors in the story of the first settlers to leave for America.

He wrote to a friend in America, *"If a quarter of a million people were going to visit the ship, almost as a shrine, in that small and almost inaccessible village in the West of England, how many people in the United States will want to see her when she has made her historic crossing of the Atlantic?"*

Stewart thought he knew the answer to that question and back in London he contacted Warwick to work out a way to be more involved. As always Warwick needed money. Stewart immediately bought £6,000 worth of souvenir off-cuts from Upham's yard. He would give these away to his insurance clients in New York and across America.

Twentieth century craftsmen wielding seventeenth century tools put the finishing touches to a hull fit for any age.

Within days of his trip to Brixham in 1956, George Stewart was meeting with Paul Bird, Fred Glass and George Sanders in an office in New York's Empire State building. They were planning the exhibition of *Mayflower II* in New York followed by Miami and then Washington DC in the following year. The four men agreed to set up a new company called *Mayflower, Inc.* in which they would all participate.

George Stewart now had 15 companies to look after and his latest corporate venture would demand more of his time than he expected.

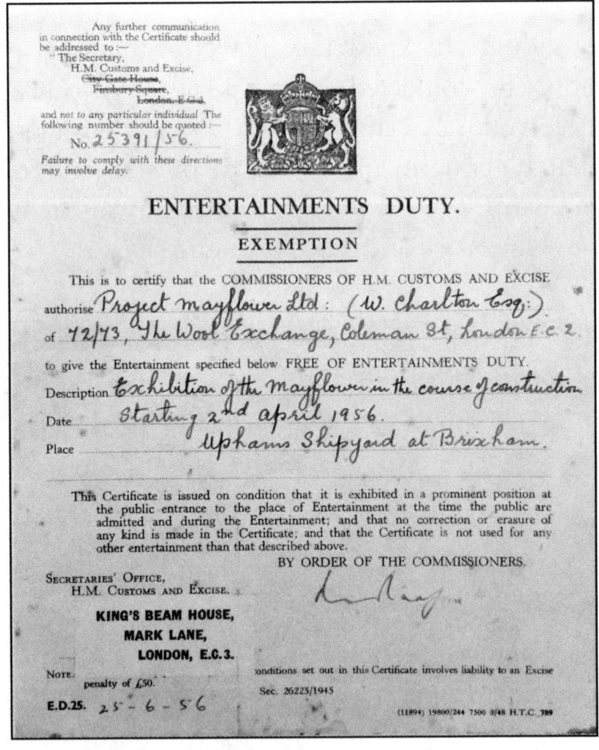

Any further communication in connection with the Certificate should be addressed to :—
" The Secretary,
H.M. Customs and Excise,
~~City Gate House,~~
~~Finsbury Square,~~
~~London, E.C.~~
and *not to any particular individual* The following number should be quoted :—
No. 25391/56.
Failure to comply with these directions may involve delay.

ENTERTAINMENTS DUTY.

EXEMPTION

This is to certify that the COMMISSIONERS OF H.M. CUSTOMS AND EXCISE authorise Project Mayflower Ltd : (W. Charlton Esq.:) of 72/73, The Wool Exchange, Coleman St, London E.C.2. to give the Entertainment specified below FREE OF ENTERTAINMENTS DUTY.

Description Exhibition of the Mayflower in the course of construction
Date starting 2nd April 1956.
Place Uphams Shipyard at Brixham.

This Certificate is issued on condition that it is exhibited in a prominent position at the public entrance to the place of Entertainment at the time the public are admitted and during the Entertainment; and that no correction or erasure of any kind is made in the Certificate; and that the Certificate is not used for any other entertainment than that described above.

BY ORDER OF THE COMMISSIONERS.

SECRETARIES' OFFICE,
H.M. CUSTOMS AND EXCISE,
KING'S BEAM HOUSE,
MARK LANE,
LONDON, E.C.3.

NOTE. ... onditions set out in this Certificate involves liability to an Excise penalty of £50.
Sec. 26225/1945

E.D.25. 25-6-56

(11894) 19800/244 7500 8/48 H.T.C. 789

Warwick invited the public to view construction of the ship, and Customs and Excise agreed to exempt Warwick from entertainments tax - much to the surprise of his legal advisors.

RESIGNATION ACCEPTED

It was a tense meeting on an unusually hot and sticky June day. After months of drafts and re-drafts the patrons had come together to establish a new constitution. Commodore Grattidge stood to address the meeting and he presented the case for the control of the *Mayflower* Project to pass to a new board consisting of some of the distinguished patrons present, as well as others. The English Speaking Union, the British Travel and Holidays Association and an Anglo-American Pilgrim Association were to be invited to nominate a board representative. The establishment would take over.

The organization would be governed by an executive committee of, say, a dozen people who were prepared to attend fairly frequent meetings. Messrs. Lowe and Charlton would be members of the Board but the control, policy and day-to-day administration would no longer be in their hands.

Before Commodore Grattidge sat down he gravely intoned a warning that unless these proposals were agreed he would be obliged to resign as a patron of the *Mayflower* Project. Warwick jumped in before anyone else could speak with his shortest recorded speech. "Resignation accepted", he said simply.

Commodore Grattidge, who had rarely experienced such rapid rejection before, was shocked into silence. Warwick proceeded to talk about plans for the next few months and the meeting soon ended in embarrassment and confusion with nothing resolved except the resignation of the former captain of the world's largest liner.

After the meeting, Lord Fraser, a man Warwick admired as a great naval officer, told Warwick quietly that he too felt he ought to resign. *"I will be available though, if you need any advice"*, he said before leaving.

Some time later, when it seemed likely that the *Mayflower* would sink without trace before sailing out of Brixham Harbor, Warwick would turn anxiously to Lord Fraser for guidance. The advice he gave would involve risking the lives of 33 men and a cat.

STAMP DUTY

Following the chaotic meeting, exasperated officials at the Foreign Office decided to continue their policy of quiet hostility to what they saw as the grubby fund raising efforts of Charlton and Lowe.

The marketing of *Mayflower II* drew fire in the most unexpected place in June 1956. The magazine *Stamp Collecting* ran an editorial which was highly critical of Warwick's plans to issue thousands of special commemorative *Mayflower* envelopes which would be mailed on arrival in the USA.

The idea, designed to raise funds to build *Mayflower* - was to invite stamp collectors to buy an envelope in advance for 7s 6d (which was approximately $1). The mail was to be taken aboard on departure and franked during the voyage. With his usual attention to the details of history Warwick designed an envelope with a picture of *Mayflower II* on the cover in the unusual deep red ink that was in common use in the 1620's.

He obtained the permission of the Postmaster General to send mail from the ship and set out to publicize the unique opportunity for keen philatelists. There would be room for only one ton of mail on board he announced, so this was a very limited opportunity.

Stamp Collecting criticized Warwick for commercializing a venture that was supposed to be a cultural affair. More importantly they accused him of breaking the law. Mail could only be sent from aboard ship by a passenger or member of the crew. The post office did not give permission for thousands of pieces of landlubbers' mail to be loaded on board then dispatched either during or at the end of the voyage.

Warwick's attorneys agreed and counseled caution. The post office might withdraw the right to frank any mail on board if Warwick continued to publicize his scheme.

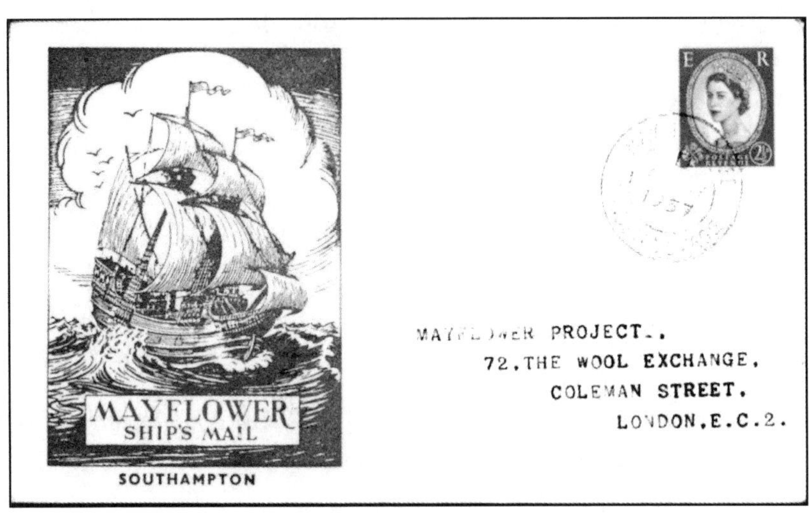

Stamp collectors were enticed to buy stamped letters from *Mayflower II*. They received the bonus of an envelope containing a copy of the *Mayflower Compact* of 1620, a document that Warwick believed was at the heart of the message of the first settlers that established a colony outside the jurisdiction of the King of England.

Warwick decided to ignore *Stamp Collecting* and the attorneys and went ahead as planned. He decided to take over 140,000 pieces of mail on board and make it part of each crew member's duties to frank some mail during the voyage.

The captain would sign each piece of mail to comply with post office regulations. The scheme raised £10,000 and each stamp collecting enthusiast got the promised special envelope which contained a copy of the *Mayflower Compact* of 1620 - and which was signed, in this instance, by captain Alan Villiers.

MAGNETIC PULL

Warwick often felt compelled to be economical with the truth when reporting on the progress of construction. Building was always proceeding "as planned" or " on time". Originally the ship was due to be completed in 1956 but Warwick reported that the sailing had been delayed until 1957 at the specific request of Harry Hornblower II. The truth was somewhat different. The progress of construction was at times excruciatingly slow and consistently behind expectations, for two reasons.

Firstly, Warwick was constantly short of cash and behind on payments to Stuart Upham. At one point he owed Stuart over £5,000 but he always made sure that any funds that came in went to the shipyard as fast as possible.

Secondly, Warwick had insisted from the first that Stuart Upham do things right rather than fast and Upham was the sort of man who didn't need to be told twice about the importance of good craftsmanship. He insisted, for example, on getting exactly the right type of timber and sometimes this would involve days of delay while he was searching the West Country for one particular piece. There were no straight lines in *Mayflower* and Upham was continually seeking out rare timber that was bent in a particular way.

There was also still no written contract between Project *Mayflower*, Ltd. and Upham's yard. Although Upham's partners were pressing for a formal document, the two principals were still working on the basis of their original hand shake over a year earlier. Warwick was confident that financial relief was at hand. By July 1956 he had all the patrons he needed to support a national public appeal. Well-known members of the church, the business world, politics, the navy and the aristocracy had all agreed to allow their names to be used. Of course Grattidge, Lord Fraser and one other had resigned and others were still arguing over the constitution and control of the fundraising organization, but Warwick found it difficult to take their grumbling seriously. *Mayflower II* was still a half-finished hull but *"she was beginning to speak for herself."*

You only had to go down to Brixham and see the visitors wandering through Upham's yard to realize the magnetic pull that *Mayflower II* was exerting on everyone who saw her.

Both English and American visitors to the shipyard where *Mayflower II* was being built, were invited to sign books expressing goodwill that would sail with the ship. Warwick insisted that American visitors received the return of their entrance fees.

Henry Hornblower and **Stuart Upham** discuss progress on the *Mayflower II* as it gradually begins to take shape, but not quickly enough for Hornblower.

Warwick had raised money from the public once before when the circumstances were much more challenging. During the war, without any establishment backing, he persuaded his soldier readers to cough up the amazing total of £8,000 for the Red Cross in one month. He did it by writing letters to himself and publishing them in the paper he was editing.

The letters appeared to be from readers who were moved by the dire financial needs of the Red Cross and each stated they were including a small donation - 10 shillings or a pound. Warwick started a snowstorm of letters to the editor that included real money for the Red Cross. He would do the same for *Mayflower II.*

SUEZ CRISIS

In late October 1956 Warwick intended to start an avalanche of donations that would make his soldier donors seem like misers. Then world politics intervened.

On July 26, 1956 Egypt, the country where Warwick had started his war time publishing career, was back on the front pages of the world's press. The Egyptian President, Gamel Abdul Nasser, announced that he was nationalizing the Suez Canal. The Canal was regarded as a vital international waterway particularly by Britain who had built it in the 19th century to speed up the sea route to Britain's eastern empire.

The British Prime Minister, Sir Anthony Eden, reacted with fury. He had been at the top of British politics for a long time and still believed that British interests should dictate world order. Warwick couldn't see how the Suez crisis could affect his *Mayflower* project and the public appeal he planned to launch in a couple of months time.

In any case his immediate concern was to fly to America to help Henry Hornblower, who was about to launch his appeal for funds for the development of a permanent berth for the *Mayflower* and the construction of the replica of the first village built by the settlers in 1620.

PERSONAL CHEMISTRY

Warwick flew to Plymouth, Massachusetts in early August 1956. He met the town officials of Plymouth and inspected the 100 acre site which Henry Hornblower's grandmother had bequeathed for the construction of a replica of the original Plimoth Settlement. He met Governors of the *Plantation* and assured them that construction of the *Mayflower II* was going well. The Plymouth public were invited to meet Warwick and the local men behind the project. The local papers reported Warwick's approval of the plans for *Mayflower*'s berthing and the development of the nearby site on the Eel River, adjoining the Hornblower estate.

"It is a natural setting for a replica of the original Plimoth Plantation," Warwick said. He went on to make it clear that the ship would be a gift from the people of England. *"It has not been built from the open check book of three or four of our wealthy countrymen but from contributions of more than a quarter of a million people throughout England".*

Warwick was thinking of the people who had paid to look around Upham's yard. Strictly speaking these people had not made donations to *Mayflower*. They had paid a fee to Project *Mayflower* Ltd. for admission to an entertainment - a guided tour of a boat yard that was building an unusual ship and Warwick had given the money to Upham. The money had come from Project *Mayflower* Ltd. which meant Warwick and John Lowe, but Warwick had no intention of splitting hairs. Displaying his trade mark optimism he added. *"We hope to arrive here next Spring with a credit balance."*

Warwick was naturally enthused at the prospect of the *Mayflower II* not only having a berth but also being part of an ambitious living museum. In the excitement of the moment Warwick was told that he would be named a governor of the *Plantation* in honor of his contribution. However, Warwick found Hornblower difficult to get along with; he felt he was anti-Jewish and anti-liberal. Since Warwick was 50 per cent Jewish and 100 per cent liberal there would be clashes with Henry on issues which had nothing to do with *Mayflower II.*

Unfortunately, Warwick often found it impossible to let any casual comment that might be open to misinterpretation, pass. At one point, on a visit to a country club as Hornblower's guest, Warwick railed against the fact that all the members appeared to be white Anglo Saxon Christians. There were no Jews and no Blacks. Did the original settlers intend to build a segregated society? Warwick wondered.

In many ways, Henry Hornblower was opposite in character to Warwick. While Warwick blossomed in the spotlight Hornblower shrunk from the public glare. Hornblower was the chief executive of *Plimoth Plantation* but he was rarely quoted or photographed except on occasions such as public hearings or unavoidable public events. Publicity was as important as food, drink and air to Warwick.

While Warwick was emotional and impulsive, Hornblower was rather cold and careful. It didn't matter if Warwick was talking, speaking or writing about *Mayflower II*; he did so with passion. Hornblower dealt with the detail. It was in his nature. He took meticulous, neatly written notes of telephone conversations and meetings for his files and if he had the slightest doubt about how to act, he consulted his attorney or his colleagues. He liked to plan carefully and be sure of his ground. He was patient and courteous and rarely allowed himself to express his feelings if they might be construed as offensive or merely disagreeable to his listeners.

Henry Hornblower had his father, Ralph, to thank for providing the seed capital to start *Plimoth Plantation,* although Warwick believed that Harry resented his father. Ralph gave him a piece of land near the Plymouth Golf Course. The land was unsuitable for development as a tourist exhibit, so Henry sold it.

Then his grandmother gifted in her will a 100 acre tract near the Eel River that was ideal for *Plimoth Plantation.* Until then the *Plantation* consisted of little more than two small buildings - a replica of a settler's house and the first fort on the harbor front. A replica of *Mayflower,* the Harriet Hornblower legacy, his grandmother's land and the $1 million dollar appeal would allow Hornblower to change all that. However, he was determined that it would be his project and no-one else's. Not even his son, Henry Hornblower III would be allowed to take any part in the *Plimoth Plantation.*

Warwick visited the Hornblower stockbroking business and to Henry's intense irritation was unimpressed. *"It's bookmaking"* said Warwick, unable to keep his opinion to himself. *"Just like the horses only dressed up a bit to look respectable."*

The fact that this was a business set up in the 1890's by an ancestor of Hornblower's, made no impression on Warwick. Nor was he impressed to learn it was one of eight major investment houses in the US. If Warwick had known more about money he would have realised he was dealing with an extremely wealthy family but even so, he was not likely to have moderated his views of the business or the man with whom he was dealing.

Henry Hornblower II was a timorous man, Warwick decided. *"An academic whose real interest is with archeology - digging for signs of Indian life - arrows and so forth."* He got on much better with Henry's father, Ralph *"who was a bit of a naughty boy."* Warwick concluded that Henry had a difficult relationship with his father. The *Mayflower* project was clearly not going to be cemented by the personal chemistry of Warwick Charlton and Henry Hornblower II.

The souvenir edition of Mayflower Mail with a picture of a souvenir medallion top left.

NEW YORK

Warwick knew little about the city of New York except that it was one of the biggest in America. but he thought it might be possible to generate a few thousand dollars by taking the ship down to New York before it was finally berthed at Plymouth. He imagined that thousands would flock to see the ship sail into the harbor and dock alongside the great modern freighters. It was at least worth exploring the possibilities on his way back to England, he told Hornblower. Hornblower declared that he was wasting his time.

Warwick went first to the British Embassy offices in downtown New York. The consular officer he met was not encouraging.

New York mobster, **Frank Costello** helped Warwick obtain a prime dockside berth for *Mayflower II* for *a* New York exhibition.

"My dear chap, the city is full of Jews, Puerto Ricans, Blacks and Irish but there are very few people of English heritage. I can't see much interest here. Boston might be more suitable."

Warwick was disgusted with the official. It was the man's lazy, blasé attitude that he hated, and he determined to prove him wrong even if his analysis had been correct. Warwick went straight back to his newspaper roots and looked up an old friend, Ralph Champion, who was working in the city as the New York correspondent of the London Daily Mirror.

Ralph Champion was researching a story on the waterfront and took Warwick to a hotel room in downtown New York to meet Frank Costello, a man who was supposed to be serving a heavy prison sentence at the time for mob related offenses.

He appeared to be having a day out and was holding court in the crowded room as various people wandered in and out. Frank Costello was amused when Warwick told him what he wanted - an official invitation from the Mayor of New York to bring the *Mayflower II* to the city. He looked at the Englishman in mild disbelief - perhaps at the sight of the bowler hat he was carrying. But he said that Warwick's requests would be met. Warwick thought it strange that Costello could speak on behalf of the mayor but he took his word for it. *"He did not look like a man you could question."*

Costello called over an assistant called Hymie Rosenbloom to deal with Warwick's problems. Warwick took an immediate liking to Hymie whom he later described as a lovely man. *" He was very thick set, almost square and he always pronounced my name War Wick."*

Hymie told Warwick that he would arrange for waterfront 81 to be available to dock the *Mayflower II.* Then he instructed

Warwick to draft the letter that he wanted the mayor to send him.

"Now" Hymie said *"What's the deal?"*

Warwick told Hymie he would bring *Mayflower II* to New York to be on exhibition. In return he wanted 20 per cent clear of the gross. Hymie was happy and gave Warwick $1,000 and two theater tickets to see the hit musical 'My Fair Lady'.

A little later, a hooker arrived at Warwick's hotel, compliments of Mr. Rosenbloom. Warwick was particularly pleased about the cash because at the time his personal funds were so tight that he wasn't sure how he could pay his hotel bill. The letter Warwick had written was duly delivered bearing the signature of the Mayor. Unfortunately Warwick had to send it back.

"I noticed in my excitement that I had misspelled the word 'honour'. I had written it the English way with a u - h o n o u r." That would never do. Anyone who saw the letter might think that it was a forgery. A new letter was sent for the Mayor's signature with the correct American spelling. Now Warwick had to introduce Hymie Rosenbloom to George Stewart, his new found friend in the insurance business, and his partners at the Empire State Building.

Warwick obtained other crucial help in New York from the American Merchandising Association. This organization specialized in importing goods from Britain and had a large number of English clients.

Warwick told the association president about the Treasure Chest scheme and his listener promptly removed a cheque book from his drawer. *"How much for the lot?"* he asked with pen poised. If only it were that simple. Once again Warwick explained that he couldn't allow an American to bail out the British project. There was nothing wrong with a little serious arm twisting however. The following week every British firm that used the American Merchandising Association received a letter urging them to invest £460 in a *Mayflower* Treasure Chest. Within a short period, 16 businesses rediscovered the spirit of early merchant adventurers and bought cargo space on *Mayflower II.*

David Patton, the Executive Director of *Plimoth Plantation* dismissed Warwick as a "crook" when he learned that the *Plantation* would receive only 20 per cent of the revenue from the New York Exhibition. Meanwhile the British Foreign Office was unimpressed with Warwick's efforts to involve British business. They were anxious to present America with a modern image and a close involvement with an historical event like Mayflower ran counter to their beliefs.

However, British business leaders were coming to a different conclusion. They were discovering that it helped to sell their goods abroad by surrounding them with "good olde English" tradition, pomp and circumstance, like the appeal to heritage and sentiment, which Treasure Chests sailing on the *Mayflower II* offered.

PULSATING WALTZ

The hull of *Mayflower II* was launched in a violent thunderstorm. There were almost as many umbrellas as seagulls swirling around in Brixham Harbor as a crowd assembled at Upham's Shipyard at 7:40 am on September 22nd 1956.

Great peals of thunder rolled down from the surrounding hills and flashes of lightning lit up the dark Devon morning. Most of the onlookers were soaked through before the ceremony started and then few of them heard anything. The weather knocked out the public address system and the driving rain made such a noise on the thin corrugated iron roof that only those on board *Mayflower II,* where most of the speeches were made, had any idea what was going on.

It didn't matter. Warwick had invited reporters from the international news agencies, as well as British and American papers and he had a surprise guest for them as they huddled in the rain.

Warwick grabbed the attention of the rain soaked media with the person he chose to launch and name the vessel, a young man called Reis L. Leming whom he had tracked down in Toppenish, Washington, USA.

Reis Leming was a former American airman who was stationed in Britain during 1953 when there was a massive flood in Eastern England. Mr. Leming had earned the gratitude of the British people by risking his life in the raging waters to save the lives of 22 people. He was subsequently awarded the George Medal by the Queen for bravery.

Warwick felt totally vindicated by the choice of Reis Leming, a man whom he had never met and who had no obvious connection with the *Mayflower* Project. *"He and his wife represented the missing decent American young people. They were almost too good to be true; modest, charming and possessed of a quiet dignity. The people in Plymouth (Massachusetts) wanted me to invite one of them or perhaps the state Governor to do the job and the patrons (in England) thought we should invite an admiral or a member of the cabinet but I thought 'what would the pilgrims have wanted if they had been making the choice?' They would have been proud of Mr. and Mrs. Reis Leming."*

Reis Leming, G.M.
silver goblet in hand, launched *Mayflower II* in a thunderstorm. Warwick's choice of this American hero disappointed several members of both the British and American establishment.

The American Ambassador, British dignitaries and politicians and dozens of other celebrities felt the rain dripping down the backs of their necks as the unassuming young ex-airman and his wife named the half-built ship and launched her into the water.

In accordance with the seventeenth century tradition that Warwick had carefully researched, he drank wine from a silver cup which he then hurled into the sea. Eric Watson, a 25 year old shipwright, dived into the sea to retrieve the cup which was presented to Mr. Leming.

Warwick had assembled the usual supporting cast of military and religious organizations to lend low cost dignity to the proceedings. The band of the Somerset Light Infantry provided the music, a male choir, the voices, and the Reverend H. T. Yeomans, the vicar of Brixham, conducted the service which Warwick had carefully prepared.

Warwick chose a rousing hymn to start the soggy event *"O God of Jacob, by whose hand thy people are still fed."* Then he set the stage with a favorite prayer of Sir Francis Drake followed by an American seaman's version of the twenty-third psalm. The message Warwick had brought back from the governor of Massachusetts, Christian A. Herter, was read, *"I am stirred by the spirit of good will that prompted your people to give so generously that will be soon sailing far away. God speed your valiant ship to our shores."*

The nautical romance of the occasion shone through the rain sodden morning. Yard foreman, George Phillips, began to chant. *"one blow, two blow, three blow...."*

Twenty hammers rang out like a sharp tattoo of thunder, driving the wedges that would, by tiny fractions of an inch, ease the full weight of the stout barrel hull onto the cradle on the slipway.

CHRISTIAN A. HERTER
GOVERNOR

THE COMMONWEALTH OF MASSACHUSETTS
EXECUTIVE DEPARTMENT
STATE HOUSE, BOSTON

September 14, 1956

To the Sponsors of the Mayflower Project and the People of Great Britain:

I salute your magnificent effort to recreate a moment in history in which your nation and mine share special pride. In bringing back the Mayflower as it was in 1620, you are reliving an immortal story of heroism in the face of adversity that cannot help but make its imprint on the world.

As Governor of the Commonwealth of Massachusetts, in which the Pilgrims chose to settle, I am particularly pleased by what you have done. We owe a great debt to the Founding Fathers. They gave us the concept of constitutional liberty on which we built the Declaration of Independence and the American Constitution.

I am stirred by the spirit of good will that prompted your people to give so generously to a craft that will soon sail far away. God speed your valiant ship to our shores! We shall take loving care of it and treasure it always as a living monument of friendship between our nations.

Christian A. Herter

Governor Christian Herter and Warwick clearly shared the same view of the contribution made to democracy of the first settlers in Plymouth, Massachusetts.

The shipbuilders sing in unison as they hit the blocks to ease the hull of the *Mayflower II* into the sea.

"One blow, two blow, three blow
Strike her hard, strike her hard
Inch a blow, up she go
One blow, two blow, three blow."

George Phillips chanted and each shipwright, having three wedges to attend to, in unison, struck once and then moved on and sang again, then moved on and then back again. There was a pause at the end of the verse; the men rested. Then they took up the chant again, with Mr. Phillips making up the chanting as he went along.

As the shipwrights trod this strange pulsating anvil waltz beside their ship, a sense of excitement built up. Few present had ever heard or seen anything like it before. The chant ended at last and the men stood back. Two on each side knocked out the great metal pins. One advanced and, with a single blow, knocked out the last remaining wooden chock.

Then, with no check, no pause at all, the hull of *Mayflower II* swept down the slipway gathering speed and launched herself for the first time on the water, bucking her stern like a bronco just once and scattering the little boats as she ran across the harbor, dragging the anchor that had been flung over her bow.

The Somerset Light Infantry played the *"Battle Hymn of the Republic"* and as the *Mayflower II* slowed and stopped and lay poised a little forward, the whole crowd gave three tremendous cheers.

The rain stopped as the unfinished mastless hull of the *Mayflower II* lay in Brixham Harbor for the first time. An important step had been taken but Upham warned Warwick that the costs would escalate as the upper planking was put in place and the cabins were completed.

Warwick couldn't wait to get back to London to put the final touches to the public appeal to raise the funds to finish the ship. The construction was several months behind schedule, in large part because Warwick had insisted on building the ship using the tools and methods of the seventeenth century.

Officials at the British Foreign Office were surprised to receive the report from Herbert Boynton. *"The ship is going to sail,"* he concluded. *"The finances have improved courtesy of British Industry which is stepping up to invest in Treasure Chests to the tune of 1,000 pounds a week. Not only that, but 5,000 visitors a week were paying to see a half completed ship, a display of ship building tools and some period costumes."* Officials in Washington and Boston now argued for a more supportive approach. D'Arcy Edmonson, a Counselor at the British Embassy in Washington, sent a memo back to the government in London stating that *Mayflower II* had become so important to the British government that it was obliged to ensure its safe arrival.

This suggestion was dismissed by Edmonson's superiors in London who countered that the government would then be obliged to take moral responsibility for the success of the project without any effective control.

The British Consul general in Boston took a different approach which his superiors in Washington and London found impossible to question.

"Whatever may be our private reservations about Charlton and Lowe and however much we may deplore the commercial aspect which the project is taking we must face the fact that on arrival, the Mayflower is going to be presented to the American people as a great gesture of British friendship towards the American people and this gesture will have special significance in New England. In these circumstances, it would, I submit, be bad policy for HMG to assume the role of skeleton at the feast." *

* Extract from *"This Somewhat Embarrassing Ship: The British Foreign Office and the Mayflower II"* Article by Ted R. Bromund (New England Quarterly Vol 72 No 1 March 1999.)

WELCOME PREPARATIONS

The leaders of the small New England town decided to arrange a big welcome party. They were anxious to celebrate but there was another consideration; they knew that for a short while the eyes of much of the world would be upon them. Their visitors were not expected for nearly a year but already you could feel the excitement that was building just by taking a walk along Plymouth harbor or down Main street.

Every week there was something new in the Massachusetts press and although it was impossible to monitor all the media reports, it was obvious that the news was spreading throughout America, through much of Europe and beyond, as far as New Zealand and South Africa.

The thirty-three visitors who were expected some time in May or June of 1957 included an architect, a doctor, a cook, a former spy, a film stunt man, several seamen, a journalist and a couple of high school kids. But it wasn't who they were that was capturing the world's imagination; it was the gift they were bringing for the American people and what that gift represented.

First and foremost the practical, conservative people of the coastal town of Plymouth saw that it represented a unique opportunity to revive the failing fortunes of their 336 year old community. Their once prosperous manufacturing town had been in decline for years. Many of the old industries had already closed and now there was little left except a financially strapped rope making factory and, of course, the cranberries which thrived in the bogs that lay on top of the impervious, granite soil.

An Englishman, Ronnie Forth, volunteered to head up the welcoming committee and no one could think of anyone better. Mr. Forth, who had lived in Massachusetts for thirty years, was an energetic man who had always been anxious to give something back to his adopted community and country.

He went to work long before a firm arrival date was fixed. A large committee of influential men and women was assembled and Ronnie Forth pushed them to persuade both the state and town to vote significant amounts of money so that Plymouth could be made ready for the big event. The harbor was dredged, new walkways were added to the seafront to accommodate the crowds and the whole town was given a spring cleaning.

Letters went to Washington to the state senators and representatives and all of them, including Senator John F. Kennedy, wrote back pledging their support. The White House agreed that either President Eisenhower or Vice President Nixon would come to Plymouth to participate in the welcome, and across America, ordinary people, including Native American Indians, accepted invitations to take part in the festivities.

SUEZ CRISIS : WAR INTERVENES

The actions of the British government in late October put an end to any possibility of a public appeal for *Mayflower II.* Those actions also caused so much damage to Anglo-American relations that for a few weeks, the very idea of the *Mayflower* goodwill gesture appeared ludicrous.

In early October, Egypt's President Gamal Abdel Nasser precipitated an international crisis when he nationalized the Suez Canal. The canal ran through Egyptian territory but had been built by the British and was viewed by both British and French as an international waterway that was vital to international shipping and trade.

On October 29, 1956 without informing their allies - the United States - the Israelis launched an attack on Egypt designed to re-take the Suez Canal. Immediately, the British and French governments called on both sides to stop fighting but in the same communiqué announced that they would be sending in a joint military force no matter what happened.

The world immediately saw through the diplomatic posturing for the conspiracy that it was between Britain, France and Israel. The situation was not improved by the fact that lawyers had advised the British prime minister that Nasser was not acting illegally, provided that he kept to his promise to keep the canal open and allow international shipping continued access.

President Eisenhower, who was facing re-election in less than a week, was furious. He was placed in an impossible position by his British friends. The Russians were cracking down in Hungary at the time and he was denouncing their imperialism. Now, how could he defend the Imperialism of the British,

French and the Israelis? Even worse, Eisenhower's foreign secretary, John Foster Dulles, had been carrying out delicate negotiations with Egypt, which would now be in ruins. Dulles had been resisting Egyptian requests for US funds to build the Aswan Dam but was trying to avoid pushing Egypt into the arms of Russia.

Warwick thought the Suez crisis could develop into another World War and, if that happened, of course his project would be wrecked. The apparently grandfatherly US president made it clear to the British Prime Minister, Anthony Eden, that the world's new super power would not permit such international lawlessness. The British people saw a different picture. Their sons were fighting and perhaps dying in the desert and all the God-damn Yankee president could do from his pompous electioneering pulpit was tell them to go home.

Anglo-American relations were, perhaps, at the lowest point in the 20th century and the American emissaries to London became aware that they were dealing with a once experienced and reliable prime minister who was now behaving irrationally and was perhaps weak and unwell.

Sir Anthony Eden's short fuse had been demonstrated when he asked a military aide to draw up the then secret invasion plans. The aide produced four different plans, all of which were rejected. Eden demanded a fifth plan so the aide re-presented the first. Eden accepted it then threw an ink well at his military servant. The officer responded by plunking an upturned wastebasket over the head of Her Majesty's Prime Minister.

Uncertain of Eden's reactions Eisenhower ordered the US Sixth Fleet to shadow the British navy, as if they were an enemy force.

Amazingly the crisis did not keep *Mayflower II* out of the news. The famous Daily Mirror cartoonist, Vicky, summed up the situation with a cartoon of the *Mayflower II.*

This cartoon by Vicky, one of the most popular English political cartoonists of the day, appeared in the UK and was reprinted around the world, as far away as Australia. It depicted the British Prime Minister using *Mayflower II* to help repair relations with the US.

Eisenhower prevailed. The British, French and Israeli forces quickly withdrew and the crisis passed but the *Mayflower* project had been damaged. There was no possibility of a public appeal. Almost worse, firms who had promised financial support suddenly discovered reasons for withdrawing.

Warwick decided he could do little but wait out the political storm and hope that, as people calmed down, they would now see that the need to repair Anglo-American relations was even greater than before. He took refuge in the Wig and Pen Club to wait for inspiration. It came over dessert and coffee.

Warwick could not take his eyes off Fiona McCrae-Taylor. She was sitting at a neighbouring table with some people in the movie industry discussing plans to publicize a film. She was gorgeous but there was something more about her than her good looks that attracted Warwick. *"She was elegant. She had this wonderful look of hauteur."* Warwick sent a message to her table to say that he wanted to meet her, when she had finished with the men in suits.

She told Warwick about her work as a publicist for American films released in England. Warwick had other very pressing plans for her.

He could not imagine being able to resist any request from this impressive young woman. He felt fairly certain that she had a similar effect on other men and he asked her to help him soften the resistance of the captains of industry. He told her all about the *Mayflower*, the Treasure Chests and the miserable response from industry. Now that there is no possibility of a public appeal, we must get the backing of industry, he explained.

Fiona MaCrae-Taylor was brilliantly successful at the task Warwick gave her; if a rope supplier or canvas maker vacillated over their decision, the cool Fiona would challenge them with her cut glass aristocratic accent , *"Of course if you don't have the authority to write a cheque, I will understand."* Warwick recalled in awe *"They would almost break their pens in their hurry to impress the cool young beauty with their cheque signing power."*

Warwick rang Henry Hornblower after the Suez crisis broke and his meeting with Fiona McCrae-Taylor to assure him that he was pressing on with the construction of the ship. Warwick told Hornblower not to accept reports of violent British criticism of the American government as representing the mass of public opinion in Britain. Hornblower was embarrassed. *"We are naturally worried,"* said Henry. *"But please don't think there is a bad feeling for England here."*

Warwick had previously arranged for Alan Villiers to fly to America to help the *Plantation* directors, with their one million dollar fund raising campaign. He saw no reason to change these plans and, ever the optimist, he saw the possibility of stealing some headlines from Nasser and Eden.

Alan Villiers flew over as planned and during the week he was there, never a day went by without stories of the *Mayflower* project, the *Plantation's* plans, and the basic aims of Anglo-American friendship being given prominence through the press, radio and television. Alan Villiers returned tired but triumphant, proudly carrying the front page of the Boston Globe, which gave more space to *Mayflower II* than the Suez Crisis.

DELAYED DELIVERY

Towards the end of November 1956, Stuart Upham was forced to admit that the *Mayflower* would not be finished for several more months. Bad weather and a shortage of skilled hands were adding to his difficulties. The delivery date that had been set for December 31, 1956 was out of the question.

This threw Project *Mayflower* into financial confusion once more. John Lowe had negotiated with the Port of London Authority to exhibit the *Mayflower II* at St. Katherine's Dock, next to the Tower of London, a prime tourist site. Detailed plans had been produced for the exhibition in early 1957 including a reconstruction of seventeenth century London, adjacent to the berthing place. Advertising space had been provisionally booked and Warwick had circulated all the patrons and other supporters with details of the plans.

"Never mind, dear boy", John Lowe counseled. *"We can still go ahead; it just means the sailing will have to be delayed maybe for a year while we exhibit the Mayflower at Southampton and London. It will all work out for the best,"* said John. *"We can still sail off for the States with a clean slate."*

Warwick was being tugged in a different direction by Ronald Forth, the Englishman who had been appointed chairman of a National Reception Committee for the *Mayflower II.* He had $70,000 at his disposal and had gathered together an impressive group of people to help ensure that the ship was greeted by something more enthusiastic than the stony silence that awaited the first settlers in 1620.

Forth wrote to Warwick with details of his plans which included ten days of celebrations. There were to be parades, of course, nightly performances of the Pilgrim Operetta plus an official welcoming ceremony set for noon, Saturday May 25th, 1957.

Warwick was impressed with Ronald Forth's energy but horrified to see a firm date for the arrival, but he recognized that he may have been partly responsible for Mr. Forth's over confidence. During his visit to the United States Warwick had told him that he expected to arrive at the end of May and not later than the first week in June.

Warwick learned that the government of Massachusetts had voted nearly $300,000 for the dredging of Plymouth Bay Channel which was to be carried out prior to *Mayflower II*'s arrival. The money was also to be used to construct a cement walk around the lone reconstruction of an original Pilgrim House adjacent to Plymouth Rock; and a fence was to be built for the crowd's safety.

Forth had persuaded Plymouth council to allocate $25,000 to the event, on top of the state funds and he told Warwick he was planning to erect a temporary stand to accommodate several thousand people.

Warwick, normally optimistic to a fault, felt driven to use the cautious phrases of a civil servant as he began to write his reply to Forth;

"We realize, if only from our own experience, how important it is that you should have as much notice as possible of our arrival. However, we would point out that setting the precise moment of landfall for a seventeenth century sailing ship without auxiliaries, after a 3,000 mile journey, can only be done within certain brackets, and to go further than this would merely run the risk of unconsciously misleading your organization."

No doubt tiring of his own vacillation Warwick finally caved in to his irrepressible optimism and concluded, *"We are advised that as far as can be foreseen the week of the 25th of May is the safest to post for the time of arrival."*

Warwick also heard from Paul Bird, the Bostonian President of the group that was organizing the reception and exhibition in New York. Plans in the Big Apple were well advanced for the summer exhibition at Pier 81. The New York Convention of Visitors' Bureau had become involved and *Mayflower II* had been adopted as the central theme for the annual summer festival.

They were expecting over three million visitors during the ship's five month stay in New York before she was formerly handed over to *Plimoth Plantation.* For Warwick there was no debate about delaying the sailing in order to balance the books with an exhibition in England. The *Mayflower II* must sail the minute she was ready. Alternative sources of money had to be found.

The pressure to leave also meant Warwick would have to cancel plans to sail the ship to several south coast cities. Weymouth, Boston, Dartmouth and Southampton offered to give the *Mayflower II* a ceremonial send-off and some had already put in considerable advance planning.

The city of Southampton, in particular, was extremely keen to be involved and two members of Parliament from that city were on the *Mayflower* board of patrons. Warwick could no more disappoint these cities, who wanted to see his ship, than he could turn down the most unsuitable applicant for a crew member's place.

He behaved, he confessed, in a somewhat cowardly fashion and asked Alan Villiers to deliver the news. *"Villiers,"* he recorded *"did so in his usual forthright manner."*

There was, nevertheless, a storm of protest, the patrons from Southampton resigned and of course there was more press coverage.

MUMBO JUMBO

By November 1956 even Warwick's attorneys were advising him to adopt a new constitution for Project *Mayflower* Ltd. Mr. Jennings of the East London firm of Allen and Overy wrote to him expressing his frustration that Warwick had declined to heed his advice.

"Since Lord Fraser and others resigned I have tried to make it clear to you and your fellow-directors that in my view the proper course to adopt would be to vest control of the project in an independent body."

The lawyer agreed that no public appeal for cash had been made but argued that the project was essentially national and public in character and therefore ought to be treated as if the funds were indeed public. Mr. Jennings gave Warwick the emphatic advice to document very carefully any costs that he or John recovered from income.

This was just legal mumbo jumbo to Warwick. *Mayflower II* was now his life. How could he allow his life to be dictated by a group of individuals who didn't understand what a freewheeling, "flying by the seat of the pants" operation he ran? It would be worse than giving a bunch of men the right to decide when you went to the toilet every day.

Warwick's reluctance to broaden *Mayflower*'s control may have also been due to the fact that he really didn't understand what a board of directors did. He had never been a director or a shareholder of a company before, had no interest in corporate law and had no idea what the purpose of a minute book was. Business law simply was not a part of his extensive vocabulary.

He did know that he, John Lowe and their office staff, still had to eat and they had to be able to take money out of their business, as and when there was enough to spare. Now that the *Mayflower* was occupying virtually all their time, the only real income came from *Mayflower* promotions such as *Mayflower Mail*, the sale of *Mayflower* coins, stamps and so on.

Furthermore, the government seemed content to deal with Project *Mayflower* Ltd as it was currently constituted. In April of 1956 Her Majesty's Customs and Excise authorities had granted Project *Mayflower* freedom from entertainment duty. They had granted tax exemption status even though Project *Mayflower*, Ltd. was not a registered charity and there was technically nothing to stop Warwick and John Lowe from keeping any money they made from the public exhibition at Upham's yard.

In 1957 Warwick pulled off an even bigger coup by persuading the tax people to permit Project *Mayflower* Ltd. to give the ship to America for a nominal sum. At the time there was ruthless government control of UK assets. Individuals had to get permission to take more than £10 in cash abroad. It was mildly shocking for the civil servants to be presented with an application from a private company to give away a sterling asset that could not be valued at less than £100,000.

Warwick saw that one of the tax men that was due to adjudicate the case bore the name of Penn. *"Penn"*, Warwick kept repeating quietly as they mulled over the legal brief on the case. *"Penn. That's one of the most important names in the history of America. Did Mr. Penn have any relatives in Pennsylvania?"*, Warwick inquired, then joked. *"Of course if you do, I know you will not allow it to cloud your judgment."* A few days later Warwick received formal approval to give away the substantial sterling asset to a dollar area.

EMPEROR'S ARCHITECT

Andrew Anderson-Bell was sitting in his house in suburban Addis Abbaba, the capital of Ethiopia, drinking tea in the heat of the late afternoon. The Scotsman was gently mulling over his future which he hoped would be as exciting as his immediate past.

He had thoroughly enjoyed his work in Africa for the Emperor of Ethiopia. As the Emperor's personal architect and city planner he had been given enormous freedom to design the development of the city. Now, in late 1956, the exciting creative part of the work was done and he was considering fresh challenges, including a high paying position half way around the world in Peru, on the eastern corner of the South American Continent.

As he sipped the cooling tea, a friend tossed him an English paper he had brought back from a recent trip to London. Anderson-Bell read one of Warwick's stories about *Mayflower II* and between sips of tea, he changed his plans. He had to sail on that ship.

Anderson-Bell made his way across Europe and eventually reached London, without his luggage. He attended his interview in the bizarre well-worn attire that he had traveled in for weeks - a soiled green jacket, faded corduroy trousers that had been made popular by the Eighth Army and brown suede shoes. His long hair was still bleached blond from exposure to the fierce African sun.

Scottie, as Anderson-Bell was known to his nautical friends, had plenty to offer. He had served as an officer in the Merchant Navy and after leaving the navy had continued a life as an avid sailor but could sense that his interview with Villiers was not going well. Eventually Villiers volunteered that he had already assembled his crew. Unless someone dropped out he saw little prospect for taking Anderson-Bell on board. However, Scottie was invited to have a second interview with Warwick and to keep in touch. Later Scottie felt Villiers had been put off by his appearance, *"I think he thought I was gay."*

However, he gave Warwick a very different impression. To him the handsome Scot came across as a serious ladies man. Anderson-Bell joked that he would like to sail to America so that he could find a rich American girl to marry, which appealed to Warwick's love of mischief but honest purpose. A week later Scottie was the last member of a crew of 33 to be appointed.

Villiers had selected the sailors with the exception of certain places that Warwick had allocated for special reasons.

The exceptions included the two boys - one English and one American who had been selected through national competitions organized by the Boys Clubs of the United Kingdom and the USA at Warwick's instigation. Warwick also felt it was important to have at least one direct descendent of those that sailed on the original Mayflower.

Sub-Lieutenant John Winslow, a Royal Navy jet pilot fitted the bill perfectly. He was an experienced sailor and the son of the man who had dedicated the keel. He could trace his ancestry back to four Winslows who were early settlers. One, Edward Winslow, had used his printing press to prop up the cracked main mast on the first voyage. Warwick also needed places for a *Life* magazine photographer and himself, and he had sold a place to a Wig and Pen Club member who was desperate to straighten out his errant son. An equally desperate Warwick who needed funds to pay his staff, had agreed to take the boy on board for £3,000.

Villiers already knew the core of the crew because several had sailed with him around the world on the Joseph Conrad and other tall ships. Villiers was confident they could handle the challenges of the *Mayflower*'s sails and complicated rigging.

Jan Junker

An ex-British spy during World War II, now Third Mate on the *Mayflower II.*

Jan Junker, the third mate, was perhaps the most experienced crew member. He sailed in a square rigged ship every year to deliver supplies from Denmark to Eskimos in Greenland.

Junker was a Danish national hero. He had been a British spy during the war operating behind enemy lines. He was captured by the Germans, tortured and condemned to death. Fortunately, the paperwork confirming his sentence was lost, and his *"play it by the book"* captors delayed the execution while a search was made. The war ended before the missing paperwork was found, so Junker was allowed to live. A grateful king of Denmark appointed Junker a Royal Captain, an honor that meant that he held a lifetime position of paid service under the patronage of the king.

Villiers had finished the crew selection process, when Babs Brennan - the wife of the owner of the Wig and Pen Club approached Warwick in early 1957, during one of his regular visits to the club. She reminded Warwick of his earlier promise to make her husband Dick the ship's cook. *"It will break his heart if he doesn't go"*, she begged. Warwick remembered his earlier commitment to Dick but Alan Villiers had appointed Walter Godfrey , a man with whom he had sailed before, to cook's duties. Babs upped the ante. *"If you don't take Dick, it will kill him."*

Warwick had to tell Alan Villiers they would be sailing with two cooks, with Dick Brennan, the owner of the Wig and Pen Club, in the position of assistant cook. The restaurant and club boss didn't care what he was called; he was on board.

However, no women would sail on the *Mayflower II*. Several young women, some with sailing experience, had applied to become crew members, but in post-war Britain, women were rarely given equal consideration to men.

Warwick defended the absence of women in the crew by hiding behind the fact that he had delegated crew selection to Alan Villiers. However, when pressed, it became clear that his passion for liberal values did not extend to women's rights.

The selection of women might have given the authorities an excuse to delay, or even stop, the ship from sailing, he claimed. To be fair, it was an era where the idea of a woman Prime Minister was absurd, where women were paid signficantly less than men for the same job, and women were encouraged to confine their instincts for adventure to nurturing roles, such as teachers, nurses, secretaries or shop assistants.

ANTIQUE BUSINESS

Hymie Rosenbloom announced his intention to visit London. Warwick was desperate to make a good impression so he arranged for Hymie to get a tour of Buckingham Palace, the London home of the Queen of England. It was, to say the least, highly unusual for a stranger to be accorded such an honor but Warwick knew the Queen's press secretary, Commander Colville quite well.

After the tour, as the two men made their way in a taxi down Pall Mall towards Trafalgar Square, Warwick could sense that Hymie was not over-excited by his brush with royalty and he asked him what was wrong. *"Well War Wick,"* Hymie said, choosing his words carefully and slowly, *"This is the antique business and I don't have much interest in it. What I would really like to know is where a guy can get a little action in this town."*

Warwick ordered a steady stream of escort girls to be sent to Hymie Rosenbloom's room until the day he left town. Hymie would show his gratitude sooner than either man expected.

In March 1957, a nationwide shipbuilding strike threatened to blow the *Mayflower* construction timetable seriously off course. The powerful British Trade Union announced plans for a national strike. Warwick turned once more to his Fleet Street contacts. He knew the News Editor of the Daily Worker, Britain's only Communist journal. The paper had a tiny circulation but a great deal of respect in the British Labour Movement to whom it gave unqualified support.

Warwick's friend on the Daily Worker gave him an introduction to the most important players in the shipbuilding union and he went along to their London headquarters at

Transport House. The leaders were meeting behind closed doors discussing the proposed strike. Warwick marched past the press waiting in the corridor and burst into the room to state his case. He begged the startled union leaders to consider exempting Upham's Brixham yard and therefore *Mayflower II,* from the national strike order. It couldn't be done, he was told.

"Would it help you politically - with your membership, if I got you a request from your American counterparts?", asked Warwick.

Well, perhaps, yes, it might, they conceded. Warwick raced back to his office and got on the phone to his new found friend in New York, Hymie Rosenbloom. Hymie organized a letter from the US International Brotherhood of Seaman, addressed to the British Union. The letter expressed support for the strike but requested a special exception for the *Mayflower* yard *"in view of the special nature of the project and its importance for Anglo-American relations."*

The British union leaders gave Warwick a verbal agreement to exempt *Mayflower* workers from the national strike but the local unions could not believe the news when Warwick called them. It took several more phone calls between the various local unions and union headquarters, before everyone agreed to abide by the unique union ruling.

The following Monday there was a deathly silence in every shipyard in Britain except one, where the workers kept chipping away at oak beams with their seventeenth century adzes and other tools. Eventually the strike was broadened to affect 2,500,000 men. The effect was dramatic as the eyes of the nation were focused on the tiny shipyard in Brixham that the hard nosed union leaders had allowed to stay open.

Warwick issued a statement to the press:

The decision of the Confederation of Shipbuilding and Engineering Unions to withdraw strike notices at the Mayflower yard is a magnificent gesture. When Mayflower sails she will not only represent the finest of British craftsmanship, but also carry the goodwill from the shipyard workers of this country to the shipyard workers in the United States.

Mayflower was once more on the front page of every newspaper in the country.

PIG IRON

Finally, in April, Stuart Upham was ready to put the completed *Mayflower II* in the water for first time. The tall, narrow, four-storied vessel glided down the slipway, rolled unsteadily and looked as if she would sink straight to the bottom of Brixham harbor. The crowds scattered from the harbor front, in fear for their lives as the ship listed over to 45 degrees. Captain Alan Villiers, who was on board with his two sons, yelled to his boys to climb the rigging if the ship went over. Professional seamen held their breath, along with the big crowd of onlookers, as *Mayflower II* hung over to one side for what seemed like an eternity. Slowly the ship steadied and returned to an upright position.

A Perilous Launch

Everyone at the launch looks on in concern as the freshly launched ship scurries across Brixham harbor and lists over dangerously at 30 degrees. This event would lead to the establishment of the "50:50 Club".

Stuart Upham, the builder, diagnosed the problem. The completed vessel was very top heavy; he ordered extra ballast immediately. However, the press were already dictating their stories and questioning whether *Mayflower II* was seaworthy.

The influential sailing correspondent of the Daily Mail gave *Mayflower II* no better than a 50:50 chance of making it across the Atlantic. Others quoted sailing experts who said they would not risk their lives by sailing out of Brixham harbor in *Mayflower II.*

One of Warwick's early backers, Admiral Lord Fraser was at Warwick's side. Although he had resigned as a patron of the project he remained good friends with Warwick. Fraser calmly dispensed some very practical advice. Of course *Mayflower II* has some design faults, he said. All ships of the time had. Make sure Upham loads her up with plenty of extra pig iron as ballast. That will lower the center of gravity and make the ship more stable.

Admiral Lord Fraser of North Cape

The much respected Lord Fraser advised Warwick to sail as soon as possible.

Why did he suggest cutting short seaworthy trials?

"The other thing is, if I were you, I would keep the sea trials as short as possible." Warwick said nothing while he considered the implications of the great sailor's advice. The public would get very concerned if they thought that *Mayflower II* might not make it. The government safety people might feel obliged to step in and stop the sailing, until design changes were made,

for which there was no money. Warwick was also concerned about his captain's reaction.

Alan Villiers was expecting at least three weeks of sea trials and was certain he would discover some 'kinks' that needed adjusting. Villiers was responsible for the lives of the men on board and it would not be surprising if he insisted on a proper safety check of the ship's seaworthiness. Warwick went to see Villiers, prepared, if necessary, to accept his resignation and appoint Jan Junker captain.

To Warwick's relief, Villiers was also convinced they should sail without delay. He too was worried that safety conscious officials might feel pressured to order endless checks and delays. "*Thirty tons of ballast should do the trick*", he told Warwick. "*These ships were built to sail laden with cargo. Every crew member should have the opportunity to withdraw*". None even considered doing so. One of their number, Dr John Stevens, replied to the prophets of doom by forming a 50:50 club - *"For sailors who risk their lives on Mayflower II."*

In America, some observers in Virginia wondered if the frightening pictures of *Mayflower II* were a plot designed to steal the thunder of the celebration of the 350th anniversary of the founding of Jamestown. The Baltimore Sun declared the incident a *'discourtesy to Jamestown. Why does Mayflower II take to the water and steal the show by threatening to capsize at almost the very moment that Virginians are opening their celebration?"*

Within a few days *Mayflower II* set off for a journey of several thousand miles across the Atlantic Ocean after only 3 hours of sea trials, mostly spent pottering about in Brixham Harbor. Warwick comforted himself with the thought that the ship was insured for £80,000.

REAL BEAUTY

One observer, who saw *Mayflower II* at anchor in Brixham Harbor, remarked that she was not just unstable but disappointingly small *"like one of the tiny fishing boats in Brixham harbor."* Another said she looked like a little lifeboat crowned with a wooden stockade. That criticism was never voiced again. Her small size became a major part of her attraction and most agreed with Stuart Upham who kept repeating, *"She's a real beauty. She's a real beauty."*

People stared in wonder and marveled that the original settlers had crossed the Atlantic in such a small, strange ship. The main hull of *Mayflower II* measured 90 ft long and was 25 ft across the widest point of the beam. For a small ship she was surprisingly tall - 40 ft from the keel to the top of the taffrail. The ship drew 13 ft of water and had a tonnage of 183 tons, by the measurement rules of 1582. Modern experts calculated that she displaced 238 tons of water.

Warwick believed that although it was interesting to describe her measurements, in the end it was as informative as measuring the width of the smile on the Mona Lisa or the height of the Statue of Liberty. It was the way she made an observer feel that counted. Almost everyone who saw her felt she was authentic.

Others, including the man who was to captain her, felt she was alive in a way that no iron ship every could be. The materials that were used to construct her had a lot to do with that. One mile of flax had been used to make her wings, the sails that were the ship's only means of power. The workmen who fashioned the deceptively light sheets to catch the wind,

Mayflower Mail

1957 (No. 4) THE JOURNAL OF ANGLO-AMERICAN RELATIONS 25 CENTS

SAILING EDITION

HERE SHE IS!

As soon as *Mayflower II* emerged from dry dock Warwick had this picture on the front page of another edition of Mayflower Mail.

referred to the raw flax as soft and billowy like the tresses of a woman's hair. Even the rope makers talked about *Mayflower II* cordage in romantic terms. The finest high grade Italian hemp was imported by the Scottish firm Gourock Ropework.

William Baker, the ship's architect, made all his research available to the rope firm and the management talked to retired workers, some of whom had made ropes for wooden ships.

Mayflower II was covered in ropes, over 400 of them measuring nine miles in total and made to different specifications for the different jobs they were required to do. Some had plenty of give or stretch in them and were 'alive', while others had none and were described as dead. The circumferences varied and some ropes had to be woven thick at one end and thin at the other.

No tree in England grew tall enough to supply wood for the masts and Oregon Pine from Canada was found. The tallest was 80 ft. The rest of the wine glass shaped hull and structure was English oak.

The main beam was cut from a massive English Oak which had arrived at Upham's yard measuring 116 cubic feet. After it had been cut to the required shape, it was less than half that volume. There were similar levels of wastage with the smaller beams because it was not easy to find crooked oaks that were curved exactly as they needed to be.

The finished hull looked too tall, like a four story apartment on water, which is what *Mayflower II* was. The basement was the main hold, where the general cargo was stored. The next level up comprised the tiller room at the rear and *"tween decks."* During the voyage of 1620 most of the 102 passengers would have lived crammed together *"tween decks."* This space probably had only 4 1/2 ft of headroom in the original version. Baker designed *Mayflower II* to have 12 inches greater headroom at this level to take account of the taller height of modern man.

Above *"tween decks"*, at the back of the ship was a third layer of four rooms. The fo'c'sle at the front housed the ordinary seamen and the hearth for cooking. The three at the rear included one for the ship's officers and another, the great cabin, for passengers of importance.

Perched right at the top above the keel on the fourth 'floor' was the captain's cabin.

Captain Villiers and his helmsmen would find a steering wheel to guide the ship. It had been added at the insistence of the Ministry of Transport safety officials. The Ministry had wanted *Mayflower II* fitted with lifeboats but Warwick resisted that requirement on the condition that she carried inflatable life rafts.

In fact the modern *Mayflower* faced one important extra danger - the 20th century Atlantic was now a busy place and there was a real possibility of collision unless the ship were able to make its position known, so the safety officials insisted that a radio be on board. This meant that a small generator was required to provide power - and the generator could also be used to provide a limited amount of electric light.

DESPERATE DEPARTURE

In the week before *Mayflower II* was due to sail, the ship had captured the imaginations of almost everyone who saw her. Lady Astor, the member of parliament for Plymouth was one of the few that felt able to resist the vessel's charms. *"Personally I can't get very excited about the Mayflower"*, she said in a strange tape-recorded message of good luck to the crew, adding by way of explanation. *"I'm a Virginian. I only wish it were taking me back to Virginia."*

Lady Astor was an American born socialite who had become Britain's first woman member of parliament. Warwick had found her annoying on previous occasions. *"During the war she got upset with Monty because he wouldn't shut down all the brothels in allied territory. She was a pain in the neck."*

Lady Astor's muted enthusiasm for the voyage did no harm; it simply gave the press on both sides of the Atlantic another angle for their daily stories about *Mayflower II*. The Times of Gloucester, Mass entered into the spirit of the occasion. *"The Mayflower crewmen, dressed in tunics and stocking caps of 17th century vintage, chuckled at Lady Astor's remarks and quaffed ale like their predecessors..."*

Right up until the moment of departure, both Warwick's partner and his first backer tried to persuade him to delay. John Lowe used the gentle understated tones with which he argued any case. *"It would be so much more comfortable, dear boy, if we exhibited Mayflower in London. She could leave for America next year debt free."* Fenston brought a businessman's perspective and sharper tongue to the proceedings. Upham could be paid but there were other serious last minute costs - £2,000 for extra ballast, £1900 for victualing the ship and £5,000 for the crew's wages and the cost of their repatriation. How were these bills going to be met?

The ***Mayflower II*** under sail.

Warwick felt a desperate urgency to leave. *"If we don't leave now the interest we have generated in America may decline"*, he argued. *"We have promised Hornblower and the people in Plymouth that we would sail in April,"* he told Fenston during a last minute meeting aboard the *Mayflower* to discuss money. *"The plans for a permanent berth depend entirely on our arrival this summer. They are waiting for us. We cannot let them down. We will clear up any debts from future revenues from the American exhibition."*

In the end Warwick probably got his way not so much by the use of hard-headed logic, as by pouring every ounce of emotional energy into willing Felix Fenston to do it his way. If necessary he would have thrown himself to the floor.

EISENHOWER'S AMERICA

The United States that was getting ready to lay out the welcome mat was going through a period of strait-laced family life. The men who had returned home from the war had started families and a baby boom was on. The new postwar families needed better surroundings, which led in time to a housing boom and a movement from the built-up cities towards the fresh air of the clean leafy-green suburbs. It was an age of rediscovered innocence.

A grandfather figure, Dwight D. Eisenhower disguised his intelligence, determination and strength and presided over the country in a reassuringly calm and downbeat manner. In the occasional crisis, Americans turned on the TV, saw Ike's ready grin and knew that everything must be all right. Black and white television was giving way to color which made everything look better.

Ray Kroc had just started a new type of restaurant in Chicago which aimed to offer fast food. It was called Macdonald's. General Motors announced that they had developed air conditioning for cars. Every week, families crowded around their television sets, to watch their favorite series including "I Love Lucy" and "Davey Crockett". Flying saucers were spotted in Kentucky and Americans picked up and dropped one fad after another - hula hoops, 'coon skin caps, drive-in movies, crew cuts and sideburns.

Elvis Presley was considered unfit for family viewing and was shown only from the waist up on his first nationwide TV appearance. Then clean-cut 22 year old Pat Boone arrived on the scene to reassure parents that Rock n' Roll wasn't as dangerous and degrading as some were saying.

There were worries of course. The Korean War ended in 1953 and there was a tense "cold war" with the Soviet Union. Families built bomb shelters in their backyards and cellars in case the country got into a nuclear war with the communists; and there was, as there always is, a measure of poverty and injustice. A young preacher called Martin Luther King Jr. was beginning to address racial injustice with an eloquent inspiring voice, but for most of the country, most of the time, life was good and uncomplicated.

People were ready to celebrate their history and their good fortune. On behalf of everyone in the United States, Ronnie Forth was getting Plymouth ready to rock, for the arrival of the foreign visitors.

Henry Hornblower describes plans for the new replica of the village built by the first settlers in 1620. Warwick (behind Hornblower) and members of Plimoth Plantation Board listen intently as Hornblower explains how the bare land outside Plymouth is to be transformed into a living museum after, the arrival of *Mayflower II*.

STINGING TOAST

Three days before *Mayflower II* was due to set sail, the undercurrent of rivalry that had been simmering between Warwick and Hornblower flared into the open. It came at the end of two weeks in which Warwick had made a desperately hard effort to impress Hornblower who had flown over to witness the start of the journey along with fellow Governors, Bill Brewster, George Olsson and Arthur Pyle.

Warwick set up a two-week-long tour for Hornblower that would have whetted the appetite of a monarch or a millionaire. There were luncheons and dinners at Claridges and other five star restaurants, trips to the theater, shopping at Garrards, the Crown jewelers, tours of some of the great ancestral homes and meetings with the leading politicians of the day, in the House of Commons, Britain's parliament.

Warwick oversaw each item in Hornblower's crowded itinerary and with his sense of history, included a morning playing bowls on Plymouth Hoe, just as Sir Francis Drake, England's most famous sailor of the first Elizabethan age, had done. Warwick assigned his persuasive assistant, Fiona McCrae-Taylor, to chaperone Hornblower.

Hornblower was so impressed with Fiona McCrae-Taylor that he invited her to come over to America to witness the arrival of *Mayflower II*. Warwick was having none of that. *"I decide which of my staff should go to America,"* he told Hornblower. *" Fiona, good though she is, is a recent addition to my staff. There are several more deserving cases."*

Warwick's reprimand carried the faint suspicion of jealousy and petulance. He had a more substantial bone to pick with

Hornblower and it occurred after Hornblower had paid muted public tribute to Warwick at a dinner to celebrate the imminent departure of *Mayflower II.*

Over 300 people crowded into the candle-lit cellars of the wine merchants James Hawker & Co. which were decorated with rhododendrons, roses and spring flowers. Ships lanterns provided a nautical atmosphere while waitresses, in pilgrim costume, served a series of gourmet dishes, including roast duck and orange salad, English trifle and Devon clotted cream, and English and French cheeses. The food was accompanied by a series of fine wines, including one that the Wine merchants who were hosting the event regarded as worthy of the name *Mayflower* wine.

The honored guests included the Mayor of Plymouth and other local VIPs, patrons of Project *Mayflower* Ltd, the crew of the ship as well as Henry Hornblower and his fellow trustees of *Plimoth Plantation.* It should have been a moment of great relief and celebration for Warwick but he sat tensely, barely speaking, at one end of the top table. He was tired and with three days to go, was worried that something could still happen to stop the sailing. Perhaps the Ministry would re-appraise their safety certificates or one of the creditors would step in and slap a lien on the ship.

During the last few days there had been a long list of unexpected costs and Warwick kept insisting on doing things right without regard to the expense. While he was entertaining the directors of *Plimoth Plantation* at Claridges to the finest food money could buy, his landlord turned up at his rented apartment in a fruitless effort to collect the overdue rent.

However, Warwick was tense for another reason. Hornblower had been asked to toast Warwick at the end of the meal, as the founder of Project *Mayflower*. Hornblower voiced his objection to this description. After all, he himself had been working to get *Mayflower* built since 1947 and had provided the plans for construction of the ship. Then there was the issue of who was in charge? Felix Fenston, like Hornblower had the title of president and Fenston might even help in Hornblower's own fundraising, to build a replica of the first settlement back in the US.

At the same time, Hornblower was really upset to learn about the cargo to be loaded onto the ship. Ninety-two Treasure Chests, all bearing examples of British craftmanship to be put on exhibition to promote British trade, seemed like crass commercialism to Hornblower II. What had they got to do with a living museum? To Warwick the support from industry was both vital and something to be celebrated, a way of recognizing and repaying the breadth of support from British industry. Later, Warwick would reflect that these were the early days of corporate sponsorship which would become the norm in a few short years.

In the end, Hornblower went ahead with the toast but his words were chosen with surgical precision praising Mr. Warwick Charlton for *".. activating a dream that had materialized*". Warwick was stung. He was being toasted for his role as a catalyst; he may have been necessary for the ship to be built but he was not an essential part of the process.

When Warwick's turn came to speak, he was in no mood to produce soaring phrases about the need to nurture Anglo-American relations. He made a quick joke that his wife was thinking of divorcing him and citing the ship as the correspondent, then sat down. The following day he wrote a note which was delivered to Hornblower at the hotel where he was staying in Plymouth.

"For the record I have never claimed to have been the only one to have thought of re-building Mayflower, but I can claim, for what it is worth, to be the one who did. Having said that, I might add that I have never sought to make this an occasion for personal publicity, although some has come and will come to me inevitably. There are many others who have helped me and whenever possible they have been recognized publicly."

Warwick drew Hornblower's attention to a special supplement that was produced that week by the Western Morning News to honor *Mayflower II*. Included in the thousands of words about *Mayflower II* was the following front page comment;

"Mr. Charlton is the first to confess that he is not the only person to have this idea - a similar scheme was mooted in Southampton at the time of the Festival of Britain but nothing ever came of it. Somewhat similar ideas have been put forward in America but with the same lack of success. Perhaps a similar fate would have befallen Mr. Charlton's brainchild if he were not a super optimist.." What looked like sugar to Warwick may have felt like salt to the shy American who had tried and failed for ten years, to build *Mayflower* with significantly greater financial resources at his disposal.

In fact, *The Western Morning News*, one of Britain's oldest and most respected regional newspapers, gave Harry Hornblower and his colleagues a little more to digest along with the large full English breakfasts of fried eggs, bacon, sausage, beans, potatoes and fried bread offered in their local Plymouth hotel.

The paper set out the aims and objectives of the two partners in the second *Mayflower*. The News reminded its readers of the importance of the first voyage of the *Mayflower* which resulted in the signing of the *Mayflower* Compact, in which, among other things, the original pilgrims undertook to *"enact just and equal laws and ordinances."*

There would be a re-enactment of this major step towards building democratic societies, when *Mayflower II* arrived off Cape Cod. Indeed, the paper reported that *"Like her great predecessor the new Mayflower plans also for a more enduring monument, for from her voyage will be formed a trust which will establish scholarships for study and student visits to forge more firmly the links of a common heritage."*

Revenue for the scholarships would accrue from exhibiting the ship, as well as films and books. The news reported that *"It is emphasized that the establishment of a trust for educational purposes is the primary purpose of the scheme."*

The Western Morning News

Saturday, Complimentary Mayflower Supplement April 13, 1957.

Mayflower II.–a ship which symbolises goodwill between two great peoples of the world

THE new Mayflower is a symbol of the common inheritance of two great nations. Where her predecessor four hundred years ago carried pilgrims to worship and settle in an almost unknown land the Mayflower of 1957 perpetuates their descendants' fundamental goodwill to each other.

In her building and voyage has been caught the romance and daring of the original pilgrims but like her great predecessor the new Mayflower plans also for a more enduring monument, for from her voyage will be formed a Trust which will establish scholarships for study and students' visits between the two countries to forge more firmly the links of a common inheritance.

To carry this out a non-profit-making company, called Mayflower Project, has been formed in Great Britain and is working with Plimoth Plantation Inc. in America. The Plantation is re-building the original Pilgrim settlement in Plymouth, Massachusetts.

MONEY FROM VOYAGE

The money to provide scholarships for studying Anglo-American relations and sponsoring travel between the two countries is to [illegible]

ford's Journal [illegible] the Mayflower Pilgrims, he realised that here was the very idea for which he had been searching—to build a second Mayflower and send her across the Atlantic.

NOT THE FIRST

Mr. Charlton is the first to confess that he is not the only person to have had this idea—a similar scheme was mooted in Southampton at the time of the Festival of Britain, but nothing ever came of it. Somewhat similar ideas had been put forward in America too, but with the same lack of success. Perhaps a similar fate would have befallen Mr. Charlton's brain-child if he had not been a super-optimist and a man who was not prepared to drop what many regarded as just a piece of idealism, never likely to reach fruition.

For nearly ten years he propounded his scheme to various people and organisations in this [illegible]

[illegible] and returned with the berthing problem solved—and what more appropriate place could have been found than that, within a couple of miles of the spot where the original Mayflower had been moored?

Not only however, did this trip solve the berthing question, but also that of plans for the new Mayflower. Mr William A Baker, an American marine architect and an official of the Bethlehem Steel Company and who is an authority on ancient ships, would provide

estimated at £100,000, and after much thought it was decided not to launch a public appeal for funds, although because of the nature of the project that might have been thought the natural thing to do. However, at the time one or two other public appeals in this country had met with ill-fortune and it was decided that it would be wise not to subject the project to any risk of that nature. The ultimate decision made was to obtain the support of commerce and industry —which indeed was forthcoming— and also to raise funds by such schemes as an exhibition to the public at the Brixham shipyard. This latter was a great success and many hundreds of thousands of the general public have paid to see Mayflower II building more than sufficient money has been raised to build the ship.

With Mr Baker's blue-prints available, Mr Upham was able to start planning, but before the actual work began there were many problems to be solved. The greatest was the supply of timber, but by the co-operation of people all over the Westcountry the builder's demands have been met. Some of the trees have weighed up to ten tons, with an [illegible]

One of Britain's most respected regional papers, **The Western Morning News**, published a special souvenir edition to mark the sailing of *Mayflower II*. The News highlighted the intention to use income from exhibiting the ship in the USA to fund educational exchange scholarships.

MUTINOUS THOUGHTS

The next disagreement was with Captain Villiers, over a last minute addition to the crew. Warwick persuaded a film-maker he ran into, called Aubrey Baring, to make a film of the voyage. Baring was part of the family that owned the successful international banking firm of Barings, and Warwick thought the name was important but Baring didn't maintain his interest, leaving at least one spare place on board..

In the end, the *Mayflower* Transit Company agreed to step in to sponsor the cost of BBC cameraman Julien Lugrin, plus an assistant as well as the production and editing costs. When the two men turned up to board *Mayflower II,* Villiers refused to let the assistant cameraman on board. Lugrin explained that the equipment he was using was very heavy and difficult for one man to move around the ship, particularly in high seas.

Lugrin was an experienced film maker and he knew what was involved, but Alan Villiers would not be persuaded even though the assistant was standing forlornly at the dockside with his bags packed. Alan Villiers was making his own 16 mm film for National Geographic and although Lugrin was shooting in 35 mm and had a much more ambitious shooting script, he must have figured Lugrin could do it on his own.

Lugrin was so upset by Villier's attitude, that he threatened to withdraw. *"If I can't do the film I have planned, I'm not going"*, he flatly told a distraught Warwick. Lugrin was only concerned about producing a quality product - he and the second photographer had agreed to travel and work for 1 shilling a month - the fee for a mariner and chronicler in the 1600s but Villiers remained adamant that only one photographer could travel.

"Any film would be better than none", Warwick begged repeatedly. Lugrin succumbed to Warwick's pleas and would begin his solo film work by following the *Mayflower II* in a patrol boat as she sailed out of Plymouth Harbor. Finally, he was hauled aboard the *Mayflower II* together with his bulky camera equipment. Captain Villiers was there to help him on board. *"Gee, I didn't realize this stuff was this heavy "*, he said to Lugrin, who had to fight to gain control of some mutinous thoughts.

A worried Warwick (top table near camera, right) had little appetite for the fine food served at the dinner to celebrate the imminent departure of *Mayflower II* to America. Harry Hornblower is far away at the other end of the top table as he prepares to give a carefully worded toast to Warwick .

CHURCHILL'S GIFT

While Warwick, Hornblower and Villiers conducted their testy exchanges over cream teas in the smartest hotels along Plymouth Harbor, the crew loaded the Treasure Chests that had provided much of the finance. They also hauled aboard bags containing 140,000 special *Mayflower II* envelopes. They would have to be stamped by the crew in quiet hours at sea. Lastly, there were the gifts. Warwick had a special watch for President Eisenhower, there were the books full of names of people who had paid to go to the shipyard exhibition, including a book full entirely of residents of Plymouth and 100 autographed copies of *"A History of the English Speaking Peoples"*, donated by Sir Winston Churchill. Warwick had Randoph Churchill to thank for organizing the gift, although his father, who was desperately concerned at the low ebb of Anglo American relations, took little persuasion.

Warwick was touched by the support he received from Randolph, whom he regarded as a good friend. He found Randolph both courageous and radical and believed that Winston could have lost nothing by listening a little more carefully to his son's views.

During the war, when Warwick needed support from above, Randolph had often helped out. On one occasion the Air Force refused to help drop copies of his wartime papers to the troops near the front, so Randolph cabled his father, the Prime Minister, to seek his support for the newspaper drop. Randolph was so furious with the obstinate Air Force, that intentionally, he did not encode the message. This meant that the contents of the cable would become known to the enemy. The cable concluded with a damning indictment of the British Air Force's attitude. *"Unfortunately Air Force not air minded."*

Just before the ship sailed, Warwick got a windfall. Representatives of the prestigious French photo magazine "Paris Match" approached Warwick for permission to do a photo-story on the voyage. He had been trying to interest them for a long time. Now he had to tell them, no, he had already sold the exclusive rights to film the voyage to "Life". But then he thought about it for a second and offered a solution. *"The voyage doesn't start until tomorrow. You can go aboard now and get your pictures. If you are careful with your camera angles no-one will know that Mayflower II is not on the high seas."* "Paris Match" gave him £10,000 for the privilege of boarding *Mayflower II* for two hours. "Life" had bought the rights to the whole journey for £1,000.

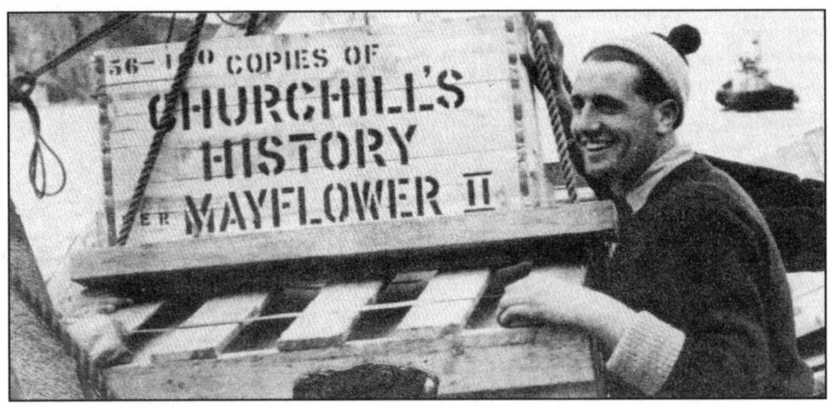

"To *Mayflower* from Winston Churchill"

Perhaps the most treasured item carried aboard *Mayflower II* were 100 copies of Sir Winston Churchill's *"A History of the English-Speaking Peoples"* inscribed by its distinguished author, with the words quoted above.

FELINE PILGRIMAGE

Directors of Plimoth Plantation (right) listen stern-faced as Warwick prepares to speak at the departure of *Mayflower II* for America. The reason for glum looks would become apparent on the other side of the ocean.

The directors of *Plimoth Plantation* looked strangely serious as they listened to the mayor of Plymouth wish Warwick a safe voyage. Ten thousand people crowded the shore line, the crew were all on board, itching to set sail and Warwick and his Captain, both dressed in seventeenth century costume, stood in front of the microphones to accept the good wishes of the British people.

Hornblower and his colleagues knew that Warwick would face challenges in America, on top of any presented by the Atlantic Ocean. They had talked to Fenston and they knew he planned to try and take charge of *Mayflower's* financial affairs as soon as the ship arrived. Hornblower, Brewster and the others had all visited England regularly to urge an early sailing date, in spite of the fact that the ship would set sail leaving a trail of debts.

They knew that she could have earned income in England before setting out across the Atlantic. They knew that several towns, including Dartmouth, Southampton and Boston were anxious to play host to her as well as London where she would be certain to draw massive crowds at St. Katherine's dock. They knew that George Stewart, the leader of the group planning the New York exhibition, had helped out with a bank guarantee for $40,000: it was to be repaid from exhibition fees.

Even as the *Mayflower II* lay in Plymouth Harbor ready to set sail, they were witness to the last minute frantic money-raising efforts to ensure that the builder Stuart Upham was paid. Upham was so entranced with the ship he had built, that he would probably have let her go without receiving full payment, but Upham had a more hard-nosed partner called Holman, who would not release her until the yard had received every penny it was due.

It took a last minute meeting on board, between all concerned, which ended with Felix Fenston signing a check for £10,000. Only then, when Fenston, Warwick and the others emerged from the captain's cabin with broad smiles, were Hornblower and the other directors of Plimoth Plantation certain that the *Mayflower II* would sail in April 1957 as they had urged.

Hornblower tried to get a list of the outstanding debts but if Warwick knew, which was unlikely, he wasn't saying. Of course Hornblower had been talking privately with Fenston for some time and Warwick's first backer gave Hornblower a clear understanding that he was also the largest single backer.

Warwick and John Lowe were certain that they had invested significantly more than Fenston but they had been forced to go to Fenston at critical times and beg him to act as a banker. Fenston told Hornblower that much of the money he had supplied, was in the form of a loan whereas Warwick had always believed it to be a gift. Everyone took comfort in the fact that Warwick had organized the New York exhibition of *Mayflower II*. Soon after she arrived in Plymouth, she would set sail again for the 'Big Apple', where it seemed certain that substantial revenues would be earned. After that there were plans to take her to Miami for the winter, then back up to Washington.

In the summer of 1958, when the ship would be back at her permanent berth in Plymouth, everybody and everything should be all paid up. *Plimoth Plantation* would have a replica of the *Mayflower* for nothing, but there were just two strings attached. All income would go into a separate account, and any surplus revenues would be devoted to fostering Anglo-American relations. Hornblower wanted to cut those strings and Fenston seemed happy to help him do it.

Both Warwick and Villiers looked perfectly at ease as they spoke briefly in front of the public address system. At the last minute someone from the crowd stepped forward and pulled a tiny kitten from inside her coat. *"The ship has to have a cat. It brings good luck"*, she said, offering the creature for the voyage.

As Warwick and Villiers were rowed out to *Mayflower II*, the crowds cheered, boats sounded their horns and a small ball of black fur with white socks began a feline pilgrimage to a new land. Villiers asked if the last minute addition to the passenger list was another publicity stunt. For once, Warwick had nothing to do with it.

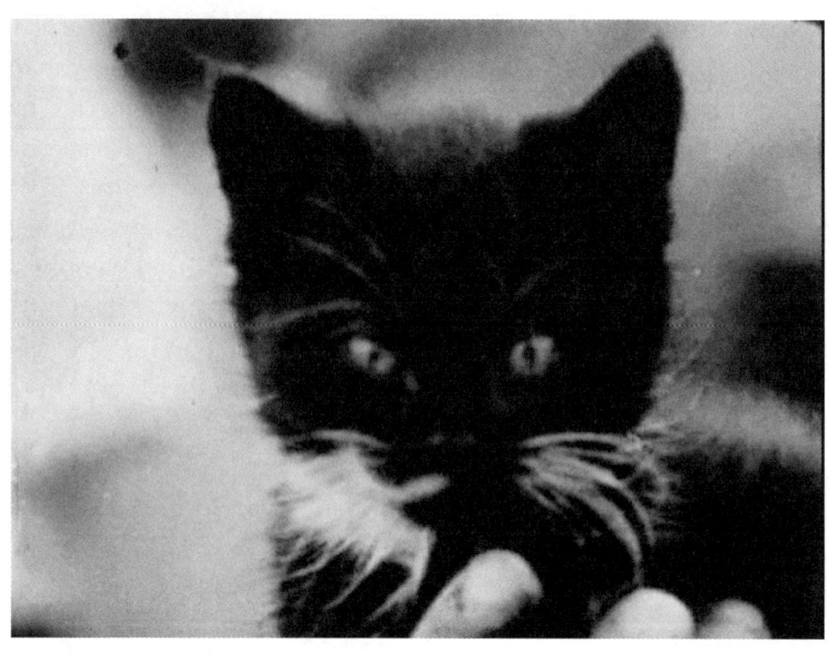

Felix the Kitten
Presented to the ship by a spectator in the crowd to bring good luck to the ship and all who sailed in her.

SMILING TIGER

As Warwick and his captain were rowed out to the boat Warwick felt a great weight slipping from him. He was leaving behind, for a few weeks at least, the constant worry about finding money for the *Mayflower*. Everything else about the project had been fun but the search for money had drained him.

The long search for a backer had yielded an initial contribution of £500 from Felix Fenston. That was a year's wage for some men but Warwick hadn't stopped to consider what a paltry sum it was when Fenston had made that commitment. When Warwick walked down the stairs of Fenston's elegant London home with the cheque burning a hole in his pocket he passed the stuffed head of a tiger on the wall. Fenston was a big game hunter.

Warwick looked at the tiger and thought it was smiling at him, perhaps, he imagined, it was because the tiger knew Warwick had a grueling hunt ahead to assemble enough money to build the ship.

Warwick cast his mind back to the late summer of 1955 when he had put together only £3,000. The keel was laid and the world had been told that the ship would sail the following year. Six months later in December 1955, the ship consisted of a keel and one miserable rib. Warwick's attorney reported that bills had accumulated totalling over £10,000.

The production and sale of "*Mayflower* Mail" at the Daily Mail National Boat Show brought in a few thousand pounds at 2 shillings a time. In May of 1956 Warwick had managed to pay Stuart Upham only £5,000 and owed him another £5,600 for work done. By August, Fenston had produced another £4,500 and other contributors had put up £5,000, but by then work at Upham's yard was gathering pace. There was a weekly non-stop hunger for money and he couldn't tell Stuart Upham to slow down anymore. The ship was supposed to have sailed in 1956. Henry Hornblower had arrived from America to check progress and begged Warwick to commit to a sailing date of April 1957.

Warwick had found Hornblower's arguments persuasive. Henry and the other people in Plymouth, Mass. had organized a nationwide public appeal to raise one million dollars. It was set for the summer of 1957. The money would be used to provide a permanent home for the *Mayflower II* and build a re-creation of the first pilgrim settlement on the land bequeathed by Henry's grandmother. But, according to Henry, the success of the American plans all depended on the sailing and arrival of the *Mayflower II.*

John Lowe had not been convinced. He had arranged for the *Mayflower II* to tour England before setting sail across the Atlantic. The ship would visit Southampton then sail around the south coast, up the estuary of the Thames into the mouth of London, the biggest city in the world. *"It can earn millions during the summer, dear boy"*, John told Warwick in his usual quiet and gentle manner. *"She can sail next year with all her debts paid and there will probably be a little left over."*

John had arranged a berth for the *Mayflower II* at a prime site in St. Katherine's Dock. Everyone with any connection to the project agreed with John's logic - except Warwick who had become possessed with the need to sail as soon as possible. They would find the money to finish the ship and sail in the spring of 1957 he told John.

And somehow they did. The Brixham Exhibition produced £14,000, the souvenirs £6,000, *Life* Magazine paid £1,000 for rights to film the voyage, a commemorative medal brought in a few thousand, the commemorative stamped envelopes a few thousand more, the Treasure Chests £40,000 and right before the ship sailed, *"Paris Match"* came up with £10,000.

Altogether, the money-making schemes raised over £80,000 and Warwick had poured every last penny into completing the *Mayflower*. However, there had been additional expenses apart from the cost of building the ship. Altogether the project had cost over £150,000. Warwick figured he was at least £70,000 short.

A choirboy sneaks away from the launching service to catch a glimpse of *Mayflower II* as she settles in Brixham harbor.
Warwick captured the boy's sense of wonder for an edition of *Mayflower Mail.*

QUIET GOODBYE

Warwick knew he was leaving debts behind, as he was rowed out to *Mayflower II*. In the costume of a seventeenth century soldier,he tried to reassure himself with the thought that, *"I'm not so different from the first Pilgrims who set sail in 1620. They were laden in debt after the voyage and had to work for seven years to pay off their merchant venture backers"*. On reflection, it was not exactly a consoling thought.

Warwick had never been to sea under sail but he thought it would be an uneventful affair, time to rest up and recharge his batteries. Some members of the Press wondered whether the *Mayflower II* would make it but he could not understand why not. Hadn't the pilgrims made it all those years before and they had women and children aboard? He even urged his captain, Alan Villiers, to follow the more dangerous Northern route across the Atlantic. Villiers preferred to go south if possible.

"You know Warwick we are not just going for a spin around the bay", he warned. *"This could be a dangerous voyage. You can never second-guess the sea."*

Warwick thought he was being given the usual stuff that old salts used to rub their superiority into landlubbers, but he was not going to interfere with his captain's judgment.

Warwick didn't meet most of the crew until a couple of nights before the ship sailed, when there was a farewell dinner in Plymouth for everyone who was to go on board. The dinner was hosted by Michael Farr who made Plymouth Sloe Gin.

The crew were all keyed up, ready to play their part in the *Mayflower* adventure at last. Warwick, on the other hand, was simply relieved to get away for a couple of months at least, from the responsibility of being the *Mayflower II's* captain on shore. Many of the crew found his carefree attitude that night irritating and some even wondered what his role had been in building *Mayflower*, and if he were some sort of interloper.

"Perhaps it is ignorance on my part", Warwick told them, *"but we opened up the whole world with ships like this. What is the problem?"* Several weeks later, as the ship's crew struggled to keep the *Mayflower* upright in a force 9 gale, his question was answered.

As the ship set sail, Warwick shook off his nervous tension. In his diary he wrote;

"We had come a long way together, Mayflower and I, and now it was time for other hands to tend her and supply her needs. As I stood for a moment and looked around the faces of her crew, and Alan, fretting away, I felt proud that she was in the care of the finest hands in the world."

If Warwick gave a thought to potential storms at sea and equally violent storms of a different sort in America, he made no mention of any concerns in his diary. The ship, beautiful as she was, had been built to centuries old standards, that were no longer accepted as safe and she had not been properly trialed.

However, here was Warwick, a man who possessed a life-long fear of flying, to the point where he could induce panic in an entire cabin of a large plane, yet his diary shows a moment of calm and reflection as *Mayflower II* eased her way out of Plymouth harbor and the English Channel.

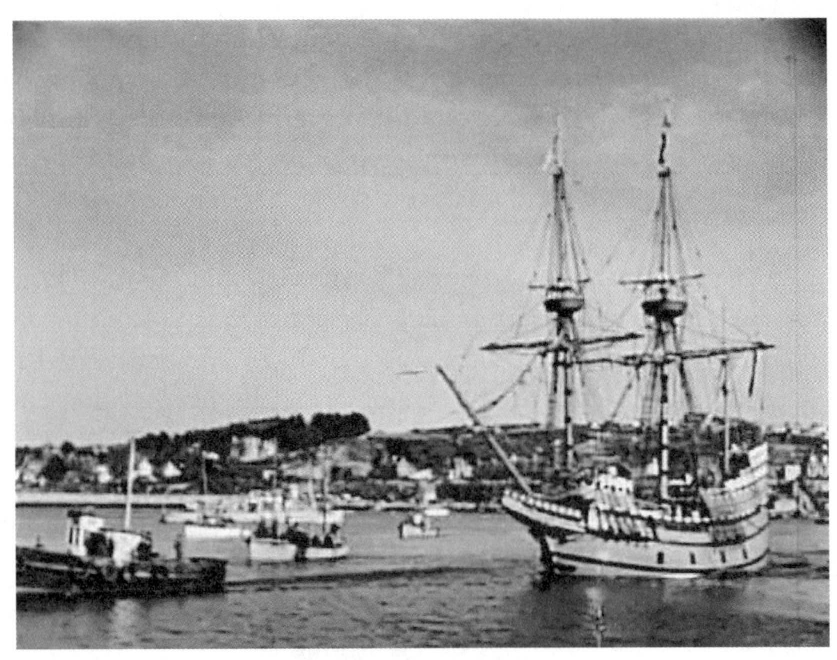

Mayflower II prepares to leave England for America.

Warwick stood on the poop deck and counted the flotilla of small craft seeing the *Mayflower II* off from England. There were sixty-seven rowing boats, launches, dinghies, yachts - all the paraphernalia of an English harbor, dancing court to the *Mayflower II* under sail.

On one boat, Warwick spotted his office staff. Miss Jeans stood very upright, little Miss Beck beside her, and Mrs. Grimmet's red hair distinguished her when distance made their faces pink blurs. John Lowe, even then in black jacket and pinstripe trousers, was in the tug escorting the *Mayflower II* out of the harbor.

When the moment came to cast off from the tug, it arrived so unexpectedly, to Warwick at least, that he barely had time to call: *"See you on the other side"* and John's response was lost on the wind. For the rest of his life, Warwick would regret not listening more to the gentle tones of his partner in the *Mayflower* adventure; John's calm but persistent pleas to wait, exhibit the ship in England and pay off all debts before setting out for America. John's quiet goodbye was almost lost on the wind, then replaced by the Captain's gravelly voice shouting orders.

STOWAWAY BULL

Warwick began his diary of the journey *"The movement in the ship is as though she knew her moment had come, the purpose of her birth, to leave Plymouth, Drake's Island astern, cup the wind in her sails and make her way as her predecessor had done, across the waters of the implacable Atlantic."*

"The crew braced the yards and let go her sails; they caught enough of the light air for her to sway and to move on her own. She was under way very quickly, her course west-south-west. Stuart Upham joined me on the poop, his blue eyes dancing with pride: 'The secret of a sailing ship is rhythm, everything giving in unison', he said. 'Rigging, transmitted to the sails, spars and hull, all working together to give her a hat full of wind.' The proud builder braced himself as the ship swayed, looking up at the topmast: "She's a very lively ship - not a groan in her, tight as a fiddlers bitch."

Even on board the *Mayflower II,* Warwick could not forget his thirst for publicity. He arranged for a man to come on board and pretend to be a stowaway. The idea was that after a couple of miles out to sea he would emerge and disembark. Cameras would be on hand in a following boat and the Press would have yet another front page *Mayflower II* moment.

Unfortunately the first mate, Godfrey Wicksteed, quickly discovered him and thought he was a real stowaway. Wickstead was a headmaster on shore and he dragged the interloper to the main deck as if he were a schoolboy caught cheating in an examination. In their enthusiasm to purge the ship of the unwanted passenger, the crew became a little overexcited, and were a bit rough with the poor chap as they threw him overboard. It was all a little silly, Warwick thought.

Villiers noted that there was a motor boat trailing *Mayflower II* ready to pick up the stowaway and he concluded that Warwick had something to do with the incident. Villiers was angry. He took his captain's duties very seriously and that morning had personally inspected every nook and cranny of the ship.

Warwick got his story though. He had set it up with Hughie Green, an old friend who was host of a television talent show called "New Faces." The face of the stowaway duly appeared on Hughie's next show singing a new song, "I wished I'd sailed on the *Mayflower*."

Not long after the *Mayflower II* cast its stowaway overboard and cut loose from its tow, the captain assembled all hands amidships and the master addressed them sternly. *"Now, lads,"* he said, *"We have to get down to the business of delivering the ship to America. The bull and the publicity are behind us!"*

The Captain's speech was, of course, wasted on the one man for whom the remarks were meant but for the rest of that day at least, Saturday April 20 1957, Warwick was too exhausted to think of another promotion. He crawled into his bunk, too tired to undress, pulled the blanket over himself and was soon sent to sleep by the gentle swaying of the ship.

SUPERCARGO

The next day Warwick was already beginning to worry how long it would take to clear the English Channel and even how long to complete the journey. Villiers gave Warwick a short course in the difficulty of predicting a journey under sail. *"We could be here for a few days, we could be here for weeks. It has taken sailing ships months to clear the jaws of the Channel."*

Warwick was classified as supercargo on the ship's manifest. He was not a part of the crew but he was anxious to share in their duties. Captain Villiers assigned him to join the watch of third mate Jan Junker but he told Warwick that he should not feel obliged to attend every watch. *"You have had a hard time and you are tired"*, Villiers told Warwick. *"We are all fresh and ready for action"*. Villiers also spoke to Junker and told him not to treat Warwick as anything other than a volunteer who was free to opt out of any duties.

Warwick's nervous energy permitted no relaxation. On the fourth day at sea he breathed a sigh of relief in his diary. *"At last our little ship is well out into the Atlantic, making five knots, with 174 miles of passage behind us."*

On the fifth day, Villiers broke the news that he had decided to take the southern route which meant a longer voyage of over 5,000 miles compared to some 3,000 miles that the original *Mayflower* had sailed. Villiers gave several reasons for his decision. He could not be certain of the ship's behaviour in a gale, the knight for the main lift was split and could only be strengthened with iron, the 'give' of the old fashioned rigging worried him, the saddle of the main topsail mast had jumped mast - and he wanted to get the ship there in one piece.

There had been virtually no sea trials, he reminded Warwick, and a few days more sailing on the southern route was nothing against the unwarranted risk of ice, fog and gales on the more direct, but more dangerous, northern course. After all, there were thirty three human lives and a cat on board, as well as a valuable cargo.

Warwick quickly recovered from the disappointment of learning that the *Mayflower II* would take the long southern route. Soon after his talk with the captain, Adrian Small, the second mate, announced that the ship had made good progress - 147 miles from noon to noon. Warwick immediately started calculating how long it would take them to get there. Later that day, Jan Junker tried unsuccessfully to stop Warwick from fretting.

"We could reach the trades and nothing could happen," he told Warwick as the two men stood outside the chart room. Warwick was aghast. *"You are joking?"*, he inquired of Junker.

"No", the Dane said seriously, smothering a smile. *"Nothing is certain in a sailing ship. We could get a force six or seven in the trades, but nothing could happen. We could be becalmed. That happened to me in 1947 and it could happen again."*

The following day, only the sixth at sea, Warwick was his normal anxious self, calculating the possible arrival date. He recorded for posterity the unshakable optimism that had carried him this far.

"Adrian Small, the second mate, told us at midday that the ship had logged 148 miles during the previous twenty-four hours. This provoked a discussion, the first of so many, on the possible duration of the voyage. I went right out on a limb as a thirty day man and said the ship would make her Plymouth landfall on May 26th."

As Warwick took the slow route to America, Henry Hornblower and his fellow directors made their way back to London's Heathrow airport. As they boarded the plane back to Boston, they discussed the vital role *Mayflower II* would play in persuading American donors to subscribe the $1 million they were seeking, to build a replica of the first Pilgrim Village.

This village, of course, would be different from the first settlement in that extensive car parking would be required, along with a reception area, as well as shopping and other facilities for the anticipated half a million tourists a year.

However, they were worried about Warwick. They had heard his riffs on socialism and the ways communists raised money, they had witnessed his last minute desperate scramble for funds and they were there on the dockside watching in bewilderment as 92 so-called 'Treasure Chests' were loaded onto *Mayflower II*.

The Americans were appalled at what they condemned as the commercialization of the venture and they wanted nothing to do with exhibiting the British goods that would be arriving in a few weeks time. They had established a non-profit to build a museum.

Then there was Warwick's revolutionary ideas about almost everything to do with the project; his refusal to allow the British Ambassador and the Boston based British consul to be part of the welcome ceremony; his insistence on a competition to identify a cabin boy, when one of the governors had been anxious to volunteer his son for the honor and his personal slight to the governors who were not invited to participate in the ceremonies to launch the ship. Then there were the consistent concerns about Warwick and John Lowe's character and their motives .... concerns that were shared by British government officials.

To top it all, Warwick had organized a tour of the *Mayflower II* down the East coast to Newport, Rhode Island and then on down to New York and Miami of all places, where it would be open to visitors for 95 cents a person.

Back in Boston, the trustees shared their concerns with the welcoming committee. In short order Tom Riley, a senior writer at the Boston Globe, learned of the criticisms, including the planned exclusion of British government officials from the celebrations.

Stories would soon appear that would cause embarassment to the Anglo-American community in Boston who were used to golfing together at the local country clubs and wining, dining and scratching each other's backs when it came to business.

MAYFLOWER MESSAGES

After a dozen days at sea, Warwick felt obliged to pull another stunt. He had managed to avoid most of the modern safety regulations including a request to carry lifeboats, but the maritime authorities insisted that the ship wear reflectors and carry a radio. The modern Atlantic was a much busier place than the ocean of 1620. He persuaded the ship's wireless operator, J.D.Horrocks to shut down the radio for a couple of days or so. Warwick was worried that the world would forget about *Mayflower II*. Maybe if there were radio silence, people would wonder where they were.

Perhaps he had forgotten his own judgment on *Mayflower II*, perhaps his constant search for publicity for the ship had become ingrained but the stunt was totally unnecessary. When the finishing touches were being put to *Mayflower II* in Upham's yard, Warwick had observed that he had a new advocate.

"The Mayflower is beginning to speak for herself."

Once at sea, the ship's hypnotic voice carried across the oceans of the world and found an echo in the most unlikely places. While Warwick fretted that the world might have forgotten *Mayflower II*, the Iraq Times of Baghdad, the Bulawayo Chronicle of Rhodesia, the communist Daily Worker of London, the Otago Daily Times of New Zealand, the Kalgoorlie Miner of Western Australia and countless other papers around the world, were reporting the every move of *Mayflower II*.

When she didn't move and lay becalmed for days in the windless Atlantic, the world's media reported that too. Her exact position was plotted more carefully than if she were a category 10 hurricane.

The ship's voyage encouraged media discussion across a whole range of subjects. In one Australian paper, a lively debate developed between various church leaders, about the religious beliefs of the separatists and Pilgrims. In other papers, arguments about women's rights were prompted by the absence of females on board.

Fashion editors rushed to bring out pilgrim dress designs and food editors reproduced recipes for *Mayflower* Deviled Corn Pudding and other delicacies of the 1600's. American and British papers in particular, treated their readers to a history lesson. Even art editors got in on the act. *Mayflower's* journey was inspiring readers to submit poems, while others produced paintings and models.

Magazines that dealt with antiques focused on furniture of the early Americans, stamp magazines featured the *Mayflower II* special covers and business editors speculated about US-British trade. In classrooms, American and British school children in particular were entranced by the voyage and university students dressed up in pilgrim costume to raise money for charity. *Mayflower II's* voyage was celebrated in village fancy dress parades and big city carnivals.

Mayflower II also started a debate about Anglo-American relations which were in a dreadful state after the British Government's appalling disregard for American interests during Suez. Shortly before the ship set sail, 100 British Government members of parliament tabled an anti-American motion which embarrassed Government leaders even further.

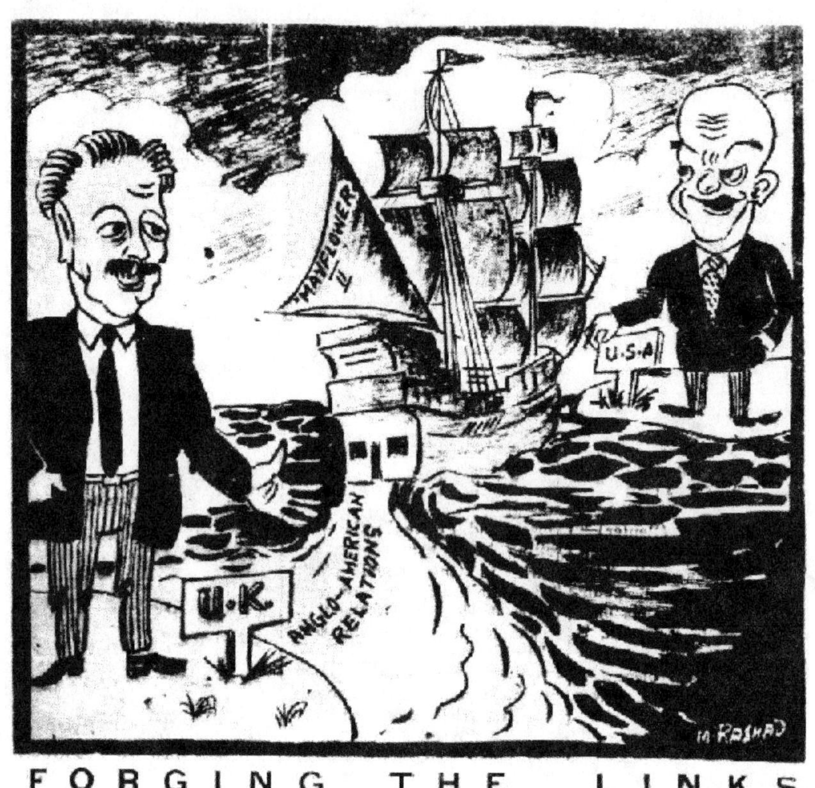

The *Mayflower II* voyage replaces discussion of the Suez crisis. Harold McMillan who took over from Anthony Eden as Prime Minister after the Suez crisis is depicted nudging *Mayflower II* on its way, in an effort to mend a frayed friendship between the two old allies.

"Improvement Foreseen in British - US relations" headlined the New Zealand Christchurch Star Sun; *"Mayflower II, a symbol of Anglo-American ties"*, said the Ballarat Courier of Australia. The same message was reprinted from the Rhine Valley to Rio in Portuguese, Spanish, German, French and Italian.

GRADUATION CEREMONY

Warwick gradually got to know the crew better. He developed a deep respect for Jan Junker, the third mate. Jan didn't say much but he was the sort of man who didn't need to say anything to communicate the feeling that he knew what he was doing. Jan had a Master's ticket, as proof of his sailing skills, and had worked on sailing ships for many years in difficult seas. Warwick thought himself lucky to be assigned to Junker's watch.

There were other real sailors like Peter Padfield, Joe Powell, Adrian Small, Jack Scarr, Harry Sowerby and David Thorpe, who all helped Warwick as he began to learn the foreign art of sailing and sailing terms.

Warwick *"intimidated the hell"* out of one member of the crew, Joseph Meany. Joe was the American cabin boy who had been selected to go on the voyage, as winner of a national competition organized by the Boys Clubs of America. Former US President Herbert Hoover, was chairman of the selection committee. Warwick upset some of the people at *Plimoth Plantation* with his insistence on a national competition because at least one governor had a member of his family who was anxious to travel as a cabin boy.

Joe, who was from Waltham, Massachusetts was only 17 at the time of sailing. His job on board, along with Graham Nunn, the other cabin boy, was to act as a "go-for" for officers and non-crew members such as Warwick and the film crew. Before Joe Meany got on a plane to England, he had been quietly given an extra job on board by Walter Haskell, the editor of The Plymouth Old Colony Memorial. Haskell was anxious to get some exclusive pictures of the voyage and had given Joe several rolls of film with instructions to take as many pictures as possible. Joe soon found out from Warwick that *National Geographic* and *Life* magazine had exclusive rights to cover the journey but Joe's inability to take pictures for Walter Haskell would lead in a few weeks time to one of the most bizarre stories ever to appear on the front pages of a serious newspaper.

Young Joe Meany found Warwick a disciplinarian and *"a bit of a pain in the ass"* and intellectually overwhelming but he gradually began to hit it off with the older man. Warwick organized a graduation ceremony for Joe at sea, when it became clear that the *Mayflower* would not make it to America in time for Joe's real high school graduation.

Joe Meany

The American cabin boy is congratulated on his 'at sea' graduation by Graham Nunn, the U.K. cabin boy.

Together with a couple of crew members, Warwick fashioned an improvised cap and gown and another crew member, Andrew Anderson-Bell, produced a scroll, recording the event.

It was presented to the overwhelmed young American, one Sunday after the regular Sunday morning prayer service, close to the day that his classmates were graduating in America.

None of the experienced sailors could recall a crew where there was so much mutual respect. Crew members called officers 'Sir' and officers addressed crew members as 'Mister'. If someone saw a job that needed to be done, they did it before, not after they were asked. A sense of teamwork developed. The exception was Warwick and Alan Villiers.

Somewhere across the Atlantic, although both men admired each other, they realized a clash was inevitable. The first sign of competition came with the cameras on board. When Villiers wasn't giving orders to the crew, he was using a video camera or taking stills. The *Life* photographer and Lugrin were doing the same for Warwick.

At least one crew member thought Warwick was *"living on his nerves"* during the voyage. In his log of the journey, Peter Padfield wrote, *"When things are going well he is happy, and anything new, such as signaling to another ship at sea, has him hopping up and down with excitement. But in periods of calm and little progress when we are way behind schedule for the ceremonies that have been arranged in America, he worries and will appear on deck at all hours of the night, and early morning, smoking cigarettes and asking everyone how much longer the voyage is going to last, or what can be done to hasten progress. We don't know. The wind is a fickle mistress."*

NERVOUS ODDBALL

During the windless days, cramped together on the 90 ft long 25 ft wide *Mayflower,* crew members prodded each other to display their storytelling skills. Some of the experienced sailors had already been to sea together; the strangers, like Warwick, were interesting mysteries to be coaxed into revealing information about themselves.

Warwick gave them stories with plenty of entertainment value. When asked about his wartime dramas he remembered a barman in an officers mess. *"The man had too much to drink one night and started calling a senior officer a silly bitch."* Warwick put the out-of-control enlisted man on a charge and was shocked when the barman insisted on a full court-martial. That night a long line of officers visited Warwick's desert tent at Montgomery's headquarters, pleading for clemency. The barman apparently had become very close friends with several of them and they were terrified at the prospect of a public trial. Homosexuality was illegal in those days. Warwick solved the problem by recommending the barman for promotion to full sergeant; a step up in rank that mysteriously involved immediate transfer to another unit in another country.

Although the crew members enjoyed listening to Warwick's reminiscences many regarded him as a bit of a nervous oddball. A few years later, at least one crew member was astonished to read the following verdict on his wild-eyed companion, in a scholarly review of the second world war;

"Captain Warwick Charlton will go down in history as one of the most original journalists and the most original editors of all time. Charlton saw the war as the first People's war fought by civilians in Army uniforms, not by professional soldiers. He saw it as a right of

the soldiers to know what was happening at home and at war and was frequently at odds with his superiors and the censors.

"His 8th Army News was started at the time when the 8th was demoralized and in danger of defeat while the prestige of the Desert Fox, the German General Rommel, was at its peak. Montgomery only became (the leader of) 8th Army because of the accidental death of General Gott after one day in office, but the young Charlton saw Montgomery as the man who was to be the saviour of the British Army in the Western Desert. He and his close friend, Geoffrey Keating, saw it as a duty to build the image of Montgomery to counteract the defeatism arising from Rommel's image.

"Such personality promotion was cordially disliked by the War Office and it meant that Charlton and Keating were forever on the fringes of official displeasure by the War Office. Indeed Charlton was court-martialed for disclosing unfavorable criticism of Keating over his image promotion of Montgomery. Even though Charlton was successfully defended at his court-martial it was to have a serious effect on his career. No less a person than the Secretary of State saw that he was shipped out to the far East when General Montgomery was moved to Europe in preparation for the D-Day invasion of France."

On the eighteenth day at sea Warwick's diary began excitedly. *"We have broken our record! The run for the twenty-four hour period was 160 miles."*

The next day brought more excitement:

"Our run till noon has broken yesterday's record: 164 miles! I thought the news so good that I could not keep it to myself. "

On day twenty, there was a change of mood:

"It really is no use counting your mileage on a sailing ship! Yesterday, heartened by a record day's run, I was cock-a-hoop: Then in the evening the wind began to drop and during Jan's watch only fourteen miles were recorded. A punishment for presuming on the benevolence of the wind gods!

"All night the ship crept over the ocean like a heavy wooden monster waddling, oh so slowly, heaving wearily from side to side with her sails flapping like broken wings. This morning the wind freshened a little but by noon our run was only 116 miles."

There was further cause for Warwick to sprinkle exclamation marks of alarm throughout his diary. The previous day the captain had volunteered the opinion that they were probably past the halfway mark. Warwick was ecstatic. Twenty four hours later, the first mate issued a correction - there was still a day to go to pass this invisible marker.

The slow progress of the ship allowed members of the crew to spend more time on their daily task of stuffing 140,000 envelopes with copies of the *Mayflower* compact, each one signed by Captain Villiers.

Warwick would calm his concerns about the lack of wind by striding up and down the deck and launching into speeches about the importance of the envelope stuffing. The ship we are sailing in is just the vehicle, he would explain. It is no different from dozens of other ships that carried the early settlers to what was to become the United States. What was different about the *Mayflower* was the agreement or compact that those who sailed in her signed before disembarking.

In some ways it was a complete accident, Warwick would point out. The *Mayflower* was bound for Virginia where a settlement had already been established under the rule of the English

King. Instead storms drove them off course and they wound up many miles north on the barren shores of Cape Cod.

They were short of provisions, winter was fast approaching so sailing down the coast to Virginia was out of the question. They had no choice but to disembark on an empty stretch of land where no law existed, but some saw an opportunity, and to quote Bradford's Journal, *"determined to use their own liberty, for none had the power to command them."*

Many aboard the original Mayflower had already lived in a community that had an agreed set of spiritual rules. These were separatists who were believers in the separation of the Church and State. They had fled England and the rule of a King who was also head of the Church. For several years they lived in Holland in the town of Leiden. Now the 41 men aboard the first Mayflower committed to abide by a set of laws that were agreed by the community.

This, Warwick would point out, was astonishing in the 1600s where royalty and religion ruled supreme. This was the stirrings of modern democracy.

"And that is the message we are delivering to the world," he would tell anyone within earshot.

On the twenty-first day at sea, the ship was almost becalmed. Warwick was so depressed that he decided to take his time over his morning washing, brushing his teeth endlessly in the hope that the salt water would do them some good.

He spent an inordinate amount of time looking at himself in the mirror and noted with some satisfaction that the facial hair he had started growing on the voyage was a definite improvement. *"I noted that my mustache suggests some Tartar ancestry, and my beard promises to be dashing, but how dashing depends on the duration of the voyage."*

"I am beginning to learn about the sea," Warwick wrote on day 25, *"to understand why Alan and the other experienced sailors on board, listen to me working out average speeds and arrival dates as though they were humouring a child. All the ocean charts, weather forecasts and past experience count for little; the sea has its own unpredictable moods."*

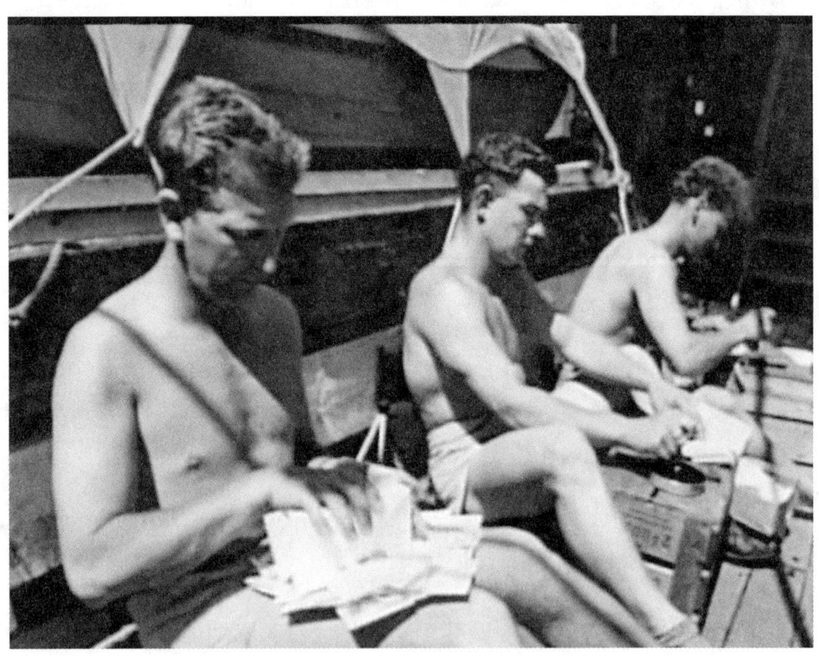

Members of the crew franking some of the 140,000 pieces of mail taken on board for the trip, thus providing stamp collectors throughout the world with unique first day covers.

PHILOSOPHICAL DISCUSSIONS

The last few days had been hard on Warwick. For 24 hours the ship had been becalmed and Warwick looked up aghast at the drooping sails. Boredom set in. It was a feeling he had never imagined possible on *Mayflower II*. He began a discussion with Jan Junker that became philosophical. "*Anything can become boring,*" said Jan, who recounted how he had felt when he and other captured war-time spies were tortured. *"At one point I had been subjected to so much, I actually became bored"*, said Jan. *"I only wanted them to get it over and done with."*

The *Mayflower II* lies becalmed in the Atlantic. It was a period of great anxiety for Warwick, as he worried about arriving on time.

Warwick agreed. During war, he had often found the rapier point feeling of danger in his stomach replaced with the ache of infinite boredom. He recalled for Jan a time when he took part in the invasion of Sicily. He should have been alive with adrenaline coursing through his veins but the invasion followed two years of intense and unpredictable desert warfare and the report he filed as the landing took place, had all the excitement of a relaxed holiday tour guide. It was published in the *Times of Malta* on June 23rd, 1943.

"The landing craft in which we are, is an American built craft and like many other vessels in our convoy was sailed across the Atlantic by British crews for the invasion of Europe. The captain of our ship tells me they are the smallest vessels to have made the Atlantic crossing by themselves.

"Sicily is only four hundred yards away. There is a pall of black smoke hanging over a hill to our north; there are now so many ships closing to beaches ahead that it looks like a monster regatta. Now that we are closing in we can see fires burning, a few wrecked vehicles and on the land in front of us nothing is moving except a solitary tree stirred by the wind."

Although he was dictating his news story while the invasion was taking place he did not forget to credit America with supplying some of the ships.

SACRIFICIAL LEECHES

Warwick proved he would do anything for a little publicity when he offered himself as the sacrificial meal for some leeches that Doctor Stevens had brought on board in a jam jar. The Doctor thought they would remind the crew how far the medical profession had advanced since the 1620s when such creatures were used to draw blood, in an attempt to cure the sick. Warwick was held down while his bare chest was covered in tomato sauce for the benefit of the cameras.

After giving a lethal dose of his blood to Doctor Stevens' leeches the two men spent more time together and realized that they

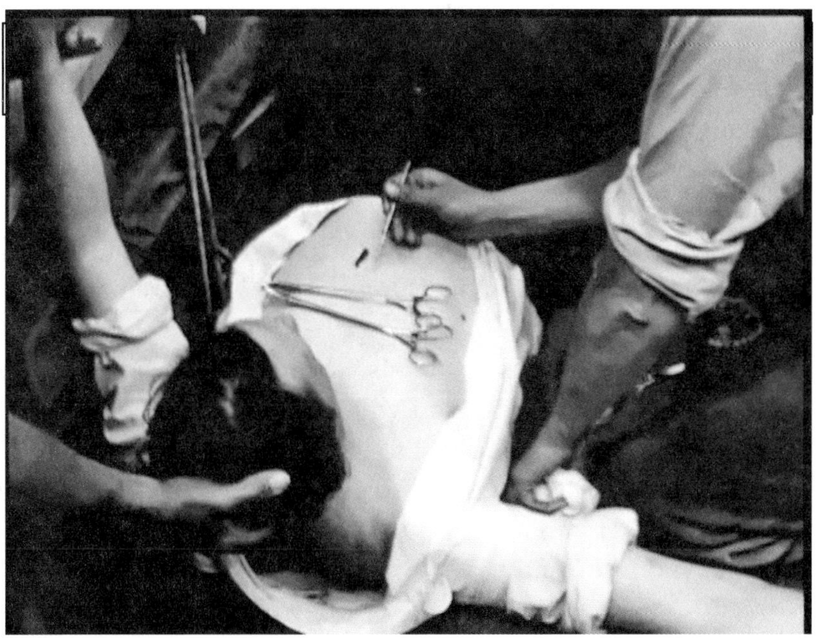

Warwick offers himself to feed the leeches. Was his blood too strong?

shared common ground. John Stevens was South African and Warwick had cousins who lived there. Warwick had visited elsewhere in Africa to cover the troubles in Kenya, that had led to independence. He had followed the terrorist group known as the Mau Mau deep into their territory, with only a photographer as company.

They were safe during daylight but an ambush was certain after dark. On the way back to a government controlled township, they came to a fork in the road. The sun was fading fast and Warwick and his photographer had to guess which way would lead them home. *"We chose correctly,"* Warwick told Doc Stevens. *"The other way would have led us straight into a terrorist camp and certain death. I found that fork in the road more intimidating than any of Hitler's bombs."*

Warwick also covered the wildlife of Africa in a visit to the Serengeti. The story he wrote drew a phone call from Aldous Huxley who was one of many naturalists alarmed at the vanishing wild life of Africa. Huxley sought Warwick's advice on a symbol for a new world wide movement to protect wildlife. What about a Lion? Or a cheetah? Or a zebra?

Forget about African animals, Warwick advised. The intelligentsia will be with you whatever your symbol but to be successful you need to appeal to the ordinary man and woman who reads the Daily Mirror. You need something really cute and cuddly. Try a Panda. Huxley adopted the symbol for the World Wild Life Fund.

On board *Mayflower II* there was a cute and cuddly animal in the form of Felix the kitten and Warwick used Felix to provide an ink stained paw print at the end of a document signed by the crew. The document was inserted into a bottle and thrown overboard with a message that whoever found it could claim a dinner at the Wig and Pen Club in London.

Years later a Norwegian would arrive at the Wig and Pen to claim his prize of roast beef and yorkshire pudding.

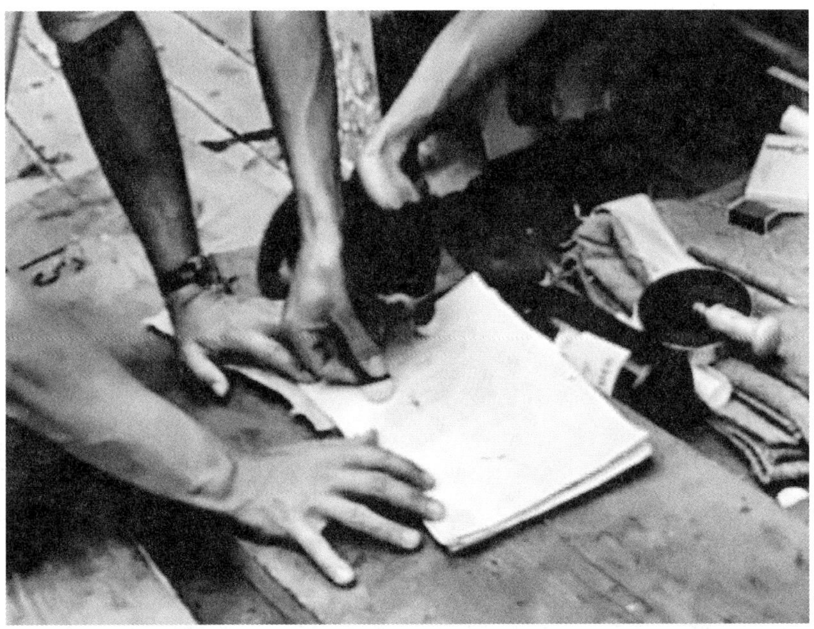

Felix the Kitten adds his paw print to the paper signed by the ship's crew, before the document was sealed in a bottle and thrown overboard.

MILLIONAIRE LIVING

After 31 days at sea Warwick finally seemed to relax, for a few moments at least. In his diary for Monday May 20th he laid bare his sense of well-being.

"Every so often I say to myself: I must remember today and all the moments of today, because they have been the happiest and best. The feeling is not prompted by any particular incident or spectacular sight but rather by a heightened sense of well-being, of feeling especially alive. Today was such a one. We were making about four knots; the ship seemed almost to glide along with scarcely any movement, certainly no sway, through the flat blue waters.

Warwick (left) and his friend Dick Brennan (right) heave hard on a rope. *"This is millionaire living"*, Dick Brennan declared.

Dick (Brennan) said to me as he stood, arms folded, outside the galley, warming himself in the sun: 'Warwick, this is a millionaire living,' and I, feeling the caress of the wind, a feather's touch which kept us cool, nodded agreement. There was of course, the normal ship's routine to carry out: we have begun painting the ship. I took a pot of white paint and a wonderfully long pliable brush and thoroughly enjoyed myself, tongue in cheek, lost somewhere between brush and paint and the surface of the wood, and thought that even the ship's painters could feel as Gauguin did about the pleasures of painting."

After 34 days at sea, with the trade winds steadfastly refusing to blow, Warwick and *Mayflower II* were becalmed 1800 miles from Nantucket Island. *"The beautiful sea is more often marked by drifting golden weed than whitecaps of breaking water,"* he wrote in his diary. *"Steady, slow progress is all very well but it can get on your nerves and it is beginning to get on mine."*

Warwick did not know it, but he was beginning to get on the nerves of some important folks in Boston. A story had appeared in the Boston Globe, poking more than gentle fun at the apparent exclusion of the British embassy from the welcome ceremonies planned for the arrival of *Mayflower II.* Tom Riley taunted the organizing committee at the end of a conspicuously placed story in the Boston press:

"What say you gentlemen? Think you might be able to find a spot on the platform down at Plymouth? Might be a nice gesture you know."

An embassy official was obliged to issue a tart statement to the effect that the government had nothing to do with the ship. In an effort to soothe hurt feelings, an embarrassed and angry Ronnie Forth, the head of the welcoming committee, organized a British Charitable ball at the Sheraton Plaza Hotel in Boston, *"To herald the arrival of Mayflower II."* It was probably just as well that Warwick was absent because Ronnie Forth used the event to honor the British government authorities that Warwick had condemned as unhelpful, or useless.

Ronnie Forth had been a longtime friend of the staff at the British consulate in Boston. He had got to know the senior officials well, as chairman of a special committee which organized a ball to celebrate the coronation of the Queen in 1953. He had also led a number of Anglo-American charitable events.

It was unthinkable that they be excluded and he could not understand Warwick's logic which seemed locked in a bygone era, when the original pilgrim settlers had been seeking to escape from countries ruled by monarchs and militaries.

So with the *Mayflower II* still at sea, the British VIPs mingled with their American counterparts including the Governor of Massachusetts, the Mayor of Boston and the U.S. Senators, Leverett Saltonstall and John Kennedy.

The British attendees included Her Britannic Majesty's Ambassador, his Excellency, Sir Harold Caccia K.C.M.G, Robert H.K.Marett, C.M.G., O.B.E the Consul-General of Boston and officials from the English Speaking Union. Among the sponsors of the event were Mr. and Mrs. Henry Hornblower II and Henry's parents Mr. and Mrs. Ralph Hornblower.

The honored guests danced till midnight and were treated to the sounds of the Caledonian Scots Pipers. Ronnie Forth did not need the call to battle of the blood curdling bagpipes. He had organized enough. Warwick Charlton could organize his own accommodation, he told the Hornblowers.

While Ronnie Forth was soothing the ruffled feathers of the British Embassy officials, Henry Hornblower was using the imminent arrival of *Mayflower* to solicit funds for *Plimoth Plantation*. In a lengthy letter to the Editor of the Pittsfield Eagle, he set out the plans for *Mayflower II* once she arrived which included a trip up and down the East coast before returning to Plymouth around Thanksgiving.

And using italics for emphasis he wrote that it was *"a gift of the people of England to the people of the United States."* and that a portion of the proceeds from exhibiting the ship *"will be used to establish an exchange scholarship fund for American and English Students."*

Hornblower expressed his pride that the ship was to be entrusted to the care of his organization and concluded:

"We are seeking free will contributions, large or small to help build the 100 acre Pilgrim village at Plymouth. The cost of the re-creation will be one million dollars. Contributions may be sent to Post Office Box 1620, Plymouth, Mass."

The letter was illustrated with an artist's impression of the *Mayflower* moored opposite the village *"as a centerpiece of the exhibit."*

PITTSFIELD, MASS. EAGLE
MAY 2 1957

Mayflower's Home Port

To the Editor of THE EAGLE:—

We would like to clear up a point or two in connection with the voyage of *Mayflower II*, her destination and permanent resting place.

The *Mayflower II*, under the command of Capt. Alan Villiers, set sail from Plymouth, England, April 20, bound for Plymouth, Massachusetts, where she is expected to arrive and be welcomed on May 25, God willing. She will remain on exhibition in Plymouth Bay, just off shore from Plymouth Rock, for a two-week period.

Following this two-week exhibition and celebration, the *Mayflower II* will sail to New York where she will be exhibited during the New York Summer Festival. A portion of the proceeds from this exhibit will be used to establish an exchange scholarship fund for American and English students.

The *Mayflower II* will return to Plymouth, Mass., in the fall and be turned over by her English builders to Plimoth Plantation, a non-profit, educational, historical organization, *as a gift of the people of England to the people of the United States.*

Until that "turn-over date" (sometime during Thanksgiving week) the *Mayflower II* remains the property of the English group which concieved the idea of building the replica of the famous ship, raised the necessary funds through free will gifts of small amounts to build it, and directed and financed the voyage from Plymouth, England to Plymouth, Mass.

The governors, trustees, and advisers of the Plimoth Plantation Village organization are grateful to the British sponsors for the generous gift of the ship to the people of America. It is a people-to-people gesture of friendship, and we are proud to have been selected by the British group to receive the ship and retain it for all time for America to see as part of a reproduction of the first Pilgrim village in America, now under construction at Plymouth, Mass.

In the interim, we are seeking free will contributions, large or small, to help build the 100-acre Pilgrim village in Plymouth. The cost of this re-creation will be one million dollars. Contributions may be sent to Post Office Box 1620, Plymouth, Mass.

HENRY HORNBLOWER II,
President, Plimoth Plantation.
Plymouth.

Henry Hornblower II attempts to set the record straight as the *Mayflower II* is en route to America. This was far from the end of the story.

DANGEROUS MOMENT

On the forty-eighth day - Thursday the 6th of June, Warwick finally registered a respect for the ocean in his diary. By this time he had been through a range of weather, from a strong blow to being becalmed. Now, as far as he was concerned, the dramas of the voyage were virtually over; they were sailing along at a good clip and all that remained was for someone to shout *"Land Ho"* from the look-out.

He wrote in his diary: *"For the second time in this voyage I had the feeling I was flying, the physical feeling of flying, and for a moment it was so real I shared the ecstasy of the birds."*

Warwick went to bed, a man content, but was soon woken by the motion of the ship as she pitched and rolled heavily. *"I heard the sound of running feet on the quarter-deck, shouts, and the unmistakable sound of rain beating down upon the decks. I ran out to find we were caught in a wind of gale force and a confused, angry sea with waves like the crude hands of some pre-historic monster clawing out to catch us. The captain was on the quarter-deck, his beret incongruous with his oilskins, the rain streaming down over his eyes. He stood legs apart, quite calm, glancing around unhurriedly, taking in the situation, deciding upon action.*

"Then he bellowed an order in his rasping see-saw voice, which carried through the wind: "Take in the topsails, lads." We had all subconsciously turned to him waiting to see what he would do and responded to the command as though we had drilled to meet such a situation. Jan gave the orders and all hands hauled away, lashed by rain struggling to maintain balance as the ship fought with the wind and the seas. I pulled away at the greasy ropes, sandwiched between two naked seamen.... the topsail yard was stuck! ....we pulled until our arms and backs ached, the quarter-deck slippery underneath, the

ship swaying so that she came up to meet us and there was a real danger of falling overboard... the wind was strong enough to snap the topmast.....until the storm passed the Captain did not change his position just behind and to the left of the helmsman...he only used the words absolutely necessary excepting that he called us 'lads'."

When the ship was out of danger Warwick recorded in his journal that the Captain came below decks to thank him for his effort. *"There was a moment when we could have been in trouble,"* Alan Villiers admitted. Warwick thought that the period of danger was a lot longer than *'a moment'*.

There would be no sleep for anyone that night. Warwick talked to his film maker Julien Lugrin about the movie that was to be made with the film he was taking of the voyage. Both men had no choice but to talk reassuringly to each other. They were both, literally, lashed in their bunks as the ship bobbed helplessly on the great seas.

In America the film was to be turned over to a film editing lab that *Mayflower Transit* had selected to edit the footage down to a 20 minute film. Some of the footage would be unusable because it included shots of naked sailors but there would still be plenty of good material left to produce a good movie.

Warwick, however, had taken a totally un-commercial approach; he was grateful that *Mayflower Transit* were prepared to pay the editing, production and distribution costs and insisted on only one thing; that copies of the movie should be available to schoolchildren free of charge.

Warwick did not record all his thoughts during the storm. They were after all too ludicrously optimistic even for him to commit to paper. Years later, he admitted that he had thought that it would be OK if the ship went down. It was insured; he would use the money to build a better ship next time. It did not occur to him that he might perish with the vessel. During the storm his biggest fear was that the other crew members might somehow get to hear his obscenely loud thoughts about the insurance money, above the noise of the raging winds.

An artist's impression of *Mayflower II* in the stormy seas that it faced as it neared American shores. A storm of controversy would be waiting for it on shore.

CHANCE MEETINGS

As the *Mayflower* approached the coast of America Warwick once again asked Dr. Stevens to shut off radio communications. At Plymouth, where the Press, radio and television were talking of nothing else except the *Mayflower* and her arrival date, the added ingredient of the radio silence ensured that the suspense was too much to bear.

In the Boston Globe, Tom Riley increased the anticipation of the *Mayflower II's* arrival by speculating that tourist income to the region could easily double from the current $425 million to over $850 million in 1958. *"The billion dollar mark was in sight"*, he said, quoting Henry Hornblower's plan to appeal to children with the *Mayflower II* and *Plimoth Plantation* exhibit. The interest of children would encourage families from the middle and far west of America to make New England, and Cape Cod in particular, a vacation destination. *"The interest is already there"*, said Hornblower who reported that one classroom in Ohio sent in a donation to *Plimoth Plantation of $1.16*.

A local radio station asked a trustee of *Plimoth Plantation,* Bill Brewster, to join them in a search for the silent ship. Brewster set off with the radio reporters in a launch to find the silent *Mayflower II.* They were gone all night and although they knew where the *Mayflower II* had last reported her position it was morning before they saw a plane circling in the sky far off on the horizon. *"No plane would do that normally, it had to be the Mayflower,"* said Brewster.

He saw Stuart Upham first; then up popped Warwick with his razor in his hand, shaving cream one side of his face. He was so excited to see his friend from Plymouth that he kept shaving while he talked and forgot all about the goatee beard that he had been carefully cultivating during the voyage. In the excitement of the meeting it was shaved off. The visitor unloaded fruit and cigarettes but did not go aboard. On the way back the advance welcome party ran out of gas and were obliged to radio the Coast Guard for help.

On June 10th, Warwick was particularly agitated. *Mayflower* was suddenly becalmed. There was discussion about the need for a tow and Warwick became upset when the crew, now proud of their ability to sail *Mayflower II*, resisted the idea. *"Warwick Charlton is anxious, as ever, not to disappoint our reception committee"*, noted Peter Padfield.

On land the media coverage built up to a drum beat frenzy. Ronnie Forth checked and rechecked the welcome plans, to ensure that nothing was overlooked. Each visitor was allocated to a family in Plymouth and there was no shortage of volunteers anxious to make their guests feel at home. Beds were made ready, steak dinners were planned, spare automobiles were set aside and young girls connived to take part in the romance of the occasion.

On June 11th, Warwick had cause for excitement. At 5.45 am the massive cruise liner, the Queen Elizabeth, glided by the *Mayflower II* very slowly. Warwick could not get over the sight of the largest passenger ship in the world and the most ancient little predecessor alone together on the ocean. He walked around the decks, shivering with excitement, constantly nudging other crew members and repeating. *"Isn't this wonderful? What a lovely sight."* Peter Padfield thought Warwick was about to evolve wings, another crew member Jumbo Goddard thought he was going to turn into a jelly.

Ark Royal crossed paths with *Mayflower II.*

DANGEROUS WATERS

Mayflower II arrived into an American harbor on June 12 1957, rather unceremoniously - at the end of a long tow rope, courtesy of the Coast Guard. The thin curled claw of sand that is called Cape Cod and has the quaint little port of Provincetown at its fingertip, is surrounded by dangerous waters. There was virtually no wind and this modern *Mayflower* had a schedule to keep.

Also, Captain Villiers knew that hundreds of wrecks dating back to ships of the 1600's, such as the *Sparrowhawk,* had foundered very close to the deceptively innocent, sand duned shore.

Close to the journey's end, with a massive reception committee waiting in Provincetown and thousands more a few miles across the bay in Plymouth, it was time for the proud sailors to be practical.

At Provincetown, literally dozens of Press representatives swarmed aboard and Alan Villiers and the crew got a taste of the instant celebrity that was to be their lot for a few weeks at least. For most of the crew it was overwhelming and inexplicable to have journalists hanging on their every word. No one was left alone. Even Felix the cat was interviewed at length by newspapermen, searching desperately for a new angle.

One of those reporters with a feline interest was Walter Haskell, who was furious that Joe Meany had not been able to take the pictures of the voyage he so desperately wanted. He was perhaps venting his frustration when he decorated the front page of his paper, *The Old Colony Memorial* on June 20th , with a first person record of the journey by Felix the Cat. Felix was quoted extensively about his history; the lady who handed him over 12 minutes before the ship sailed, the cabin boy to whom he was entrusted, his difficulty in getting his sea legs, life on board, including an accident that resulted in one leg being put in a splint by the ship's doctor and the day he was nearly washed overboard. The story was placed at the top of the front page, along with a picture of Felix and direct quotes from Felix continued on page 5.

Other journalists were looking for trouble and in a day or two would find it. They all knew and resented the fact that *Life* magazine had been given an exclusive and would publish their account of the voyage on the following day.

John Lowe and **Warwick Charlton**. Journalists swarm over the ship to interview the crew, only to discover that they had signed contracts forbidding them to talk to the media. The angry media would soon find another story.

Several reporters seized on the young American cabin boy, Joe Meany, as a fresh face and a new story.

Others photographed the formal re-enactment of the signing of the "*Mayflower Compact*" which Warwick had promised the citizens of Provincetown would happen there, rather than Plymouth.

Warwick and Alan Villiers crowded around Provincetown native, Harry Kemp, the frail seventy year old "poet of the Dunes" who was given the honor of supervising the signing ceremony. It was one of the last times Warwick and his captain would appear in the same picture frame. From that point on Warwick would begin to go a separate way from Alan Villiers and the rest of the crew.

In fact, Warwick jumped ship immediately and was flown down to New York to appear in his seventeenth century costume on a TV show. Afterwards, he posed for the cameras as he was kissed on both cheeks by the comedienne Lucille Ball and the actress Jayne Meadows, before flying back to Provincetown to rejoin *Mayflower II* for the triumphal last 30 mile journey into Plymouth Harbor.

Arrival of the *Mayflower II,* June 13th 1957 at Plymouth Harbor.

IMITATING ART

On Thursday June 13th, the last day of the voyage, and the last day before Warwick would exchange the simplicity of his life at sea for some troubled times on land, he made an extensive entry in his diary.

"We left Provincetown at five in the morning with the pilot on board. An hour later we let go the tow and set all sail, and an east wind took us across Cape Cod Bay. There was a dream like quality to Mayflower's stately, measured progress. The early morning mist lifted in grey gossamer ribbons, revealing the placid harbor, a setting so formal it seemed an example of nature imitating art.

"A gay armada of several hundred boats of all shapes and sizes was attracted to us, spreading out across the water like an unruly fan as each jostled and fussed excitedly with the others' wakes for a better position. There were yachts, cruisers, trawlers, snarling little motor boats - even a canoe and a houseboat with an outboard motor attached, battling bravely along behind us. I tried to think of a simile to describe the scene; a mother hen and her chicks? No, for Mayflower had too much grace. A well loved grandmother with her grandchildren? No, for Mayflower was too young and pretty, and had too much dignity for a true family occasion. I gave up, defeated by my own excitement and the indescribable noise.

"Every boat that had some means of adding to the racket did so; whistles, sirens, foghorns, rattles and even cannon, while jet aircraft swooped low above and around us, and from the shores of the bay where we could already pick out people waving and running, there drifted the sound of car horns. By 10.30 we were off Saquish Point and surrounded by a forest of masts. For the last time the crew, to a great cheer, ran up the rigging to the yard arms, and in the billowing

sleeves, woolen caps and buckled shoes of their seventeenth century costume, took in all the sail.

"We had to pick up our tow again to get into Plymouth because of the narrowness of the channel. The tug came alongside at too sharp an angle and its superstructure, radar equipment, mast and searchlight, began to grind against our spritsail yard. Watching from the quarter-deck I saw one of the tug's crew apparently crushed between the yard and the tug's mast. It was Joe Lacey, always the first to react, who hurled himself out on the yard, straining at the canvas and braces, attempting to force the two apart. Then he himself fell, recovered and came back holding his side. We discovered later that he had cracked a rib. Miraculously we sustained no other damage from our tangle with the tug, and her seaman, who seemed in danger of being crushed, was unhurt.

"Overhead, helicopter passengers peered out from plastic bubbles and Alan asked the Coast Guards to shoo them away: 'They make it impossible to pass orders,' he said. The closer we came to land the more it seemed that everything that could float in Plymouth was out there to welcome us.

"A few minutes before twelve o'clock we made fast at the buoy and swung slowly around in the harbor so that the thousands of spectators on shore could see us, and the crew in turn could gaze in astonishment at the vast throng on shore. A thousand terns swarmed over the tip of Long Beach and turned sharply towards the harbor. The sun peeped through the clouds as though it did not want to miss the spectacle."

SWASHBUCKLING TOUCH

"After about an hour a cannon boomed, and at its signal the shallop, which had been built by Plimoth Plantation for the occasion, sped out from the shore to meet us. I went with Alan and the first landing party to the ramp at the side of the Plymouth Rock.

"As we were rowed towards the shore I glanced at the captain with whom I had been so proud to sail, sitting beside me with his black Pilgrim hat in his hand, and thought how like the younger Churchill he looked, with his air of imperious determination. He half turned, and slipped a quick, almost furtive glance back to Mayflower, idling gracefully at her buoy, and in the second before he set his face once more I believe his mind went willingly back to the quarter-deck, with planking beneath him and the sails set full above and the long blue horizon beyond the restless bows - and no official reception, no 'flamin' publicity.

"I, too, looked back as the shallop came to the steps. I remembered how we cursed Mayflower's discomfort, her motion and how we laughed at them. I remembered her inconveniences and the sheer delight and happiness she gave us, the power a sailing ship has of making you feel really alive; the short wild days and the long quiet ones.

"We walked up the steps to be greeted by Ellis Brewster, the descendent of Ruling Elder William. Dozens of television and film cameras whirred, flashbulbs lit us briefly, and a man in Pilgrim clothes beat out a long roll on a drum.

"I remembered the gay spirit of the crew; practical jokes and the laughter; friendships formed from the most trivial - and the most important - causes; words here, a joke there: and as our lovely ship dipped gently to her anchor in the sheltered waters I felt a wave of

sadness sweep over me to Edgar's voice stirring in my memory: "Her's a real beauty, I'll tell you! A real beauty!"

A drummer ushers the *Mayflower II* captain, Captain Villiers, followed by Warwick and Cabin Boy, Joe Meany.

Warwick chose to arrive in the uniform of Miles Standish who was the sole military man aboard the original *Mayflower* in 1620. He admired Standish, whom he regarded as a key to the survival of the colony during the first terrible winter.

Standish organized scouting parties to look for a place to settle, explored the neighboring woods and made the first potentially dangerous contacts with the Indians.

Warwick looked the part as he waded ashore in an ox hide jerkin and pants, with ornate shoulder pads and braided button fastenings. His shirt had large white linen cuffs and collar and the outfit was set off with ornate boots and a wide brimmed hat that looked stylish even in the 20th century. A thin mustache gave Warwick a slightly rakish look, although the goatee beard that he had accidentally shaved off, would have added a final swashbuckling touch.

Ellis Brewster stretched out his hand and said: "Welcome to America!"

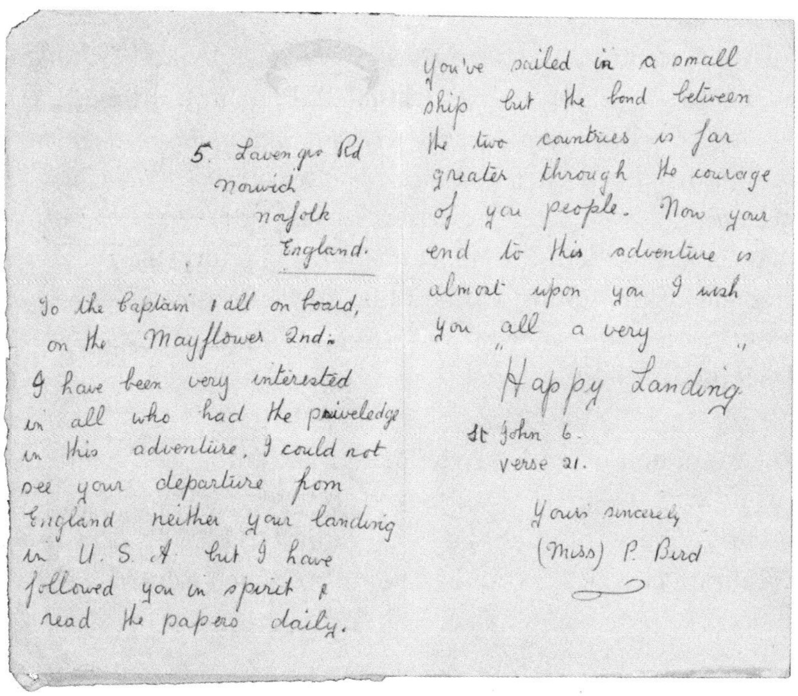

5. Lavengro Rd
Norwich
Norfolk
England.

To the Captain & all on board, on the Mayflower 2nd.

I have been very interested in all who had the priveledge in this adventure, I could not see your departure from England neither your landing in U.S.A but I have followed you in spirit & read the papers daily.

You've sailed in a small ship but the bond between the two countries is far greater through the courage of you people. Now your end to this adventure is almost upon you I wish you all a very "Happy Landing"

St John 6.
Verse 21.

Yours sincerely
(Miss) P. Bird

One of the hundreds of letters that arrived in the Captain's cabin after the arrival of *Mayflower II* in Plymouth habour.

TROUBLED TIMES

The voyage of *Mayflower II* was over. Warwick didn't realize it but his troubles with *Mayflower II* were really only just beginning. Everything changed in America. Alan Villiers went off to spend the night as the honored guest of Harry Hornblower and the rest of the crew were whisked off to homes throughout Plymouth.

As they went their separate ways Warwick looked at his crew members all handsomely outfitted in Pilgrim costume. *"After 56 days at sea he could see they had only one thing on their minds. They were fit. Even when the ship was becalmed they had been swimming. The only women they had seen were mermaids."* Warwick watched the reactions of the crew as they were greeted by the young women of Plymouth, pink cheeked and beautiful in their pilgrim costumes and thought *"My God, they are animals of prey."*

Accommodation for Warwick had apparently been overlooked but he was too tired and relieved to worry; he was happy and slightly amused when he was found a bed in a museum building. His night would be complete when John Lowe's wife joined him.

First though, before Warwick was bedded down in the Howland House Museum, he was greeted by two of the people who had supported him, John Sloan Smith of the *Mayflower* Trucking Company and Bill Connor the Daily Mirror columnist whose short commentary had propelled Warwick to get on with *Mayflower* himself. John Sloan Smith had a special stand built to ensure that his company and staff had the best view to welcome the ship and *Mayflower* trucks were waiting to carry the Treasure Chests to various exhibitions in stores around

America. Sloan Smith distributed to his company a special commemorative program packed with information on the *Mayflower*, the way she was constructed, details of the builder, captain and crew and articles supplied by John Lowe and Warwick. The trustees of Plimoth Plantation could barely conceal their concern at what they saw as an intrusion of a commercial interest into an historic event.

In the days that followed, Alan Villiers and his crew were fêted by the welcoming committee like conquering heroes, while Warwick was somehow off to one side. He thought he understood why. He told himself that he was like the writer and director of a play. He had done his bit. Now it was the turn of the actors to enjoy the spotlight. The star of his show was Alan Villiers and the crew were his cast, reaping the applause of the audience.

It was also to be expected that some of his fellow journalists would be furious at him for selling the rights to the voyage to *Life* magazine. It wasn't surprising that they lashed out at him at the first opportunity. He would probably have done the same in their shoes.

He didn't realize, however, that he faced a deeper problem; that the people he thought were his partners, were nothing of the kind; he was not welcome in Plymouth. They wanted his ship but they wanted nothing to do with him or his ideas and had been hard at work to ensure that they got their way. Over the next few days and weeks they would step up their efforts to write him out of the *Mayflower II* story.

Almost immediately, Warwick swapped his romantic period costume for a business suit and tie. The problems he faced were of a 20th century nature. The modern Press were much more curious than the shy Indians that initially hid deep in the

New England forest; they were swarming all over the ship and the shore, seeking answers to a number of questions. Some were frivolous.

For twenty-four hours they reported that the ship's log had been stolen and wanted to know why. The ship's captain, Alan Villiers, was reportedly furious. In fact Warwick had taken the log and given it to his friend Dick Brennan who was to rush it by hand down to the offices of Warwick's New York publisher, Little Brown, & Co. There it was photocopied and returned immediately. Warwick would need that log as a reference in the book he had been commissioned to write. He still owned the ship, he was officially listed as supercargo which meant he had total control of all commercial transactions and he saw absolutely nothing wrong with his action.

The Press took a different view and reported verbatim a sharp exchange between Villiers and Warwick that was overheard by a crew member. In a couple of days the incident was forgotten but the rift that had been simmering between Villiers and Warwick was now out in the open and real enough.

NICE BOYS

Just as the world's press reported the good news of the successful journey, they now gave extensive coverage to the bad. The more serious allegations concerned unpaid bills that were owed to suppliers to *Mayflower*.

The Adelaide Adventurer of South Australia reported:
Bills amounting to thousands of pounds, although guaranteed, were not settled when the Mayflower II left Britain two months ago. "We have been financially embarrassed," a spokesman for Uphams, the old established boat builders who did most of the work, said yesterday.

The list of unpaid debts included £6,000 for ropes and rigging, £470 for sails and £3,000 for seasoned oak timbers. Ernie Lister, a Brixham tugboat skipper, told the Press he was owed £307, his fee for towing the *Mayflower II* out to sea. Other reported claims included £1,196 for photographs and £1,820 for drinks.

One particular debt in Brixham Harbor struck an emotional note : Molly Fulton, an elderly widow who kept a rooming house, was apparently owed £102.90. She had rented rooms to four of the crew who apparently left for America without paying. *"They were such nice boys"*, she was quoted as saying.

John Lowe, who for once appeared in the spotlight, offered words of reassurance to the creditors. The *Christian Science Monitor* quoted John Lowe as saying that:

"Arrangements have been made to cover all remaining commercial liabilities."

Lowe pointed out that 12 days after its arrival in Plymouth, the *Mayflower II* would set sail for New York where it would be on exhibition and return to Plymouth on Thanksgiving Day. But the English Press treated the outstanding debts as a national crisis. Warwick had wanted to stay in Plymouth to present Vice President Nixon with a gold medallion with a tiny watch inside, but he felt he had no choice but to deal with Fenston and the English Press who were, by now, baying for his blood.

Vice President Richard Nixon was surrounded by some of the crew members as he welcomed the arrival of *Mayflower II*.

Twenty thousand spectators sweltered in the grandstands for hours until the drums and trombones from marching bands signalled the arrival of a smiling, waving Vice President Nixon, perched atop a big convertible. He led a parade, one and a half miles long, of 20 marching bands and 60 historical floats as they paraded through Plymouth. The Vice President was followed by an impressive collection of New England and American political leaders, eager to pay public homage to *Mayflower II*, including the new Governor of Massachusetts, Foster Furcolo,

Massachusetts Senator Leverett Saltonstall and Senator John F. Kennedy. The Vice President was rowed out to inspect the ship at anchor but Kennedy, the handsome young junior senator, demonstrated his skill at subliminal advertising, when he toured *Mayflower II* and was photographed at the helm of the ship. Two years later he would be at the helm of the entire country when he beat Richard Nixon to become the next President of the United States.

In one of many separate celebrations, 2,500 music lovers were treated to a pageant in honor of Captain and Mrs Villiers. The quiet, reserved John Lowe was in the audience but he went almost unnoticed as Villiers received as much applause as the performers. Afterwards the captain handled his new celebrity with aplomb as he was introduced to each of the cast. *The Old Colony Memorial* reported his every word including his observation that *"the costumes and lighting were magnificent."*

Warwick commissioned the Staffordshire pottery firm of William Adams & Sons to produce a set of *Mayflower* dining china.
Henry Hornblower II and colleagues dined on these plates on their visits to the Wig and Pen club.

Ronnie Forth had reason to be quietly satisfied with every detail including the bouquet for Mrs Villiers.

On Wednesday June 19th, *The Brocton Times* announced that Warwick Charlton had excused himself from the two weeks of celebrations in progress, to fly back to England. They quoted him as saying that he expected to pay every bill, certified as reasonable by an accountant. Warwick expected *to "clear the slate by July 1st."* This undertaking was verified by George P. Olsson a member of the Board of Directors of *Plimoth Plantation.*

Warwick pointed out to other journalists that if he had kept the *Mayflower* in England for a year *"she would probably have sailed to America in the happy position of having a surplus. But I am sure that position will be reached in the next few months."*

A few days later, the *Boston Daily Record* was one of many papers that speculated that the creditors of *Mayflower II* might cause the ship to be impounded. *".. if action is started in the Federal Courts. In that event a US Marshall would board the ship in Plymouth or wherever she was berthed, seize the Mayflower and place a caretaker aboard until the court case has been settled."*

BLUNDERBUSSES READY

Almost immediately afterwards, Felix Fenston told the Press that he was calling on John Lowe and Warwick to resign and he packed his bags and left for New York and London, without saying goodbye to his hosts. In London he wrote a letter of apology to Hornblower and explained that he intended to organize a meeting of the patrons of Project *Mayflower*. Warwick and John Lowe were to be invited to the meeting and asked to step down. In New England, Fenston left a stream of newspaper headlines behind him.

He became instantly known as the financial 'angel' behind *Mayflower II*. The Boston Daily Record gave front page treatment to the call for Warwick's resignation. The paper reported that Felix Fenston was threatening to withdraw his financial guarantees to Project *Mayflower* Ltd. Fenston said he had advanced the project $98,000 of which $56,000 was in the form of a guarantee and $42,000 in cash loans. Other media, on both sides of the Atlantic, created a storm of controversy.

Some commentators were more concerned about the principles behind the scheme. The plan to take *Mayflower II* to New York appeared to some reporters to be profiteering - an attempt to cash in on American fondness for their own history.

Alistair Cooke, the respected BBC radio commentator, wondered if the *Mayflower II* was tainted with commercialism because it was bearing chests designed to increase British trade. Bill Riley, the principal commentator for the Boston Herald, weighed in with a similar attack. It was, he said, *"A coldly calculated and completely organized plan to wring every possible dollar from a supposed gesture of international friendship."*

Riley and virtually all the other reporters representing the New England Press were incensed that the *Mayflower* was to be exhibited in New York so soon after arrival.

Someone was trying to make a million bucks out of *Mayflower,* they said in disgust. The Governors of *Plimoth Plantation* got behind their stockade walls with blunderbusses ready to defend themselves against charges of profiteering. The publicity shy Henry Hornblower was appalled at the searing spotlight that shone on the imperfections of the venture.

"We have no financial connection with either the London or New York Mayflower projects," Hornblower told the press. *"We have not become involved beyond supplying blueprints for the ship and agreeing to accept her when she is delivered to us on Thanksgiving."*

That was not quite correct. The agreements covered more than supplying blueprints. The governors and members of Plimoth Plantation had visited England on multiple occasions and had followed the progress of the ship's construction.

They were aware of the challenges in fundraising and the support from industry. They were also aware that the English had been encouraged to keep the ship in England for perhaps another year when London, Southampton and other port cities offered to raise money from exhibition fees.

They were aware that everyone connected with the *Mayflower,* except Warwick, wanted to delay sailing. They were also witness to the desperate last minute plea for cash to settle at least some of the remaining financial obligations, but it had not seemed to be in the American interests to contemplate delay.

For a start *Plimoth Plantation* had persuaded senior Massachussets politicians to get the President or Vice President to a welcome parade and had obtained funds from the local council and state to improve Plymouth harbor and various roads.

They were also anxious to raise the $1million they needed to turn a bare piece of land into a replica of the original village and they recognized the contribution that Project Mayflower was making to their own progress. Henry Hornblower had written in his 1956 report:

"Two issues of Mayflower Mail, published by Project Mayflower, were received during 1956 and helped greatly in keeping members of the Plantation and other interested parties in the United States, as well as England, informed on the progress and construction of Mayflower II. Publicity on TV, radio, in newspapers and magazines received wide report both in the United States and elsewhere in the world. (This) showed that Project Mayflower has able directors for that purpose. The Plantation benefited greatly being associated with publicity on every occasion."

Both gifts and membership had risen sharply in anticipation of the ship's arrival. In addition, *Plimoth Plantation* would soon seek to become heavily involved in the New York exhibition and the so-called commercialism that was being roundly condemned by the Press. For now, somebody had to assume the blame for the unpaid debts, and that person was Warwick Charlton.

Nobody connected to *Plimoth Plantation* had anything good to say about him or for that matter the unassuming John Lowe. One governor remarked, *"God help us from our friends."*

Hornblower meanwhile heaped praise on Alan Villiers. *"He is a gentleman who is trying to be helpful to our project."* Villiers returned the compliment. *"The Governors have convinced me they are a group of ethical men and from now on my main concern will be to see that justice is done by them."* Captain Villiers did not make clear what injustice the Governors of *Plimoth Plantation* were suffering, nor how he planned to repair the perceived problems.

Even while the celebrations continued the *Boston Globe* reported that *"certain interests wanted Lowe and Charlton dumped to rid the ship of unfavorable publicity and aspects of commercialism. Meanwhile the Mayflower II sits solemnly on America's doorstep sunning and sleeping as the south wind sings; 'Hush little ship, don't you cry: you'll be a museum piece bye and bye."*

SERIOUS MONEY

By coincidence Felix Fenston and Warwick were on the same flight back to London. Fenston would later claim that Warwick offered to resign during the flight. There was another coincidence.

Warwick was not the only person in Plymouth short of cash on June 19th 1957. On the day that he flew back to London to face the English creditors, Hornblower gave a short speech to his campaign workers who were beating the bushes for the $1 million needed to develop the replica of the first settlement. At the time they were only one-third of the way towards getting the total needed.

In a talk to friends of *Plimoth Plantation,* Hornblower underscored the importance of *Mayflower II* to what he believed would be the best living museum in America. *"It is one thing to hear how the pilgrims lived in the Mayflower, cold or hot as the weather dictated, tossed by storms, jammed into impossibly small quarters, wet and thoroughly miserable. But when you step onto and go below the decks of Mayflower II, history really comes to life."*

Hornblower ended his talk by emphasizing that *Plimoth Plantation* was free of commercialism. *"As you know this is a non-profit corporation dedicated to the telling of this story. For many years, a handful of persons - the Plantation Governors and a few friends - spent most of their spare time at this job, compensated only by the satisfaction of doing it."*

As he gave the pep talk, Hornblower and his colleagues were developing a plan to ensure that they would get complete control of *Mayflower II* and her income. The plan, they believed, required the support of Fenston and the other creditors. They would be offered repayment of their debts from the income *Mayflower II* would generate. In return for this, the combined statement of intent that had been agreed with Warwick and John Lowe, would be quietly forgotten.

Two days earlier, only five days after *Mayflower II's* arrival, Hornblower's attorney, Lothrop Withington, wrote a detailed memo to Fenston's New York attorney to make the case for dealing with income from *Mayflower II.* There seemed to be little need for a separate foundation, he argued.

"In numerous discussions with your client Felix Fenston, he agreed that it was unlikely that there would be any surplus [of funds] for at least three years. After you have read the articles of Organization and By-Laws of Plimoth Plantation, I think you will be satisfied that their purposes are sufficiently broad to provide all the advantages which can be obtained from the creation of another charitable Foundation."

At the time of this memo, Felix Fenston had the purely honorary title of President but he had no executive position. Nor did he own any shares in Project Mayflower Ltd. He had, however, given money to the company as well as financial guarantees on the company's behalf. If it could be shown that some of the financial backing was in the form of loans, he would have rights along with the other creditors.

Hornblower understood that Fenston intended to exercise those rights to take executive control of the company at the earliest possible moment.

Warwick, on the other hand, believed that the millionaire Fenston was re-appraising his involvement in the *Mayflower* project. He had provided the money to help Warwick get started because he thought that it might buy him some respectability. At one point he even thought that he might get a knighthood out of the exercise.

On his visit to America, Fenston suddenly realized what a major event the *Mayflower* had become. He had seen the massive interest in New England, felt the excitement in New York and read the stories of politicians elsewhere in America, pleading for *Mayflower* to visit them. The Governors of states bordering the Great Lakes region were mounting a campaign to attract *Mayflower* to their shoreline cities.

Warwick decided that Fenston's business instincts told him that not only could he get his money back but there was some serious money to be made.

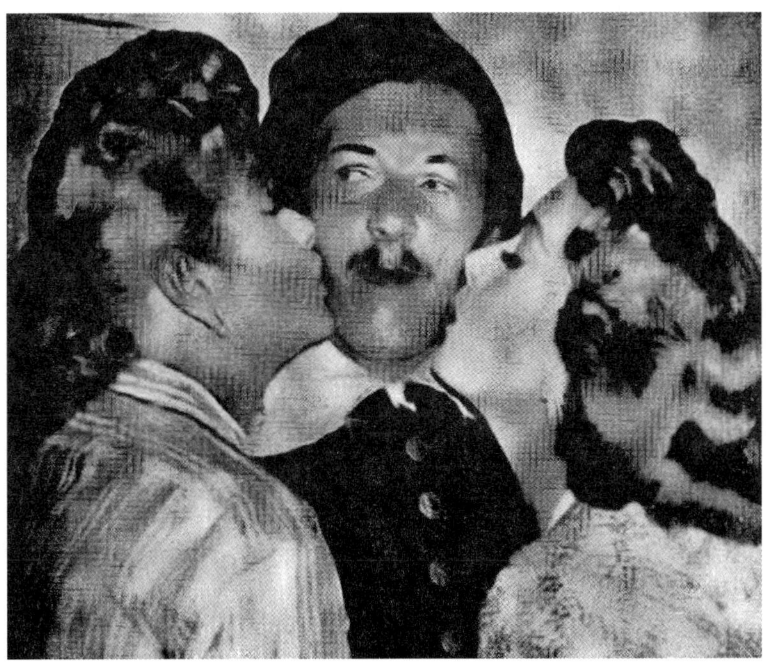

TV megastar **Lucille Ball** (left) along with fellow actress **Jayne Meadows** thank Warwick for appearing on their TV show. The printed press were less generous with their affection.

EMBARRASSING GIFTS

Captain Alan Villiers looked at the pile of letters waiting for him when he took a break from celebrations to return to *Mayflower II* as she lay moored in Plymouth Harbor. There were several hundred.

One was from Miss P. Bird of Lowengro Road, Norwich, England who had addressed her letter simply to Captain Alan Villiers, Landing at Plymouth. *"I have followed you in spirit and read the papers daily. You've sailed in a small ship but the bond between the two countries is far greater through the courage of your people."* Miss Bird quoted the bible, Saint John 6, Verse 21. There were hundreds of others, expressing similar sentiments, from ordinary citizens of both countries, as well as dozens from leaders of the United States among others. Steve McNicolls, the Governor of the state of Colorado, was one of the first to write. His letter had been waiting at Plymouth Harbor since mid May. He said:

Gentlemen,

On behalf of the citizens of the State of Colorado, I extend greetings and a welcome to our shores.

Your enterprise and the gift of the superb replica of the famous Mayflower are warm gestures of friendship and mark a significant step in our common history and heritage. Welcome to America.

There were others from many of the state governors, US senators, as well as politicians of lower rank. There were also greetings and congratulations from all over the world including a message from the British Prime Minister and the Queen of

England. The Suez Crisis had been forgotten. In the days after arrival Alan Villiers confessed that he struggled to cope with his overwhelming instant celebrity.

Each time he answered a few letters, phone calls and telegrams of congratulation, more flooded into the captain's cabin of *Mayflower II.* For days he got by on just a few hours of sleep. Villiers was no stranger to the public eye and he was probably better prepared than the crew to deal with their five minutes of fame, but he still found it hard to cope with the constant attention and praise for his role as captain.

The rest of the crew members couldn't work out what they had done to deserve the steak dinners, chauffeured limousines and the genuine overwhelming hospitality of the people of Plymouth. They were cast as heroes and their opinions were sought on the reports that there might be a rift between Warwick and Fenston, as well as the tales of their debt-ridden ship.

They issued a statement through Captain Villiers that *"ownership and control of the Mayflower II should go to a public Trust `or else',"* but none of the dozens of reporters was able to report what the crew were actually threatening to do. The truth was they didn't know: they just wanted to return to the seemingly endless round of cocktail parties and parades.

One exception was young Joe Meany who had been close to tears as he was greeted at Plymouth by his mother and young girlfriend. He couldn't wait for the photographers to stop asking him to pose for pictures. *"I just want to get home,"* he told one reporter. There he would find an offer to pay his college fees for the next four years. It came from a wealthy benefactor who had been inspired by the part young Joe played in the

Mayflower adventure. Joe Meany Jr. would go to the college of his dreams, Notre Dame, after all.

The crew had one last chore between the merry making: to unload the 92 Treasure Chests that had come across as cargo. A *Mayflower* van was ready to whisk the chests off for exhibition across America. Warwick had ensured that one chest carried a special consignment of cattle feed for delivery to a cattle ranch in Gettysburg, Virginia. It was destined for the ranch owned by President Eisenhower.

There was also a Treasure Chest of gifts for *Plimoth Plantation*. As their final task, the crew had to unstrap some watches from the hull of the ship. A watchmaker had paid a fee to subject them to the rigors of a sea-soaked crossing to prove they were waterproof.

Hornblower was embarrassed by the Treasure Chest that was addressed to him and said he wasn't sure he wanted to open Pandora's box. It contained a number of valuable collectors items manufactured by British companies, which had been donated by the Plymouth Gin Company of England.

The Managing Director of Plymouth Gin had intended them for display at the new *Plimoth Plantation* but was horrified to learn that Hornblower had given the items away to various friends in Plymouth.

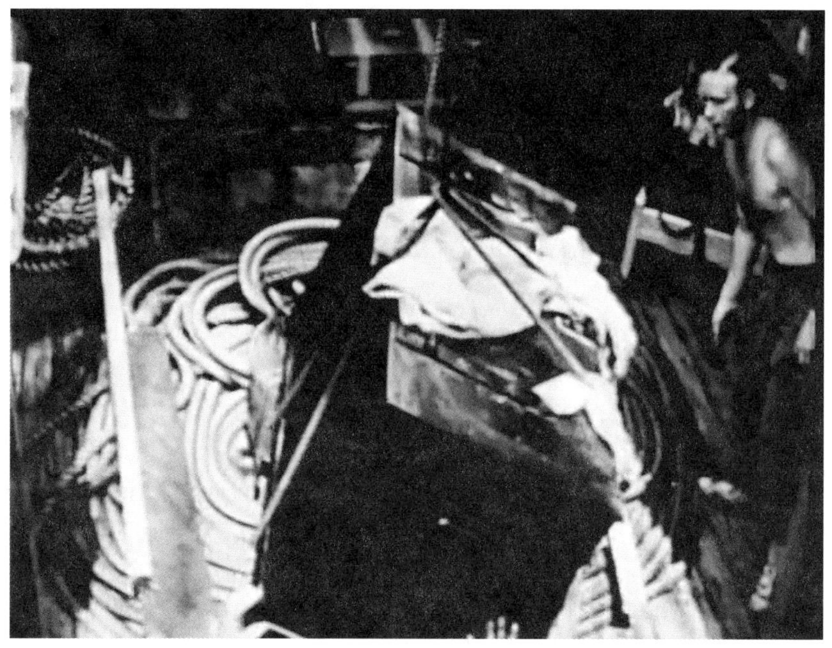

The crew unloading the **Treasure Chests**. Was this the unwelcome intrusion of commercialization into the gift of the *Mayflower II* ?

INSTANT TROUBLE

The Press was waiting to greet Warwick as he arrived at London's Heathrow Airport, a mere week after *Mayflower II's* arrival in the US. This time it was his face rather than the now familiar picture of *Mayflower II* that appeared on page one of the News Chronicle and other papers.

The journalists were interested in the developing row between Warwick and Felix Fenston and the claims of some of the suppliers that they had not been paid.

Warwick chose not to hide. Soon after getting off a tiring long night flight, he appeared on the BBC's prime time news program Panorama, hosted by Richard Dimbleby, the country's most respected presenter. During the interview Warwick reassured viewers that all unpaid bills would be settled but he went further and declared all the money involved in the *Mayflower II* project were administered by a trust. In one part of the interview, Warwick said; *"It is a lot of nonsense, we have a foundation, a trust was set up before we left England. Every cent that comes in from America goes into that foundation for the maintenance of the ship and the furtherance of the aims and objects of the project."*

This was not yet true. Hornblower had not set up the trust and although Warwick did not know it yet, he had no intention of doing so.

Warwick's attorney was so alarmed by the interview that he immediately wrote to Warwick setting the record straight and covering his back. The letter dated June 19, 1957 was marked private and confidential. Mr. D.V. Jennings stated...."*there is not, as you are aware, any foundation or trust at present in existence, although very urgent efforts were made after your departure to the United States in the Mayflower II to get this matter settled."*

Mr. Jennings also referred to a report that appeared in the Daily Telegraph which quoted a Project *Mayflower* spokesman as saying there were more than enough funds available in the London account to meet liabilities. The attorney continued; *"If this report is correct I should be glad to know what your intentions are with regard to the settlement of the various outstanding claims some of which as you know, we are handling from this office."*

Warwick announced that he was filing suit for libel against several papers but a couple of days later his own attorney wrote a formal letter to his client withdrawing his services. At the same time Price Waterhouse, Project *Mayflower's* honorary auditors, quit.

The implied criticism of Warwick became so strong that the Boston Evening Globe felt it worth dragging his mother into the scandal. She issued her usual threat to Warwick from her home on the south coast of England; she would disown him unless he fought on. The paper quoted her combative advice *"I hope he keeps on fighting; if he doesn't he won't be my son. However the guns go against him, he must not give up the ship. My message to him is to keep the flag flying."*

She was fed up with seeing her son attacked, she told the interviewer. The venture was his idea and he sailed in the ship. None of the people who are criticizing made the voyage. It was my son's faith and belief and work that made the voyage possible. *"No-one wanted to take over the ship until it was successful. That is the way of the world. My son is a true Elizabethan."*

This was about the only story that contained a kind word for Warwick. He had become the bad guy, a promoter of a scheme that had made one sales pitch too many. The Press, whether they meant it or not, was making him pay for every inch of good *Mayflower II* publicity he had squeezed out of them over the previous two years. Only *The Old Colony Memorial* of Plymouth, Massachusetts had little to say about Warwick Charlton, but they would have plenty to say about him later.

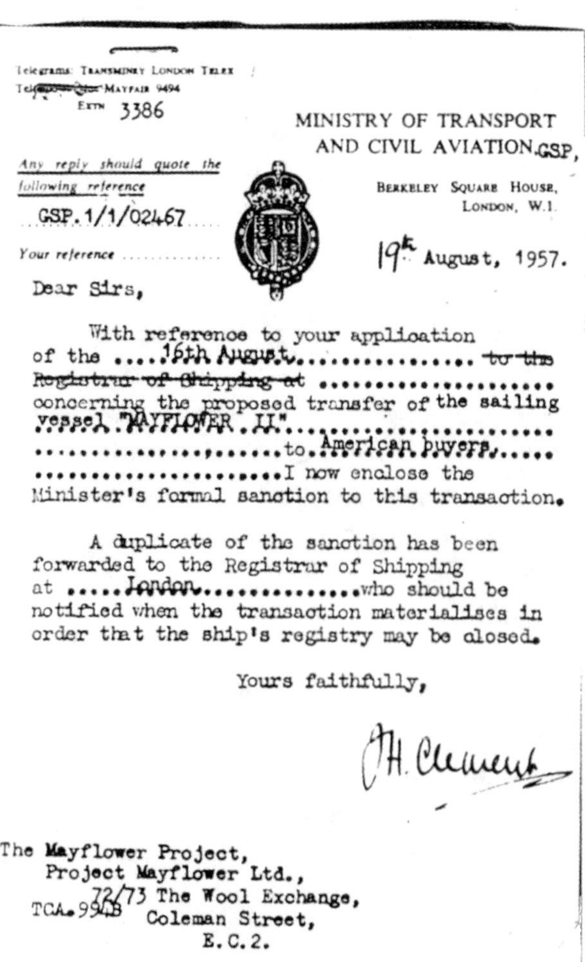

Telegrams: Transminry London Telex
Telephone: Mayfair 9494
Extn 3386

MINISTRY OF TRANSPORT
AND CIVIL AVIATION GSP,

Any reply should quote the following reference
GSP.1/1/02467

Your reference ....

Berkeley Square House,
London, W.1.

19th August, 1957.

Dear Sirs,

With reference to your application of the ....16th August................ ~~to the Registrar of Shipping at~~ .... concerning the proposed transfer of the sailing vessel "MAYFLOWER II"........................ ....to American buyers...... ....I now enclose the Minister's formal sanction to this transaction.

A duplicate of the sanction has been forwarded to the Registrar of Shipping at .....London................who should be notified when the transaction materialises in order that the ship's registry may be closed.

Yours faithfully,

J H. Clement

The Mayflower Project,
Project Mayflower Ltd.,
72/73 The Wool Exchange,
Coleman Street,
E.C.2.

TCA.9948

FRESH CRISIS

The day after returning to London to defend his actions on national television, Warwick was asked to attend a meeting at Fenston's Hill Street home at 11:30 am on Tuesday June 20th. There, in front of several of the patrons, Fenston intended to invite Warwick to resign.

The rich and the famous men assembled by Fenston, twiddled their thumbs for two hours and finally a letter arrived. It was from Warwick. He could not attend the meeting he said and had no intention of resigning. The only directors and shareholders of *Project Mayflower Ltd.* were John Lowe and himself, and John was still in America.

Fenston immediately issued a statement which was picked up by the world's Press that left readers in no doubt who was the guilty party. *"Financial Angel quits"* ran one headline, reporting Fenston's decision not to be responsible for any more of *Mayflower's* debts.

A few days later Warwick faced a fresh crisis. Fenston announced that he was seeking a High Court injunction to prevent Warwick from giving *Mayflower II* to America until the creditors had been given adequate assurances of payment.

Fenston wrote to Hornblower to reassure him, *"If we are successful in our application it would be the wish of the trustees and patrons here, that the ship should be handed over to you, as agreed, on Thanksgiving Day, subject to the filing of the American Foundation and an agreement entered into between yourselves and the Foundation."*

To Warwick, Fenston's move was a blatant attempt to gain control of the ship and her income and get all of his money back and maybe more. He believed his plan for an Anglo-American trust and scholarships would be history, if Fenston and Hornblower cut a deal.

Hornblower encouraged Fenston's bid to take over *Project Mayflower* with promises of close cooperation. He believed the millionaire businessman would continue to be a good friend of *Plimoth Plantation.*

Warwick, on the other hand, felt no particular gratitude or obligation to Fenston. The man was enormously wealthy but Warwick viewed Fenston's contribution as a relatively insignificant sum. Fenston had made his fortune during the war, while others were still fighting to ensure the freedom of the country and Warwick was always amused by the fact that Fenston had been invalided out of the army early, after falling from a bicycle. As Fenston tried and failed to obtain an injunction, Warwick flew back to the States. He announced that he was prepared, if necessary, to gift the *Mayflower* to *Plimoth Plantation* immediately.

Fenston got wind of the new move and followed Warwick once more across the Atlantic. Warwick was in Boston ready to proceed with his plan to gift the *Mayflower* to *Plimoth Plantation,* when he received a call from Felix Fenston. He was in the office of his New York attorney and after some preliminary pleasantries, suggested that the handover of *Mayflower II* should be delayed. Warwick bridled at the suggestion and refused to budge from the commitment he had already made.

Fenston handed the phone to his attorney who threatened Warwick. *"I would hate to do to anybody what we will do to you if you go ahead."* The threat guaranteed that Warwick would proceed, whatever the consequences. Typically, he answered threat with counter threat. *"I am about to go to Washington DC to talk to some of the country's top politicians,"* he shouted down the phone. *"Why don't you meet me there and we will have a public debate about your client's motive."*

By now the publicity had reached a critical mass, so that literally anything to do with the *Mayflower II* and Warwick was news. The Boston Globe reported that Warwick had spent the weekend with some Boston relatives. The fact that he had gone to Fenway Park on Saturday afternoon to watch the Red Sox play was news. Equally worthy of reporting, was the information that he had stopped at a diner on a car ride through New Hampshire and played Elvis Presley records on a juke box. *"His interest in and knowledge of American life amazed us"*, said Mrs. Samuel Bearse, one of Warwick's distant cousins. *"He knew all about Elvis, Ted Williams, Rocky Marciano and Joe Louis."*

However, the Press remained highly suspicious of the man they had dubbed "The *Mayflower* Maestro" and "Britain's number one promoter." Some journalists just couldn't believe that he wasn't making a fortune out of the *Mayflower*. Warwick defensively told the Press that he was not receiving fees for appearances he made on two top-rated television shows , *"I've got a Secret"* and *"The Steve Allen Show."* At least one member of the Press warned his readers *" to hang on to their daughters and their valuables - a modern day P. T. Barnum was on the way to town. Watch out for the smooth talking promoter with an English accent"*, he warned, without ever accusing Warwick of anything more improper that possessing charm, talent and great powers of persuasion. The story was syndicated and appeared in Boston, New York and elsewhere.

IRISH QUESTION

Mayflower II was buffeted by heavy seas as she made her way down the coastline in late June 1957 from Plymouth, to Provincetown, then on to Newport, and to Staten Island. A hurricane called Audrey had passed up the coastline and was still affecting the area.

Mayflower II
In all her glory. The little ship was said to speak for herself. However, until now, she has hidden more than one secret.

Captain Villiers had hoped to make most of the trip under sail but 40 mile an hour winds and high seas forced him to take the prudent option and accept a tow from a tug at the end of a 600 ft. long nylon wire. The ship could have ridden out the storm but Villiers had a schedule to keep. The ship had to be in New York Harbor for the reception Warwick had arranged for July 1st.

Mayflower II's New York appearance was scripted down to the minute so she had to arrive on time. She was due to arrive at Staten Island at 4 a.m. on June 30th, then leave under full sail for the Statue of Liberty where she would arrive at 10.30 am. From there, a marine escort of 500 boats accompanied her up the north river to Pier 81 at West 41st Street.

The following day was designated *Mayflower* Day in New York as the city rolled out the welcome mat for the Captain and crew. Warwick was still back in Boston and in his business suit as his crew members were engulfed in the adoration of the population of the Big Apple. *"That should make the captain and crew happy"*, he said as he flew down to New York, a day after the celebrations. Party time was over for him. Apart from the debts there was an office in England that no longer had anything to do. There were people to fire, office furniture to be sold off and a business to be closed down.

As the ticker tape and cheers rained down on their triumphal journey up Broadway one or two of the crew wondered briefly what they had done to enjoy all the fuss. So did some of the welcoming party. The New York Police Chief turned to one of the crew during the speeches of welcome and muttered. *"You know I don't know why I am here. I'm Irish and this Mayflower doesn't mean a damn thing to me."*

Alan Villiers was now the star attraction of the *Mayflower* story. He made several television appearances including one on the most popular game shows of the time, "The $64,000 Question". Villiers won $16,000 on the show. Then he flew back to his comfortable home in Oxford, England with his wife Nancy, to write his account of the voyage and edit his video for sale. The first mate, Godfrey Wicksteed, took over as Captain as the ship went down to Miami for another exhibition.

From his home in Oxford, England, Villiers wrote a warm note to Hornblower and voiced his dislike and distaste of Warwick and John Lowe in the strongest possible terms.

LAST MOVE

Every day or so it seemed, in late July, a new legal document arrived at the offices of *Project Mayflower Ltd.* They all contained the same message although the amounts differed; they were court judgments in favor of creditors of *Project Mayflower Ltd.* By the end of the month they totalled £15,000. If they weren't paid within 30 days the creditors could ask the court to appoint a liquidator. Fenston and the other creditors would have a say in the disposal of the assets of *Project Mayflower Ltd.* Of course, the only asset of value was the *MayflowerII* herself.

Warwick made one last attempt to persuade Henry Hornblower to cooperate with him rather than Fenston. He wrote to him on August 2nd and regretted that in view of the fact that no progress had been made with the establishment of a trust to administer *Mayflower's* income, he was withdrawing his offer to hand *Mayflower* over to *Plimoth Plantation.*

For once the normally calm tone of Hornblower's correspondence was ruffled. He wrote back to point out that he had raised $250,000 from the Massachusetts legislature on the basis of the agreement with *Project Mayflower Ltd.* At the same time the US public appeal had been seriously damaged by the exhibition of the ship in New York first, rather than Massachusetts.

Near the end of a three page letter he concluded; *"Mr. Withington advises me he did say we would be glad to sit down with all concerned, putting all the cards on the table, to see if we could be of any help in settling the differences, and we will still be glad to do that."* An olive branch had been offered but still no trust. Warwick surveyed the office in Coleman Street that had been the headquarters of *Project Mayflower Ltd.* Somehow it looked smaller, as rooms often do when they are empty. The filing cabinets and desks were all gone, sold to pay pressing bills. Over the last six months both he and John had forgotten about their public relations clients who had naturally forgotten about them.

There was no income and Miss Jeans and others had been let go. Warwick saw no alternative but to close down the office and reach for his typewriter. If he could get a *Mayflower* book written by the end of the year while the story was still news, perhaps he would be back on his feet.

Warwick, now close to despair, believed that *Project Mayflower Ltd.* would shortly pass into the hands of a court appointed liquidator but before he abandoned the company, he decided to make one last attempt to protect *Mayflower II* from Fenston and the other creditors.

He intended to transfer the ownership of *Mayflower II* to an American company he had established for the purpose.

John Lowe looked upon Warwick's maneuvering in a spirit of helpless despair. He would support him to the end by signing whatever documents Warwick put in front of him, but his bitterness towards his partner would grow. It became clear to John that he, like Warwick, would end up in debt.

Like Warwick, he had no personal savings or resources to fall back on, and without a public relations company, he saw no clear path forward. He decided to cease giving advice to Warwick and drifted quietly away from his partner.

TRADING PLACES

The plan involved a good deal of red tape.

The Ministry of Transport and Civil Aviation were required to sanction the move and they received the formal request on August 16th. Warwick's pleas for a quick approval were issued on August 19th and he raced off to a notary public, then to the American Consul in Grosvenor Square, to get the signature of a consular official.

While Warwick was completing the transfer, representatives from *Plimoth Plantation* were meeting with Fenston, his attorneys and attorneys for the other leading creditors. *Plimoth* representatives wanted an assurance that the English creditors would not take action to impound *Mayflower II.* They would be paid from *Mayflower's* income, they were assured.

They were not aware that *Project Mayflower Ltd.* of London no longer had an asset to impound. As the result of Warwick's actions *Mayflower II* was now owned , free of any encumbrances by The *Mayflower* Foundation, a Connecticut Corporation. The share holders of the new American company, The *Mayflower* Foundation were John Lowe, Warwick Charlton and an attorney acting on their behalf.

If they chose they could find a new home in America for *Mayflower.* The Marine Museum at Mystic was at least one possibility. By now, however, Warwick was out of money and time. He had no source of income. Three creditors were threatening court action unless they were paid immediately. He had a book to write rapidly and somehow he convinced himself he could work with Hornblower.

In early September Warwick contacted Hornblower to confirm that he was prepared to proceed, as originally agreed. He was ready to sign a bill of sale to transfer the ship to *Plimoth Plantation,* for the token consideration of one US dollar.

The offer seemed too good to be true and some of the Governors of Plimoth Plantation thought there might be a catch but Harry Hornblower knew exactly what to do, the same thing he did when any issue arose that needed a second opinion from a sharp legal mind. He picked up the phone and called his attorney Lothrop Withington, the senior partner of Withington, Cross, Park and McCann. Lothrop Withington had served the Hornblower brokerage firm of Hornblower and Weekes very well and was good friends with the family, including Harry's father, Ralph Hornblower.

Warwick was asked to attend a meeting at the law firm's offices at 73 Tremont Street, in the center of Boston. Others were asked to attend, including the people Warwick had partnered with in New York, who were currently exhibiting the ship.

Warwick was desperate. He needed $15,000 immediately to meet creditors who refused to wait. It was agreed that these funds would be made available but held in escrow, pending Warwick's delivery of documents transferring the ship to *Plimoth Plantation.* At the same time, the *Plantation* would contact all the creditors in the UK and promise to meet the debts in an orderly fashion.

Lothrop Withington sought and obtained agreement from Warwick's New York partners that in return for an advance of $25,000 which was required to support running costs at the New York Exhibition, *Plimoth Plantation,* as the new owners, would permit the group to follow up the exhbition in New

York with trips to Miami in December 1957 and Washington DC in the Spring of 1958.

Letters were sent to all parties and, for the absence of doubt, it was made clear that Plimoth Plantation would not be involved in the exhibitions beyond supplying the *Mayflower II. Plimoth Plantation's* share of the profits would be used to repay the funds they had advanced and then surplus revenue due to Plimoth Plantation would be applied to paying off the creditors in an orderly fashion.

The last piece of the plan was to ask George Stewart, Warwick's New York based insurance friend, to help persuade the English creditors to be patient. Stewart visited England regularly and also had a personal interest. At one point, in his enthusiasm for the project, he had advanced Warwick a few thousand dollars.

In all the letters that were produced, *Plimoth Plantation* made clear that they were making no commitment to meet the claims of the UK creditors. Their compensation would have to come from the revenue from Americans who paid their entry fees to walk the boards of the little ship in New York and elsewhere.

In case the group in New York were concerned about switching their allegiance from Warwick *to Plimoth Plantation,* Lothrop Withington made clear that there was a compelling reason for doing so. Just as Warwick had persuaded the UK authorities to allow the ship to be transferred without any tax levy, so, on behalf of *Plimoth Plantation,* he had persuaded the US Customs authorities to grant exemption to any tax on entry. This exemption was granted on the condition that *Mayflower II* was a museum exhibit in the possession of a non- profit.

The directors of *Plimoth Plantation* were still concerned. They would make no formal announcement until they had talked to

Fenston and his attorney in London. They found it difficult to accept that Felix Fenston had no legal right to make decisions related to the ship and that he was just another creditor who needed to be persuaded to wait.

Warwick meanwhile, had convinced himself that he could trust *Plimoth Plantation* to honor their commitments. After all, he reminded himself that when they had requested and received approval from US Customs back in 1956 for a waiver of any import duty, they had given an assurance that the ship was *"a gift from the British people to the American people."*

Back in England, on September 16, 1957, Warwick produced the various documents that Hornblower's attorneys had deemed necessary to confirm the transfer of the ship to *Plimoth Plantation*. Warwick saw no need for legal advice. For him it was important that the documents be historically correct, like everything else he did connected with *Mayflower*. So, Warwick produced the wording of the actual sale document in the archaic language of the 1620s. It began *"To all to whom these presents may come, greeting:*

"Know ye, that the Mayflower Foundation, Incorporated, a corporation duly organized and existing under the laws of the state of Connecticut, owner of the sailing ship called the Mayflower II of the burden of 260.12 tons, or thereabouts, in consideration of the sum of $1 to its hand paid, the receipt whereof is hereby acknowledged, have bargained and sold, and by these presents do bargain and sell, unto Plimoth Plantation Inc., a corporation duly organized and existing under the laws of the Commonwealth of Massachusetts, the said sailing ship, together with the mast, bowsprit, sails, boats, anchors, cables and other appurtenances thereto apertaining and belonging."

At the request of Hornblower and his attorneys, Warwick made his way to the US embassy in Grosvenor Square in London. The documents were then signed and witnessed by a notary public, then, for good legal measure, also witnessed by a US government official. They were then wired to Hornblower's attorneys who though bemused by some of the archaic language, telegramed their approval on the following day.

Warwick repaired to a cottage in Kent which a friend had offered him free of charge, as a temporary office and refuge. He would now concentrate on writing his account of the voyage. However, the Press were not yet ready to leave him in peace. He had separated from his partner, Paula, and was still newsworthy enough for his personal problems to attract wide Press attention. A copy of one Press cutting detailing Warwick's marital woes found its way to *Plimoth Plantation.*

Hornblower wrote to Villiers to keep him informed of the acquisition and Warwick's personal dramas. He had a role in mind for Villiers and wanted him on his side. Hornblower was confident *"it was the beginning of the end."*

Villiers wrote back *"I look forward to hearing details of your astonishing news. The sooner those two bastards are out of our lives the better."*

While Hornblower and Villiers were trading gossip, Warwick contacted the *Plantation* to obtain confirmation of his position as an honorary governor of the *Plantation.* George Olsson sent him a regular membership application. Warwick immediately wrote to point out the error and an honorary membership form was mailed a few days later. An honorary membership was meaningless. Warwick was getting no response to his request for the promised Honorary Governorship.

As far as Warwick was concerned *Plimoth Plantation's* acceptance of his offer locked them into the original agreements. They would be trustees of the ship on behalf of the American people; there should be a trust fund and they would not be able to use any of the income for other purposes beyond the repair and management of the ship. Warwick would be a governor of Plimoth Plantation and his appointed trustees would have a say in deciding how any surpluses were used, including the establishment of Anglo-American scholarships.

In fact, Lothrop Withington had succeeded in obtaining *Mayflower II* for Plimoth Plantation on terms that involved minimal obligations, as well as minimal financial risk. He had provided all of his considerable legal expertise over an extended period, free of charge (or 'pro bono' as the lawyers like to say). Mr Withington's only reward was a model of *Mayflower II.*

Lothrop Withington - his only reward was a scale model of the *Mayflower II,* later affectionately called *"Warwick's Folly".*

PERSONAL PROBLEMS

On the day back in September when Warwick had met with Hornblower and his attorneys in Boston, Hornblower had taken Warwick aside and asked him how much the *Mayflower* had cost him personally. Warwick really had no idea. He knew he diverted so much money that he left England with the rent on his home three months in arrears.

He knew he had poured cash fees from freelance journalism into the *Mayflower,* as well as income from some of his PR accounts but he didn't sit down and do a proper accounting. He never kept track.

Warwick thought he had spent at least $30,000 out of his own pocket in addition to the money that he and John Lowe had raised through their various fund raising schemes. According to Warwick, Hornblower agreed to repay Warwick the $30,000 as soon as the ship's revenues permitted.

Warwick was relieved but desperately short of immediate cash, even for food and accommodation. The high exchange control regulations imposed by the British Government at the time, meant permission had to be obtained to take more than £10 abroad in foreign currency, so he was always short of cash.

He decided to sell his military uniform that he had arrived in, only to find that his friend Dick Brennan, the second cook, facing similar financial restrictions, had already done so.

In November 1957 Warwick took a break from work on his book to write to Hornblower. It began;

Dear Harry,

"I was glad I spoke to you and Dave (Freeman) last week. I was beginning to feel out of touch."

Warwick's feelings were justified. He did not know it but a week after he wrote this letter there would be an official ceremony at Plymouth to be witnessed by the press and covered by live television at which *Mayflower II* would be officially handed over. The ship's ownership would be transferred to the sole ownership of *Plimoth Plantation*. Neither Warwick nor John Lowe would be present to remind everyone that their agreement called for the ship to pass to *Plimoth Plantation,* to be held in trust for the American people.

Warwick displayed his ignorance of events by quoting newspaper reports about *Mayflower II* to Hornblower. It was not surprising. For the last three months every spare minute had been spent writing his account of the voyage which was due for publication in America shortly.

Warwick wanted Henry's agreement to spend a few weeks in Miami, where the ship was due to be exhibited during the winter, autographing and promoting his book.

"It represents a wonderful opportunity to put myself on my feet financially. I have had to sell my office and contents and am finding it a little difficult to get going with nothing behind me. I would be most happy to give part of the revenue to the Plantation."

Even when he was desperate, Warwick could not resist the temptation to write well and with a sense of history. He ended his letter:

"The address at the top of this note paper is that of a 17th century cottage near to the old Pilgrim way, about nine miles from Canterbury. Just up the lane is a pre-Norman church, and out of the window where I am writing I look down the gentle curve of the Wye Valley, a completely unspoiled part of England that must have looked much the same when Chaucer passed this way."

Warwick's manuscript for *"The Second Mayflower Adventure"*, records his faith in his partnership with Plimoth Plantation, just days before he was due to hand over the ship. The book is dedicated to Henry Hornblower. He asserts that the ship was a gift from the British people to the American people and that the agreed aims of both *The Mayflower Project* and *Plimoth Plantation* were taking shape *"in the form of a permanent foundation for educational and even travel exchanges between the two peoples."*

Warwick believed that his ability to obtain permission to stage an exhibition free of entertainment tax, was due to the long term educational aims for the project. He went into extensive detail describing the design and construction of the ship, which was complemented by a diary that he had kept throughout the voyage.

However, there was no reference to disagreements with his partners although Warwick may have subconsciously hinted at the possibility of problems when he reminded his readers that the original Pilgrims *" were shamelessly exploited and swindled by some of their backers and emissaries."*

BIZARRE CEREMONY

Just before Thanksgiving the *Mayflower* sailed from New York back to Plymouth. The local press heralded her return by announcing that the formal handover would take place at an official ceremony scheduled for early morning on November 27th, Thanksgiving week. Massachusetts Governor Furcolo and other state and local leaders were present, along with the media. It was a bizarre ceremony.

Neither Warwick nor John Lowe was invited to attend. Alan Villiers was present to hand over the sale document Warwick had signed on September 16, although he was embarrassed enough to explain to the local Press that he was not authorized to represent Warwick Charlton, John Lowe, or their two companies - the UK registered *Project Mayflower Ltd.* or the recently formed Connecticut company *Mayflower Inc.* Henry Hornblower had prepared remarks in which he noted that *"the two men who were most responsible for getting this ship built couldn't be here today"* and he then read two telegrams of good wishes from Felix Fenston and Warwick.

Warwick's read: TODAY I HAND OVER MAYFLOWER II TO YOUR SAFE KEEPING. MAY SHE BE A REMINDER TO THE PEOPLE OF OUR TWO COUNTRIES THAT THOUGH THE ATLANTIC OCEAN MAY SEPARATE US, IT CAN NEVER KEEP US APART.

Hornblower then went on to praise the uncomfortable Alan Villiers and the crew for bringing the ship across the ocean. *"Mayflower II would have been a beautiful museum piece even if she had never set sail,"* said Hornblower. *"But it was your bringing her across under her own canvas that put life and reality into her."*

A few days before *Plimoth Plantation* made the public announcement of their acquisition of *Mayflower II* Hornblower's attorneys produced a document dated November 21st 1957 *"for the benefit of Project Mayflower Ltd. Creditors."* There was only one signature - Henry Hornblower's - on the document, which stated clearly that after *Plimoth Plantation* took possession of the ship it would use its best endeavors to pay the creditors, but only from the surplus earnings of the ship, after all costs had been met. In other words, the American people would clear up the debt with their $1 entrance fees: *Plimoth Plantation* would not be required to pay one cent.

There was no mention of an obligation to establish an Anglo-American Scholarship fund or for that matter any financial or other obligation to Warwick, John Lowe or *Project Mayflower*. Put simply, *Plimoth Plantation* took ownership of the ship for the extremely low cost of paying off *Mayflower II's* creditors.

The new 'outright ' ownership by *Plimoth Plantation* was ecstatically reported in the weekly Plymouth newspaper of record, *The Old Colony Memorial.* The million dollar fund that the directors of *Plimoth Plantation* had sought to raise, in order to develop a replica of the original settlement on the 100 acre property outside of the town of Plymouth, was still less than a third of the way towards its target, but there was now a solution. Surplus revenues from *Mayflower II* could be used in any way Hornblower and his directors decided. *Plimoth Plantation* was on its way and Hornblower and his colleagues intended to keep Warwick Charlton out of the way.

On November 29th, 1957, a few days after the ceremony to take possession of the ship , *Plimoth Plantation* took over Warwick's New York deal and signed an agreement with *Mayflower Ltd.* of New York, the company made up of Warwick's waterfront friend Hymie Rosenbloom, the insurance man George Stewart and their friends Paul Bird and Fred Glass.

The ten page document was, in effect, a joint venture. Both sides agreed to chip in $25,000 and the New York businessmen agreed to pick up the costs of taking the ship down to Miami in January 1958 and then back up to Washington in April, before returning to Plymouth in June 1958.

The agreement called for the New York Group to pick up all the costs of the various exhibits, including insurance on the ship of $300,000. After all costs had been met and each side had received its $25,000 back, profits were to be split 20/80 with *Plimoth Plantation* receiving 80 per cent of the net profits.

Warwick and John Lowe had been cut out of an agreement that they had originated.

LITERARY STENCH

The Old Colony Memorial had made a good start in obliterating Warwick's name from Plymouth. Throughout the celebratory weeks of the ship's arrival and the subsequent weeks before the November hand-over *The Old Colony Memorial* had consistently ignored Warwick. Hornblower and his fellow directors knew the news editor Walter R. Haskell well. Haskell reserved all his headlines and praise for the salty, plain spoke Captain Villiers and the gallant crew. *"Witty speech by Capt. Villiers dispels bad Mayflower publicity "* ran one headline. *The Old Colony Memorial* regarded anything Villiers did or said as news. When he broke into applause at the wrong place, at one of the many public functions in his honor, the incident was considered newsworthy enough to rate a separate story.

When he was presented with a baseball signed by the Brooklyn Dodgers the paper reported his advice to the assembled company *"to throw a straight ball not a curve."* Villiers was talking philosophy, the paper explained. At times the sycophantic adoration of Villiers bordered on the absurd.

"Villiers was terrific when he appeared on a television game show," said the paper. The paper noted that Villiers had answered the questions with a spirit of great confidence. Elsewhere in a three line commentary immediately underneath a story about *Plimoth Plantation, The Old Colony Memorial* made a very short but transparent attack on Warwick.

"There are too many journalists who 'make' news instead of reporting it."

Meanwhile the English establishment were making their views clear on where the credit for the *Mayflower* adventure lay.

On October 20th 1957, in the elegant chambers of the British Embassy in Washington, D.C., Her Majesty Queen Elizabeth II, held a special investiture ceremony to honor Ronnie Forth, the organizer of the *Mayflower II* welcome in the United States. She conferred on Mr. Forth the title of Honorary Officer of the Most Excellent Order of the British Empire.

On November 27th, in its front page report of *Plimoth Plantation*'s acquisition of *Mayflower II,* Walter B Haskell's story appeared under the headline *"Villiers Hands over vessel to Hornblower in Telecast Ceremony."*

After the ship was safely in the ownership of *Plimoth Plantation,* Walter Haskell ran a lengthy article in the weekly paper in which he analyzed the mistakes that had been made by Warwick Charlton and John Lowe.

"Mr. Charlton had originally intended it to be a heartwarming gesture by the people of England", Haskell noted. *"But suddenly it turned into a commercial venture. Mr. Charlton was in too deep and could not back out."* Haskell itemized the various fundraising schemes Warwick had employed to pay for the ship's construction, including the Treasure Chests, as if they were crimes against humanity. Haskell quoted Warwick as recognizing that he had made a terrible mistake in selling the exclusive rights to photograph the Atlantic crossing to *Life* magazine. Haskell agreed it was a mistake.

The rest of the American Press had been angered by their inability to gain access to the ship, except from a long distance lens. Without equal access to *Mayflower,* the Press began to dig and prod, said Haskell. *" The more they dug the more they found, and by the time the Mayflower II did arrive in Plymouth Harbor it was loaded with literary stench."*

Haskell praised *Plimoth Plantation* for the open and correct way in which they had conducted themselves and he gave voice to proprietorial pride in *Mayflower II.*

"It has been a shame that the Mayflower II has been a target of newspaper ridicule. Despite the distasteful publicity, the ship remains worldwide news. She's a lovely ship regardless, and she has proven (her) worth to Plymouth during her visit the past week. The Mayflower II is now in the hands of Plimoth Plantation. She can suffer no more harm from newspapers or magazine articles."

In early December, with *Mayflower II* safely moored in Plymouth Harbor and in the possession of *Plimoth Plantation,* Hornblower telephoned Warwick in England to suggest that his appearance either at the *Plantation* or on the *Mayflower* when it traveled to Miami might cause problems. Hornblower struggled unsuccessfully to be diplomatically vague.

He was anxious to avoid possible clashes of personalities and further adverse publicity. He mentioned Warwick's personal problems which had appeared in the Press. Some of the Governors would be embarrassed by Warwick's presence, Hornblower said, and a book promotion might revive charges of commercialism.

Hornblower concluded the phone call by saying that some of his colleagues felt it would better if Warwick not only stayed away from *Plimoth Plantation* but also from America for a while.

CAT'S GUARANTEE

The pain poured out of the pages from Warwick's six page reply written on December 9th. How could the Governors take the view they did ? He wasn't the first man in the public eye to go through a divorce and how could they take one view about his commercial activities and look at Alan Villiers in a different light. *"Villiers is a bluff, blow the man down, spray of the salt man,"* conceded Warwick. But he had earned thousands of dollars for articles, broadcasts, lectures and television appearances for his part in the project.

But he had nothing to do with the organizing of the project. *"Nothing commercial Sir, I'm a sea dog, and that lets me out. But that chap Charlton! Ah, he's another matter. He's also an author and journalist but look at the trouble he has given us. Mayflower for one thing. And so I imagine their reasoning goes. Of course it's true that I haven't been able to hand the ship over to you free of liabilities. But do they seriously think I did not want to. Indeed I had hoped to do far more, to hand her over with a surplus. It is my belief that she will not only pay her bills, but will go on earning her keep, and more besides for centuries to come."*

"I would remind those Governors who consider my presence would be harmful that I have given over three years of my life to Mayflower, all my resources, even my office and office furniture."

In case Hornblower started to feel sorry for him, Warwick concluded by stating that he was coming to America and he was going to promote his book in Miami even if he had to walk there and start his own exhibition. Hornblower wrote to Warwick again in early January to repeat his concern about Warwick's proposed appearance anywhere near either *Plimoth Plantation* or the *Mayflower*.

"While I quite appreciate the position you and John are in....at almost every press conference we are asked the question whether any part of the proceeds are going to Warwick Charlton or John Lowe."

In despair Warwick tried a whimsical approach. He wrote back on the day he received the letter to confirm that he would be in Boston on January 18th to begin promoting his book. *"This is not an unusual thing for authors to do and is not generally regarded as wickedly commercial"*, he told Hornblower. Warwick reminded Hornblower that he had never made himself out to be a rich man and he was currently surviving thanks to a £1,500 bank loan which was guaranteed by Felix the cat (who traveled on *Mayflower II*).

Warwick wrote that the active patrons of *Project Mayflower* had always intended that Warwick should receive a fee for the work he had done to be paid from surplus income *"You may confirm this with Felix the Cat . . this of course was before it became apparent that there would be no surplus income."*

Just in case Hornblower should conclude that Warwick was sinking to hysterical defeat he ended his letter with combative optimism and the cryptic warning that once he had got back on his feet financially *"you will have to be more wary of me than Khrushchev"* (the enigmatic leader of the Soviet Union).

Hornblower and his fellow governors issued a public statement about *Mayflower II "to clear up confusion and questions that have arisen about her status."* There was no reference to any ownership interest the American people might have in the vessel.

The governors were concerned that their fundraising drive would be adversely affected if potential donors thought any money they gave would be used to pay off *Mayflower* debts.

"Mayflower can take care of her own problems", said the statement boldly. *"She is an excellent vessel built in every respect to our own plans and specifications. She represents a need to raise $180,000 more in total than we had expected a year ago, but this constitutes only a fraction of what we expected to pay for her 11 years ago."*

The statement predicted that there would be significant revenues from the Miami exhibition to meet the creditors' demands and there was every possibility that by Thanksgiving 1958, *Mayflower II* would have earned enough to pay off all her debts. *"Her ownership by the Plantation represents very substantial progress towards our ultimate objectives."*

The statement concluded by asking for donations to develop the replica of the first settlement so the *Mayflower II* and *Plimoth Plantation* could become the number one visitor attraction in the region.

From time to time, the question of the ownership of *Mayflower II* by *Plimoth Plantation* would crop up, either in a letter to *The Old Colony Memorial* or a question from a confused visitor. On each occasion *Plantation* staff would patiently explain that yes, she was supposed to be a gift to the American people but that unfortunately she arrived with debts.

No one ever explained that the intended recipient of the gift - the American people - had been required to meet those debts. This would be one of the rare occasions when it could be argued that helping to pay for a gift had somehow become a disqualification from receiving it.

Richard Preston, Massachusetts' Commissioner of Commerce, evidently felt that "Commerce" was not a dirty word and supported Warwick's endeavour.

MOVING AUDIENCES

While Warwick was sailing towards America, John Lowe had tied up arrangements to sell the film of the voyage to John Sloan Smith of the *Mayflower* Transit Company. They paid for the cost of making the film and contributed £3,000 on top towards the project. Warwick had asked that the deal include a provision that the film be distributed, free of charge, to schools. John Sloan Smith, who was totally enamoured with the *Mayflower II,* was delighted to agree; at last Warwick was finding ways in which he could help. At the same time the Trucking company boss came up with a few ideas of his own.

When the ship arrived, Sloan Smith was there with his wife at Plymouth Harbor. He had a stand erected to seat several hundred company executives and their families as well as friends of the company. Sloan Smith had thousands of copies of the *Mayflower* Compact printed and distributed to the shoreline crowds by girls in Pilgrim costumes. Warwick and he had talked of the importance of the Compact - the document of governance agreed upon by the first settlers; Mr. Sloan Smith did not forget the lecture Warwick had given him; together with a copy of the Compact in Bradford's own handwriting, was the explanation that it was one of the forerunners of the Declaration of Independence and the Constitution of the nation.

Mr. and Mrs. Sloan Smith and their guests poured over the *Mayflower II* at anchor and marveled as millions would do over the next 60 years, at her amazingly small size. On Sloan Smith's instructions, one entire issue of the company's newsletter - the *Mayflower* Aero-gram, was devoted to the *Mayflower II* greeting in Plymouth.

As the *Mayflower II* went on exhibition down the east coast of America in the summer and fall of 1957, John Sloan Smith instructed his company to follow and promote the journey. As the *Mayflower II* dropped anchor in Miami the *Mayflower* Transit Company was there to greet the ship with an on-shore exhibition, in a giant tent, adjoining the mooring site.

Over half a million visitors went through the exhibition and toured the ship over 86 days. They were told the story of the construction and sailing as well as the plans for a permanent berth and soon to be constructed pilgrim village for the *Mayflower II* at *Plimoth Plantation.*

Even Warwick was impressed. *"The people of Miami were supposed to be interested only in Spanish and Latin American culture,"* Warwick told him. At a reception to promote Warwick's book of the voyage, he expressed his feelings about the first settlers so eloquently that John Sloan Smith told him *"Everyone in America should have been here tonight. I want you to tour America. My company will sponsor you and you can tell them all about Plimoth Plantation."*

For the next two years, the *Mayflower* Trucking Company sought audiences all over America for Warwick and the 27 minute film of the voyage. The demand for prints of the film became so great that the job of distribution and booking was handed over to a specialist company, Motion Pictures Distribution.

They calculated that by the end of 1958, over 15 million Americans - almost one in twelve of the entire population - had relived the history of the founding of America by watching the saga of the modern *Mayflower.* Copies of the *Mayflower* Compact followed the film everywhere. In Dade County, Florida, a school administrator requested 35,000 copies of the

Compact and reported that all were distributed to 16 schools in the county.

As Warwick's tour lengthened, the *Mayflower* Transit Company's affection for him grew. After a visit to Harrisburg, Pennsylvania, organized by the local *Mayflower* agency, W. S. Kurtz & Son, the general manager, Arthur Kurtz reported that he had kept Charlton busy from the Sunday night when he stepped off a train until Wednesday noon when he boarded a plane.

"On Charlton's Monday schedule were lectures and showings of the film "The Mayflower Story" at three public schools, a radio interview, two television interviews and luncheon and dinner parties.

"On the agenda for Tuesday were lectures at three additional schools, receiving the key to the city from Nolan Zeigler, Mayor of Harrisburg and a lecture before Harrisburg's Lions Club luncheon. In addition Major Charlton presented autographed copies of his book "The Second Mayflower Adventure" and framed autographed pictures of the Mayflower II to some of Harrisburg's leading citizens."

"Newspaper stories made much of Charlton's visit", said Kurtz *"and the publicity was good for us. Charlton works extremely hard at his job. He plugs both the Mayflower II and the Transit Company from 8 in the morning until 12 at night"*

Others noticed that Warwick found discreet ways to plug his sponsor. One Californian *Mayflower* Truck operator gave Warwick his company cigarette lighter, after listening to Warwick's talk. The next day he turned on his television set to find Warwick light a cigarette as he talked about the *Plimoth Plantation.* As he did so he held the lighter steady so the camera could catch the *Mayflower* Transit logo on the lighter.

At another meeting in Yakima, Washington, Warwick met Mr. and Mrs. Reis Leming again, the young couple that he had flown to Britain to launch the ship.

The Reis Lemings were photographed with Warwick holding the chalice used in the christening ceremony.

Warwick spent two years - 1959 and 1960 - as a road warrior, promoting *Mayflower II* and *Plimoth Plantation*. He visited 35 states but got no closer to Hornblower and his colleagues.

LOVE AFFAIRS

Marilyn Russell was impressed by Warwick but he wasn't going to have it all his own way. *"By the way, what's your line?"* , she asked *"Just so we can get it over with."*

She had met him in Miami, at a reception, where she was a producer for the local TV station. Warwick was, as usual, the center of attention but the striking, tall lady from Alabama had become the focus of his attention.

Warwick did his feeble best to feign innocence. *"I don't have a line."*

"Yes you do. Every man does."

"Well, how about coming right now to see the Mayflower? I feel very romantic and I would like to walk over the ship with you at night."

They woke up the security guard and made their way under a moonlit sky, below decks towards the captain's cabin. They had hardly got used to the cramped dark space when they were disturbed by the *Mayflower*'s angelic cabin boy, Graham Nunn. He was escorting a young woman aboard and Warwick was embarrassed to hear young Graham use the same approach that he had employed a little earlier. *"I want to show you over the Mayflower right now,"* he heard Graham say. *"It makes me feel very romantic to walk over the ship with you at night."*

Warwick attended the annual convention of the *Mayflower* Trucking Company in New Orleans and addressed the delegates. A couple of hours later the organizers became worried that the delegates were becoming bored by a series of lacklustre company talks. "*Send Warwick out again*", instructed

John Sloan Smith. Even Warwick was unsure about the wisdom of addressing the same audience with the same speech twice in one day. *"You'll find something new to say"*, said John Sloan Smith, who by now believed Warwick was capable of walking across the Mississippi.

At one point the love affair between Warwick and the *Mayflower* company nearly landed him in the trucking business. An agent in Westchester County, New York tried to persuade Warwick to become his partner and heir. *"I have no children"*, he explained. *"You could take over from me. It could be your base in America"*. Warwick nodded politely, unable to articulate the truth - that he knew nothing about business, knew nothing about trucking and was so uncertain of all things mechanical that he could not even drive a car.

At another stop, the local *Mayflower* people were so impressed with his public relations skills that they proposed he stay and set up a company called "Ideas for Industry". This had more appeal for Warwick but back in Indianapolis they were scheduling more cities for Warwick to visit and he moved on to Dallas, where they made him an honorary sheriff.

In San Francisco, Warwick finally found an audience that mildly over-awed him. Admiral Nimitz, the commander of the American Naval Forces in the Pacific during World War II, came along to one of the *Mayflower* talks; afterwards he met Warwick privately on several occasions and the two men talked about British naval history. *"I felt honored by his interest"*, recalled Warwick.

"Here was a man who had led the American War against the Japanese who, let's face it, were brutally tough opponents. They were the Mike Tysons of the Pacific and this modest self effacing sailor had managed to inject a sense of pride in the US Navy, a pride that withstood

*unremitting losses."*Admiral Nimitz was president of the Drake Navigators Guild of San Francisco at the time he met Warwick in 1958. *"The admiral knew absolutely everything there was to know about Drake and he got me so enthused that at one point during our conversation I felt that maybe I should build one of Drake's ships as a follow up."*

On the other coast, Warwick addressed an audience of West Point Cadets, but this time did not feel in the least overwhelmed by his audience of several thousand trainee officers. One of them was unconvinced by Warwick's claim that his country had a great military history. *"If that's so"*, the cadet asked, *"then how come we were able to beat Britain so easily in the American War of Independence* ?"

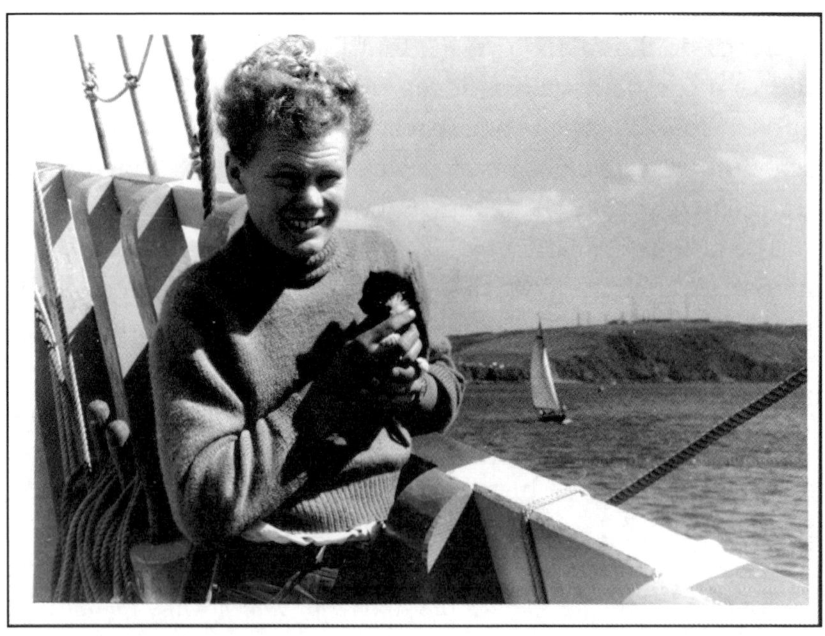

Graham Nunn, the U.K. cabin boy and **Felix** the cat.

"Quite simple", said Warwick crisply. *"On that particular occasion we weren't really trying."* The room collapsed with laughter and the battle for another audience was won.

While Warwick was entertaining the audiences in America, Commander Alan Villiers was telling his version of the *Mayflower II* story.

He remembered that the ship was very difficult to handle. *"It had the most horrible movement I have ever experienced"* but his real distaste was saved for the publicity that the ship attracted.

"Mayflower II was put afloat on a sea of baloney," he told an audience of the Royal Empire Society in London, England. *"I had nothing to do with that. My job was to sail the ship."* However, he recalled that when the *Mayflower II* was exhibited in New York he was amazed at the number of children who asked questions about who sailed on the original *Mayflower*.

With this acknowledgement, Villiers was, perhaps, recognizing that Warwick's incessant one-man public relations campaign had worked.

HOLLYWOOD CALLING

Warwick went back to England in December of 1958. He talked to Felix Fenston and some of the other *Mayflower* creditors. They had received partial payments on the outstanding debts from *Plimoth Plantation.* Warwick decided that the best way he could help make everyone whole was to go back to America, doing what he was good at - lecturing about the *Mayflower.* His talks would encourage visitors to Plymouth to tour the ship. Apart from lectures, sponsored by the Aero Transit Company, Warwick had retained an agent who was offering his services on the lecture circuit.

His exclusive manager Mae C. Hoenig produced a brochure on Warwick offering a "Living History". She quoted the National Geographic Magazine, *"One of the most fabulous journeys of modern time "* alongside an innocent looking Warwick, decked out in Pilgrim costume.

Warwick plugged away, living out of a suitcase, but as the weeks went by he became increasingly lonely. During the day and early evening there would be a fresh set of faces eager to learn the *Mayflower* story first hand and they were always generous with their applause and compliments. By night he was alone again in a hotel room, with a television set for company.

In New York Warwick was introduced to the film actor Spencer Tracy who had played Captain Jones, the skipper of the *Mayflower* in the film of the original voyage. Warwick was unimpressed with the film star who was very drunk *"and behaving like a slob."* He also met Lucille Ball who, together with her husband Desi Arnaz, were major television stars. They had a weekly half hour show called *"I Love Lucy"* and were always searching for good writers to keep the show fresh. She invited him to come out to Hollywood to work on her show.

Warwick thought it was the big chance he was looking for to get his finances back in shape and went to Hollywood at the first break in his lecture tour schedule. The timing couldn't have been worse. The Hollywood writers union had just begun a strike which went on for several weeks. The opportunity to work on the *"I love Lucy Show"* was lost.

Warwick had tried to keep in touch with Henry Hornblower while he was on his tour of the US. Hornblower wrote to him on May 16, 1958, care of the *Mayflower* Transit Company. Hornblower now had possession of the *Mayflower* in Plymouth and was trying to tidy up any debts that remained unpaid. He had sent Bill Brewster and Herbert Boynton to England to look into the creditor situation.

"I do not know if we will have any trouble with Felix (Fenston)", he wrote *"but I am certain a lot may be avoided if we have copies of your correspondence, etc."* Hornblower ended the letter on a depressing note;

"Mayflower does all right when the weather is good, but it has not been very good, so I doubt if the overall results are going to be anything outstanding." On another occasion, Hornblower wrote to Warwick again. *"I must have written to you last on one of our rainy days. Let me tell you I am still full of optimism about the Plantation's future even though attendance on the ship for the last month of July was off 30 percent in contrast with last year.....we still have that unfortunate matter of the British debts to concern ourselves with."*

Warwick went back to the East Coast to spend a couple of days at *Plimoth Plantation* before returning to the new base he had established in Hollywood. He was disappointed to see that progress on building the village was slow. It took the original settlers less time he told Hornblower, who reminded Warwick that they didn't have to build car parks and toilets for visitors. After receiving from Hornblower another sad written tale of reduced attendances, Warwick showered Hornblower with advice for attracting visitors.

"How about the Shriners, Elks, Lions, Rotarians, Optimists, Jaycees, Masons, Women's Clubs?" he wrote from Hollywood. *"Who is lecturing to these groups? I've spoken to them in 44 states and it is my experience that they want a 25 to 30 minute film, a talk that will pull them out of their seats. I have found that you have to arouse them emotionally, make them feel that the Plantation belongs to them and must be seen."*

He then went on with a laundry list of suggestions including religious services in the Plantation Fort meeting house, a Plantation Thanksgiving stamp that could be mailed on board, plus better road markers to make visitors more excited as they got closer to the ship. He also had advice for the Plantation Governors and business supporters that would cost little.

"Some of them are running businesses that are sending out millions of pieces of mail a year. Get them to send out stickers on their mail which say 'See Mayflower now.' Ask them to do the same with print and newspaper advertising they have already bought and paid for. And here is an idea for your wife, who is, I do believe, a music lover," Warwick concluded. *"Get her to see her friends in the Boston Symphony and arrange for them to give a concert in costume aboard Mayflower. Get them to play 17th century music and use the instruments of the period, too."*

The advice fell on deaf ears.

Warwick's manager kept him on the lonely road sharing his *Mayflower II* adventure with one audience after another.

THE WICKED PILGRIM

Warwick's disappointment at Plymouth was compounded by news of a story published about him in *The People,* one of England's more sensational Sunday papers.

The headline over two pages, thundered, *"Good riddance to the Mayflower Cad"* and the long and detailed story accused Warwick of a cavalier attitude to his wives and children.

They had been left destitute, the paper reported, without food or rent, while Warwick went off on his adventures. Warwick's wives actually tried to mitigate the damage *The People* sought to inflict. His first wife, Lucy, was interviewed by *The People* but, sensing that no good could come of publicly criticizing her former husband, she refused to say anything but good about Warwick, when a young reporter called unannounced at her West London flat.

Lucy's restraint brought the young journalist close to tears but her reticence made no difference to a story that covered two entire pages and painted a damaging portrait of Warwick Charlton and a heartless wicked pilgrim.

The People had a circulation of several million and was regarded as a scandal sheet that paid a fee for salacious stories - rather on a par with the American *National Enquirer* - and there was, at least, a suspicion that someone other than Warwick's family had been paid to condemn the *Mayflower* man in his absence.

The story was picked up by the wire services and reprinted in many papers, particularly in New England where it was destined to hurt most. Warwick was in despair. On September 8th, 1959 he wrote to his mother in England:

"The news has come as a terrible blow. I was in the process of the most important project... when the American version of "The People" story broke over here."

Warwick went on to say that things had been going so well that he had even turned down an attractive television offer because his advisers thought he would soon be offered much better terms.

Warwick then turned his attention to his money problems caused by the *Mayflower* project. He had tried to make the best of a very bad job he told his mother. He had come out in January after talking to John Lowe and the two principal creditors, Felix Fenston and George Stewart. *"So far as the English creditors are concerned there were about eighty of them when we landed: now, only two years afterwards they have been reduced to three main ones: Felix, George Stewart and the rope people."*

Stewart and the rope people had volunteered to make a gift of their goods, said Warwick, so the only real debtor left was Felix Fenston. Fenston had been over to the *Plantation* recently and said he would not ask for all his money back. Warwick went on:

"In the age of the Sputnik and the intercontinental ballistic missile I caught the imagination of the world, diverted if you like from the loneliness of man in the space age, to a time when he was less complicated, had fewer doubts about both himself and the world around him; an age of innocence perhaps but also one of faith and courage. The story I enacted was a simple one of water, wind, sun and sail, and people were happy to share them with us. I know they made me feel close to the beat of the pulse of life; the breath of wind, the sway of the ship moving with the sea, the slow dignity of the sunrise and sunset. At first I looked at these things apart and then I felt a part of them, and I believe, indeed I know, that millions of people shared this

release with me and laughed, "to see the sails conceive big bellied with the wanton breeze."

Warwick switched from romance to finance:

"That my company owed money when we arrived was hardly surprising: the ship was delivered only three days before sailing, five months behind the promised delivery date. I could have kept her in England for a year and garnered money for exhibitions, but I chose to sail and keep the faith with the people here who had planned our welcome. And what of the debts? Piddling really against the magnitude of the enterprise, in this day and age.

"How many buildings, hospitals, government budgets, charitable appeals go over budget and no one calls for sackcloth and ashes. Of course it was a personal financial blow for me. Everything has gone by the board for the Mayflower."

Warwick had taken the only course open to him, he told his mother. He made arrangements for the creditors to be paid from the revenues from the ship's exhibitions in New York, Washington and Miami, and stayed in America where he hoped to repair his own finances. Warwick concluded, *"of course the publicity here.....has hurt me.....but I am well, I am bubbling with ideas and energy and determined to make my way."*

In another letter to his eldest daughter Vicki, he wrote about his problems and at the same time his regrets that he had not seen more of his children.

Sheraton Hotel in Chicago
10 Feb 1960

Dearest Vicki,

You have probably seen in the newspapers that I was unable to build Mayflower and sail her to America and at the same time, pay my rent. If some things had been different the film and a lecture tour would have made some $50,000, perhaps more, but the domestic troubles of the project, not dissimilar to those of the first Mayflower, so occupied my time and my energy that I am now many thousands of miles from home, trying to repair my fortunes. This is called the windy city and the wind comes across the lake and from the great plains of America and screamsdown the wide tall streets. This is a very luxurious hotel and I am staying here as the guest of an American friend. I have about $90 left, three good suits, two pairs of shoes, half a dozen ties, some socks and handkerchiefs and an overcoat. The temperature outside is arctic! Five degrees below freezing. Tomorrow and the next day I go on television and radio to tryand promote my interests. If I can earn enough to hang on I have several projects that might secure my future; one concernsthe state of Texas and another Life magazine.

I think of you very, very often and I wish so much that things had been different and we could have seen more of each other; if I really get under way I'd seriously suggest that you come out and see me, but I'd have to get enough for a return ticket and sufficient to look after you while you were here. In New York and here it is very pricey and most times, unless I am seeing people on business, I sit in the hotel room (so as to conserve money): I either read, look at tv or stare out of the frosted windows (I am 14 floors up) at the city with its lights and busy beetle cars. I have a secret ambition, one I would give anything to to bring home, and that is for you and Randal and me to have <u>one</u> holiday together. I wonder if it could be worked out

Warwick kept going for a few months but the stories of his personal life had an effect. The offer of a television contract was withdrawn and other projects he was working on fizzled. The people at *Plimoth Plantation* were not encouraging him to visit them. They certainly saw no temporary or permanent role for him as they built out *Plimoth Plantation* and promoted *Mayflower II*. He returned to England.

PLYMOUTH ROCKS

Henry Hornblower's representatives had been in England several times while Warwick was touring America. Together with George Stewart, he had persuaded the creditors of Project *Mayflower* to remain patient and wait for their portion of surplus revenue from the exhibition of the ship.

In the end, the exhibits in New York, Miami and Washington provided the funds that were needed to repay *Plimoth Plantation* the money they had advanced, and to satisfy all the creditors on the other side of the Atlantic.

A statement of accounts circulated internally by *Plimoth Plantation* showed that the New York, Miami and Washingtom DC exhibits drew over 730,226 spectators and generated $831,170 in gross revenue. The money came from exhbition fees, souvenirs and food sales. However, this was just the beginning.

By the middle of 1958 *Mayflower II* was back in Plymouth and under the sole control of the *Plantation*. The governors were so excited that they began betting on the attendance total at Plymouth for the next full year. Ralph Hornblower made a bet that the attendance would reach 225,000. George Olsson wrote back suggesting a higher number; 250,000 paying customers before Thanksgiving. They had reason to be optimistic.

In 1958, the year that *Mayflower* arrived back at Plimouth, *Plimoth Plantation's* sales and income increased substantially. The roll of members who agreed to an annual fee of anything from $10 to over $1,000 had risen to 953, a 50 per cent increase in the *Plantation's* long term supporters.

In March of 1960 , Lothrop Withington was able to write to his clients that all the debts in England had been settled and *Plimoth Plantation* had possession of the ship free and clear of any obligations.. Many creditors were happy to accept 50 cents for each dollar owed so the final total was only $102,000 (£36,428). From now on, all the *Mayflower's* surplus income could be directed to the development of *Plimoth Plantation.*

By the end of the year, with *Mayflower II* permanently back in Plymouth, the ship generated $140,409. In addition the ship helped to attract another $65,000 in membership fees and gifts. Although only $17,785 was generated by the village, there was total revenue for the year of $307,008.

It did not take long for *Plimoth Plantation* to be transformed both financially and physically.

For more than a dozen years - since 1947 - *Plimoth Plantation's* public exhibits had consisted of just two small buildings on the harbor front - a re-creation of the first house built by the early settlers and a re-creation of the original fort.

The millions of visitors who would come to Plymouth in the next 60 years could take a step back and touch their history. There was the star attraction of *Mayflower* of course, but now there was also a full replica of the original village of 1620, spread out over 100 acres. Visitors would walk in and out of each of the 19 family houses and see a faithful recreation of the furniture, decoration and tools of the founding families.

In the neighboring fields they could watch men and women clad in seventeenth century costume, tending maize and other crops. They could watch bread-making, thatching, plowing, milking and cooking. They could see modern pilgrims recreate the first contacts with Indians, as well as town meetings, elections and the other business of the day. They could discover why this mixture of Pilgrims, separatists and strangers came to this strange new land and how they learned to cope. Then they could walk a short way through the woods and discover an encampment of native Americans called the Wompanaog. *Plimoth Plantation* had become one of the finest historical and educational exhibits in the world.

Mayflower II had made all this possible.

The Treasure Chests were seen as an embarrassment when they were loaded onto the *Mayflower II* (above) but a final accounting revealed that they were critical to the success of the whole venture.

A final accounting of the financing of *Mayflower II* appears a little like a re-enactment of World War II. The British started the effort and got so far; then the Americans stepped in and helped finish the job. Initially the help was, like the second war, carried out covertly but before long it was out in the open and the well-financed Yanks tidied things up.

Warwick thought that he could build and deliver the ship for approximately £100,000 ($280,000) but the actual cost was £194,954 ($545,873) - well over his original estimate. It is extraordinary that most of the money, starting with Felix Fenston's £500 ($1,400), was raised in approximately two years, during a time of severe austerity. It is worth noting, that at the time when the fundraising was carried out, the average earnings of men over 21 in the UK was approximately £12 ($34) a week or £624 ($1747 a year). Women earned even less.

In the end the two penniless public relations men, John Lowe and Warwick managed to raise an estimated £140,333 ($392,932). However, there was a shortfall which turned out to be £36,428 ($102,000). This shortfall came from the pockets of ordinary Americans who paid 95 cents a time to see the ship.

Plimoth Plantation's contribution was to supply the plans that they had commissioned from the naval architect William Baker plus assure his regular support during the construction process. They also worked with the UK creditors and the liquidator of Project Mayflower Ltd to persuade the creditors to accept a reduced amount.

A Project Summary.

Cash donations	£38,000	$106,400
"In kind" donations of products from industry *	£15,000	$ 42,000
90 Treasure Chests @ £460 each	£41,400	$115,920
Life Magazine/Paris Match/ and other publications	£14,000	$ 39,200
Coins/plates/various souvenirs	£10,000	$ 28,000
Mayflower stamped envelopes	£10,000	$ 28,000
Souvenir shavings	£ 6,000	$ 16,800

Brixham exhibit. 245,000 visitor fees	£14,000	$ 39,200
Three issues of *Mayflower* Mail	£ 6,000	$ 16,800
Total raised by Charlton and Lowe	**£154,400**	**$432,320**
Shortfall paid to satisfy creditors raised from US exhibition fees **	**£ 36,428**	**$ 102,000**
Plimoth Plantation contribution ***	**£ 4,193**	**$ 11,740**
Total project costs:	**£195,021**	**$ 546,060**

Note: *All Sterling figures have been converted at $2.8 = £1 sterling (the approximate exchange rate during the period).*

* 150 companies supplied material, products and services to complete the ship including provisions for the journey. Many of these requirements were given to the project including large value items such as wood, ropes and Treasure Chests. Food for the journey was supplied by the Heinz company and medical supplies from Pfizer. A full list of supporting companies is shown in Appendix F page 439.

** Originally the creditors were owed £66,628 ($186,000) but they agreed to accept the reduced sum of $102,000 as shown above.

*** This cost is listed in *Plimoth Plantation's* annual accounts for 1957.

The summary of the fundraising raises the indirect question of how Warwick and John Lowe survived right through to the sailing of the ship. All Warwick would repeat, when asked, was that he had to sail pretty close to the wind to stay in business. He lost his regular source of income - the four public relations accounts - by the end of 1955, the first year of the *Mayflower* project.

A review of the fundraising shows that Warwick and John Lowe had limited ways to support the cost of running their office, which consisted of the two of them plus three full-time assistants and then Fiona McCrae-Taylor, and at least one more employee as the project developed; a total of seven people.

The fact that the Project Mayflower bank account contained only £3 when Captain Grattidge demanded an accounting, provides a clue. The three pounds may have been the original 3 that Warwick supplied to set up the company. And he may have relied on cash from one source or another to stay afloat. That in turn may have limited his exposure to income tax and insurance.

A conservative estimate of office and staff costs would suggest Warwick needed around £30,000 during the 16 months of 1956 and 1957 to keep the financial ship afloat.

The cash donations to the Mayflower Project, all £38,000 of them, would have been enough to run the office but records show that the vast majority of that money came right at the end just before the ship was due to sail and it went to the shipbuilders and other creditors. Only Felix Fenston's initial £500 and perhaps another £3,000 may have come in earlier and would therefore, have been available to support day-to-day expenses.

The gifts in kind were, of course, precisely that, given to help build and fit out the ship. Most of the money - probably £12,000 of the £14,000 supplied by publications, came right at the time of sailing. The funds from the Treasure Chests and the Brixham exhibit went straight to Stuart Upham to keep building the ship which probably cost over £100,000 compared with the original estimate of £80,000, largely due to Warwick's insistence on using tools of the 1600s which were not in use in the 1950s.

That leaves *Mayflower Mail,* various souvenirs like ties, dinner plates and medallions but they would have cost money to produce. All these items apparently generated £32,000 which would have yielded just over £10,000 if they averaged a reasonable net profit of 30 per cent. Warwick had a number of one-off costs to deal with, which would have eaten up much of that revenue, including insurance of the Mayflower, trips to the US, entertaining the visitors from *Plimoth Plantation* and building and staffing a *Mayflower* exhibit at the boat yard.

It is difficult, in the absence of the employment of a forensic accountant, to explain how Warwick, who was not known to keep financial records, managed to make it through to the United States where concerted attacks in the media accused him of being a profiteer and destroyed his reputation. One member of the press may have had a point when he suggested that Americans should lock up their daughters to protect them from Warwick's undoubted charms but the mass of media condemnation was clearly misguided when they portrayed him as someone who was going to empty their wallets.

CHICKEN BONES

As the money came rolling in to Plimouth Plantation from *Mayflower II* exhibition fees the Plantation accounts showed the *Mayflower II* as an asset. They owned the ship.

Warwick did not know it but, at the end of 1959, he had one friend in Plimouth who refused to let go of the objectives of his gift. That man was Ronnie Forth, OBE, the Chairman of the Welcoming Committee. Both men shared a love of America but they nevertheless made for a strange pair of bedfellows.

Ronnie Forth OBE

arranged the welcoming party for the *Mayflower II* and was point man for the main celebrations that took place from June 13th onwards in Plymouth.

He and Warwick were at odds over who should attend.

Warwick, the passionate republican had made life difficult for Ronnie Forth, the committed English royalist. Warwick had caused Ronnie intense embarrassment and shame by insisting that the British Ambassador and the Consul general in Boston be omitted from any guest lists and welcoming party.

Whatever he thought of Ronnie Forth's politics, there was no doubt that the royalist had done a magnificent job of organizing both state and local funds and had mounted a stellar reception for *Mayflower II*. It was he who had constantly pleaded for a firm arrival date in early 1957. Those pleas had fallen on deaf ears with everyone except Warwick.

Now in 1960, almost three years after the ship arrived and after earning the Queen's gratitude in the form of the Order of the British Empire for staging the greeting of *Mayflower II*, Ronnie Forth was concerned that Warwick's aims, and objectives had been forgotten. He was in the perfect position to do something about it. He lived in Plymouth, held local public office and had been co-opted onto the Plimoth Plantation board of Trustees. He was witness to the impact of *Mayflower II* on the Plantation and the local economy.

He observed in one letter that the steadily rising income from Mayflower II was being squandered and misused. The place was over staffed, he complained. and he questioned the value of money spent on archeological research *"digging for chicken bones and non-descript broken pottery.."*

At trustee meetings during 1960, he reminded others that Mayflower II was intended as gift to the American people, not to the City of Plymouth or any private organization - the nature and terms of the gift was the basis on which he had raised a large amount of public money for the welcome.

He also refreshed the memory of the governors of the plan to use some of the surplus revenue from *Mayflower II* to establish a scholarship program dedicated to Anglo-American studies. He saw a wonderful opportunity to involve other non-profits especially the Pilgrim Society, an organization that he knew had an interest in cultural exchanges and the funds to support a scholarship program.

Ronnie went so far as to table two formal written motions to trustee meetings which set out in great detail how the revenue from *Mayflower II* would be allocated to maintaining the ship and other essential tasks, as well as scholarships.

In between meetings Ronnie talked to Henry Hornblower II, Alan Villiers, Felix Fenston, George Olsson and anybody else who would listen. His pleas fell on deaf ears and Ronnie Forth noted at the time, that Harry Hornblower was not happy to learn that Ronnie had written to Felix Fenston to gain his support for a scholarship program.

However, Ronnie Forth OBE did not contact Warwick, now back in the UK. Perhaps the royalist could not overcome his fundamental differences with the man who saw the importance of *Mayflower II* in heralding a new democracy, free of Kings, Queens and religious leaders.

Perhaps Warwick had expressed his views too forcefully to a civil man who was an essential part of Plymouth and Boston high society; a society where English representatives of the crown coexisted comfortably in the twentieth century with leaders of the American republic.

PROFUMO AFFAIR

Warwick arrived back in England with less than £5 in his pocket. There was nothing for him to do but earn a living and wait to hear from *Plimoth Plantation* for news of the ship, the income it was generating and the establishment of the Anglo-American trust.

It proved to be a long wait. It would come, not from the establishment but from the people who worked as interpreters of *Mayflower*, the people who had been touched by the little ship and had made it their life's work. And right at the end of his life there would be a final chapter that even Warwick might have struggled to invent.

On arrival back in England, however, his immediate thoughts were how to get through the following week. He went straight back to the Wig and Pen and met a friend from Odhams Press who offered him work on a weekly magazine called *"Today."*

He fell back into the unpredictable life of a freelance journalist and re-established his reputation for producing good stories. He still knew all the right people and when Britain's Minister of War, John Profumo, was disgraced in one of Britain's biggest post-war scandals, Warwick was there gathering first hand accounts. He managed to use his endless circle of friends, to propel himself into the middle of a political circus, that was to lead to the resignation of Prime Minister Harold Macmillan and a year later the fall of the Conservative Government.

The Conservatives had been in power for a dozen years in the early sixties and were beginning to suffer from a series of scandals.

The most damaging by far was caused by Macmillan's Minister of War, John Profumo. In the House of Commons, under the privilege of making a personal statement, Profumo denied rumors that he was having an affair with a woman called Christine Keeler. He lied, and was forced to admit his deceit and resign.

Warwick gave this picture to his daughter Vicki. He found something mildly reassuring in the occasional scandals that erupted among the pilgrim settlers. He said it helped him to imagine them as humans, prey to the temptations faced by lesser mortals, like himself. So it was no surprise to his friends, that following his *Mayflower* adventure, Warwick became heavily involved with Stephen Ward who was at the heart of a scandal that would bring down the British government.

The scandal had all the ingredients that Warwick found appealing. Profumo had been sleeping with Keeler while she was also sharing a bed with a military attaché at the Russian Embassy. The participants had met at a series of parties hosted by members of Britain's aristocracy, including the Astors. Prince Phillip was rumored to be involved. There were photographs circulating in Fleet Street of naked men and women of public note in private compromising positions.

Christine Keeler, a woman at the heart of Warwick's book on an affair involving a Russian spy and a Minister of the UK government. It would bring down the British government.

One of the consistent attendees at these bacchanalian events was an old friend of Warwick's - Stephen Ward. Stephen, an osteopath to the rich and famous, including Churchill, had introduced Keeler to Profumo.

One of the places where John Profumo and Christine Keeler used to meet, was the elegant London home of Billy Bolitho, another old friend of Warwick's. Bolitho came from a distinguished banking family and Warwick had persuaded him to lend his name to the list of luminaries supporting the *Mayflower* Project.

Warwick's friends in the parliamentary Labour party, including Tom Driberg, sought his advice on questions they might ask in the House of Commons, in order to drive the scandal into the open. The exposures and the story worked its way from small stories on inside pages, to front-page headlines in the British Press, over several months. During this time Warwick went to some of the parties and became so close to Ward, that the osteopath would not speak to the other journalists.

Finally, the establishment fixed on Ward as the scapegoat to be punished so that the scandal would go away, and Ward was charged with soliciting prostitutes - a serious crime. Ward was tried and found guilty but he committed suicide before the court could pronounce sentence. Warwick , however, had the material for a book called *"Stephen Ward Speaks"* which was rushed into print soon after Ward's death. The book began with Ward's lecherous invitation to Warwick *"You can have her if you want her."*

It is not clear whether Stephen Ward actually uttered those words or Warwick was taking journalistic license with the truth, to get the reader's attention.

The sensational opening sentence was followed by a strongly worded argument that it was the political and social establishment that was rotten, not Ward. Ward had been framed. The scandal signaled the end of the political career of Prime Minister Harold MacMillian and he resigned a few months later and was replaced by Sir Alec Douglas-Home.

However the whole Conservative party was tainted by the scandal, as well as tired after 13 years in power and a year later they were voted out of office.

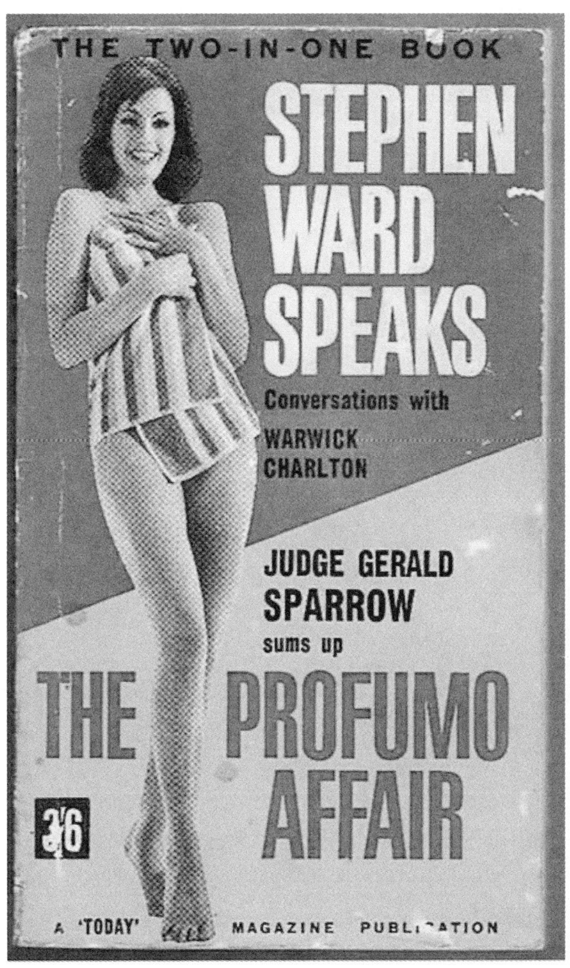

Stephen Ward took his life before he could be sentenced for living off immoral earnings. Warwick befriended Ward who, he thought, had been sacrificed by the Establishment.

Mayflower Aerogram

PUBLISHED MONTHLY BY AERO MAYFLOWER TRANSIT COMPANY, INC., INDIANAPOLIS, INDIANA

SEPTEMBER, 1957 SOUVENIR ISSUE

THIS ISSUE of the Mayflower AEROGRAM is devoted exclusively to The Mayflower II—the replica of the tiny vessel that brought the Pilgrim Fathers to America. The reasons for this issue are twofold:

When our organization first was conceived, its founder selected the name "Mayflower" to symbolize long-distance moving—and the firm has been so identified since its start in 1927. Because of this, Aero Mayflower Transit Company, Inc., its agents, and its employees naturally are vitally interested in the project that has made possible a re-creation of its namesake.

Secondly, we of Aero Mayflower are interested in, and have been a supporter of, this project because of its patriotic and religious significance. We recognize the Mayflower II as a symbol of religious freedom. We laud it as a tangible goodwill offering from the people of Great Britain to America—one which will materially strengthen the bonds of friendship between these great nations. Also, the Mayflower II has made possible a vivid and dramatic retelling of the story of events that are so vital a part of our American heritage.

It is in a spirit of appreciation for these things that we join all Americans in welcoming this gift as the centerpiece of Plimoth Plantation, Inc., our newest national shrine.

In the pages that follow, we tell the stroy of the Mayflower II as we have observed it—from the time that the idea was conceived to the arrival of the ship at Plymouth, Massachusetts, where it was formally welcomed by the Vice-President of the United States.

The front page of a souvenir edition of the house magazine of the **Mayflower Transit Company**. The company`s CEO, John Sloan Smith was a big supporter of Warwick`s endeavours, both during the run up to the transatlantic crossing and once the ship had reached the U.S.

COLOR CLASH

On a visit to South Africa to cover a story for *Today* magazine, Warwick propelled himself into a public confrontation with his old wartime mentor, General, now Lord Montgomery. While in Cape Town, Warwick read a report that Montgomery had accepted an official invitation to visit the white South African Government.

The Government, led by its prime minister Dr. Hendrik Verwoerd, was busy implementing the policy of apartheid. Warwick thought it was outrageous that Montgomery allow his name to be associated with the enforced separation of black and white and he called a press conference to make his views plain.

He called Monty's visit *"ill-judged"* and his support for apartheid, *"disgraceful."* Monty led a multi-racial army he declared. One third of the soldiers that had fought for the allies in the desert were non-whites. The Rand Daily Mail and the Press in England and elsewhere leapt on the story of a junior officer condemning his former commander.

Warwick, meanwhile, was visited in his Cape Town hotel by the South African police who invited him to make an early departure. Warwick also heard from his old friend Major General Sir Freddie de Guingand, Montgomery's former chief of staff. Warwick's outburst had been disloyal, he was firmly told, but Warwick was unrepentant.

CAREY STREET

Warwick Charlton did not make a good first impression, when he arrived at the offices of Mr. E.A. Perkins. He had phoned a couple of times to put off the meeting, claiming other more urgent business. Now he was two days late for his latest appointment with this man who said he was a senior examiner for the Bankruptcy Court.

Mr. Perkins looked up slowly from his paperwork and stared over his spectacles at the tall, imposing man that stood in the doorway. *"I am glad you are here. If you had not turned up this time I might have had you arrested."*

Warwick was as unimpressed with Perkins and his drab little office, as Perkins was disappointed in him. The only thing of interest to Warwick was the address in London's Carey Street. The name of the street was synonymous with financial ruin and had long since entered into the colorful language of the born and bred Londoner. In normal conversation in the pubs and markets of England's capital city, people would say *"If I don't do this or that I'll be in Carey Street"* as a shorthand way of implying that they would experience severe money troubles.

Carey Street would make a good story Warwick thought, forgetting for a moment why he was there. Mr. Perkins told Warwick to empty his pockets and hand over any money on his person. He had less than a pound to put on the table that lay between the two men and no watch or anything else of value. Mr. Perkins carefully noted the insignificant sum in his file and handed the money back.

Perhaps sensing that he had done more than enough to get Warwick's attention, Mr. Perkins offered him a cigarette. He explained that he intended to question Warwick extensively about his financial affairs. It could take a long time. He had three hours set aside that day but they would probably need to meet again, at least two or three times. Perhaps Warwick would like to make a local call to postpone any other appointments he had planned for the rest of the day?

Warwick telephoned the newspaper office where he worked and told his editor he was tied up. Mr. Perkins ordered two cups of tea with milk and settled down to question Warwick. He wanted to know everything, he told Warwick, about his background, his education, his income, his savings. He needed to build a full list of creditors as well as a list of any money he was owed; most of all he wanted to know how he got into this horrible mess.

Warwick had been a little subdued by the request to empty his pockets. He felt like a suspected criminal, rather than someone who had simply ignored a dusty old debt. The bare room without a picture or decoration of any kind reinforced his unease. But Warwick was not easily cowed by a number cruncher and he had no intention of making Mr. Perkins' job easy. *"I became obsessed by an idea,"* he told Mr. Perkins flatly.

Mr. Perkins patiently explained that he needed some more basic information. He quickly put together a picture of the "ideas man" he was interviewing. Warwick Charlton was a journalist and writer, and apparently very good at his profession. He had worked for the BBC and written two plays (one of which had made it to the West-End stage) without any becoming major hits. His main source of income, though, was from freelance writing.

At one time or another Warwick worked for most of the best papers and magazines published in London. He earned a pretty good salary but like most journalists spent it all. He lived modestly in rented accommodations, had no car or any other possessions of value. He appeared to have no expensive habits such as gambling or a taste for expensive clothes or holidays. He liked a drink but even a man with quiet conservative habits like Mr. Perkins knew that journalists had a reputation for living from one pay packet to another.

Even the best of reporters, including many household names, were often broke and would borrow from their drinking buddies but they rarely got involved in more serious money matters that would lead to bankruptcy. Warwick Charlton's case was not making sense to Mr. Perkins.

Perhaps Warwick had lent someone some money. Did anybody owe him a significant sum? Yes, he confirmed, he was due to receive £10,000 from someone in America.

Mr. Perkins perked up. This would be more than enough to meet the personal obligations Warwick had accumulated. Apart from £1,000 that was owed to the Inland Revenue tax authorities there were additional debts of about £5,000 for a total of £6,000. This American money, if it could be collected, would take care of everything nicely.

Warwick explained that he had given away the *Mayflower II,* the only asset his company possessed. The Americans who took the boat over had agreed to repay some of his personal expenses, when the boat generated sufficient surplus income. Henry Hornblower, the chairman of *Plimoth Plantation* had agreed that with him personally. Warwick gave Mr. Perkins a name and address to write to and they agreed to adjourn the discussion for a few weeks.

Warwick was on time for his next appointment with Mr. Perkins but his inquisitor did not have good news. The Americans strenuously deny any financial responsibility either legal or moral, he told Warwick. They claim there is nothing in writing, except one letter dated September 1957, which refers to an obligation but even that letter does not mention a specific sum and is in no way binding. *"We appear to be back to square one,"* Mr. Perkins told Warwick.

A few months later Mr. Perkins held a formal meeting of Warwick's creditors. One person showed up and after the meeting Mr. Perkins told Warwick he was declared bankrupt. Warwick could earn a living but he was required to keep the Official Receiver advised of his earnings. He could not open a bank account or obtain credit in excess of £10 without declaring his position. He could not stand for Parliament. His *Mayflower II* adventure had ended in financial disgrace. Warwick chose to shine a light on his shame in a lengthy article that was published in *Today* magazine.

"Some people in my position take their own lives," he wrote in his introduction. *"Four have done so in the past few months. They could not face the stigma and handicap of being known as a bankrupt."*

"Was I, in fact fraudulent, extravagant, over-ambitious or just unlucky?"

"Until 1954 I had earned a living writing scripts, books and articles. Then I became obsessed with an idea."

Warwick recounted his role in raising funds to build the ship and the fact that it took longer and cost more to build her. He continued;

"I sold my office furniture, my typewriter, let my rent go into arrears and finally poured even the £3,000 I earned from the book into the venture to settle outstanding debts. And when the ship got to America I handed her over to an historical trust for safe-keeping.

"Now the Mayflower is the chief attraction of a national shrine in Plymouth Massachusetts, that she inspired to be built around her. To date she has grossed nearly 1 million pounds from sightseers. Why then am I bankrupt?"

Warwick did not answer his own question but informed the reader of the details of the bankruptcy process and ended *"So going broke is not the end of the line."*

LUCKY STARS

After his final hearing at Carey Street, Warwick went to the Wig and Pen Club to drown his sorrows. In some ways it was not the best place to try and put the *Mayflower II* story behind him.

Dick Brennan witnessed the birth of the little ship, when Warwick had used the place to entertain and persuade people to become part of his great adventure, and reminders were everywhere in the historic old building, at the top of Fleet Street.

Warwick had helped Dick turn his club into a shrine for the *Mayflower II* with a series of framed press cuttings on the wall and *Mayflower II* plates and other items used regularly for dining upon. The menu reminded the journalists and lawyers, who frequented the club, of the voyage and Dick Brennan's part in ensuring that the crew ate well. American visitors loved the place with its tiny rooms, old oaken beams and sense of history. They reported from time to time that they had seen the *Mayflower II* in Plymouth and she was attracting an increasing number of visitors.

After listening to Warwick's tale of woe, Dick Brennan, decided it was time to call on the friendship he had built up with Harry Hornblower. Dick and his wife Babs had recently visited the Hornblowers in Boston while on holiday.

Every time Hornblower came to London he visited the Wig for dinner, served on commemorative *Mayflower* plates, and a chat with Dick about the ship and progress at the *Plantation*. The chirpy cockney sparrow and the conservative New Englander hit it off very well. Dick wrote to ask his friend Harry to let Warwick have some money. *"I know he is quite hopeless in lots of ways, but there is one thing he did, (he) got the ship there and handed it over. So Harry if you have had a good season, try your best."*

Harry sent his friend's letter to his attorney Lothrop Withington for advice and Withington produced a withering denouncement of Warwick and any moral or legal obligations that Hornblower might feel existed. The lawyer said it was enough that *Plimoth Plantation* had picked up *Mayflower II's* debts. The *Plantation* had no further obligation, apart from a letter dated September 11 1957.

In that letter the *Plantation* had agreed, at its discretion, to repay some of Warwick's costs if and when funds permitted. The lawyer ended, "If, out of the goodness of your heart you or *Plimoth Plantation* want to make him a small donation because he has gone through bankruptcy, I am not going to stand in your way but if you do, *get him to sign a full release of every claim of whatever nature from now until doomsday."*

Hornblower wrote back to his friend Dick a letter which had the full approval of attorney Lothrop Withington. There would be no money for Warwick - it cost us something like $150,000 to untangle the mess he created.

"We feel no obligation to Warwick - actually the shoe is on the other foot. He can thank his lucky stars he had us to bail him out."

Dick Brennan did not have the heart to let his bankrupt friend see such a positive spin on Warwick's financial situation.

"Begging your pardon, Sir, would it be cheating to take a Dramamine?"

New Yorker magazine captured Warwick`s insistence on avoiding modern aids, including radio and 20th century navigation equipment.

ANNIVERSARY PLANS

Although Hornblower had no time for Warwick he invited several people connected with the journey of *Mayflower II* to take some role in the life of *Plimoth Plantation.*

Hornblower made Dick Brennan, the second cook aboard *Mayflower II,* an honorary member of the *Plimoth Plantation.* He made Felix Fenston an honorary trustee and, when Felix died, Harry invited his widow to assume the same interest. He knew Felix had money but if Harry hoped to attract more gifts for the *Plantation* from Felix's widow, he was in for a disappointment. Mrs. Fenston, although charming, took virtually no interest in the place, visited the *Mayflower II* once in 1996 and made no financial contribution.

Harry invited one of the crew members Andrew (Scottie) Anderson-Bell to be a trustee - a position he held until his resignation in the early 1990s. Scottie had impressed Warwick with his wonderful frankness. Although a good sailor, the handsome Scottie had offered as his main reason for wanting to be on board, the prospect of meeting and marrying a rich American woman. He had been successful, and although the marriage didn't last, Scottie made Boston his home.

Harry also made Ruth Butler an honorary trustee. Ruth was part of the team in New York that had organized the 4 month exhibition at pier 81.

A year after his bankruptcy Warwick had a chance meeting in London with a member of the *Plimoth Plantation* staff. Cyril Marshall, the *Plantation's* exhibition manager, told Warwick that things were going very well. Warwick contacted Henry

Hornblower and reminded him that it had been four years since they were in touch with each other.

"It is quite extraordinary how time mellows an image", he told Hornblower. *"Almost everyone you speak to here recalls it a great adventure and in glowing terms. There was a piece about it only the other day on network TV which had as its theme Anglo-American travel. The problems which seemed so large at the time are now incidental to what was an exciting and wonderful undertaking for everyone concerned."*

Hornblower agreed that the *Plantation* and *Mayflower II* had had a good year but he was not about to mellow with the passing of years. *"We have just built a new reception center and worked ourselves into quite a debt position"*, he told Warwick in a brief note.

In the following year, Hornblower heard from John Lowe, who phoned to say that he was being taken to court for one last bill connected with *Mayflower* that had somehow escaped the liquidator. The general post office had issued a writ against John Lowe for £560 11 shillings and 5 pence for an unpaid phone bill left over from *Mayflower* days. Hornblower handed the request straight to his attorney and Lothrop Withington wrote a spirited reply which concluded that *Plimoth Plantation* had no legal or moral obligation to bail out John Lowe.

In 1967 Warwick felt hurt enough to contact Hornblower again. He ran into a crew member who told him about a tenth anniversary celebration that was being planned to commemorate the 1957 crossing. Warwick had heard nothing from *Plimoth Plantation* himself and called Hornblower to ask to be brought up to date. He had not received even an annual report.

Two years later in 1969, Warwick was still waiting for a package of material that he had been promised, together with the *Plimoth Plantation* accounts. Warwick and Hornblower's paths crossed in Chicago. Warwick was full of his new plans to build a theme park to be called Merrie England. Hornblower was in Chicago researching the history of mime.

Another three years passed and the pain of Warwick's exclusion from *Mayflower* surfaced like a festering sore that would never heal. Warwick couldn't wait to express his disgust at the information he had just learned. A letter would take too long. He fired off a lengthy telegram to Hornblower in which he expressed his hurt with bitter sarcasm:

VERY SAD TO HEAR AS ORIGINATOR OF MAYFLOWER II WHICH I SAILED OVER TO AMERICA TO COMMEMORATE 1620 VOYAGE AND TO HONOUR COMMON HERITAGE THAT YOU HAVE NOT INVITED ME OR ANY ONE OF THOSE WHO HELPED BUILD MAYFLOWER TO SHARE IN 350TH ANNIVERSARY OF THE FIRST VOYAGE. WE PAY OUR OWN WAY ALTHOUGH YOU USED TO BE OUR GUEST HERE. SINCE THE SHIP HAD PRODUCED A REVENUE OF SEVERAL MILLION DOLLARS, IT SEEMS A SHAME YOU CAN□T AFFORD TIME FOR TELEPHONE, A LETTER OR POSTCARD TO TELL US WHAT GOES ON.

NEVERTHELESS WE WISH ALL AMERICANS, ESPECIALLY THOSE WHO SHARE THE PILGRIM HERITAGE AND ESCAPED FROM TYRANNY TO FIND FREEDOM, OUR BEST WISHES. THE NEWS CAME TO ME OF YOUR CELEBRATION FROM MY SON-IN-LAW, A BOSTON AMERICAN, MORTON ROSS, WHO TELLS ME THAT ANYWAY NONE OF US SHOULD EXPECT TO SEE A LIGHT SHINING FROM BEACON HILL WHERE

MANY OF THE GOVERNORS OF PLIMOTH PLANTATION LIVE INCLUDING YOURSELF. WHAT A LUCKY THING WHEN WE SAILED MAYFLOWER II TO AMERICA WE DID NOT LOOK OUT FOR YOU TO LIGHT US INTO SAFE HARBOUR.

A reply arrived by telegram within 24 hours.

PLANS FOR 350TH NOT FIRM YET. WILL KEEP YOU POSTED. HARRY HORNBLOWER.

Warwick shows off the proposed model for his ***Merrie England*** theme park.

FORGOTTEN OBJECTIVES

Five years later in May 1975 Hornblower was spurred into action by a report from Alan Villiers. The Captain of *Mayflower II* told Hornblower that he had been invited to a small luncheon party at the home of Felix Fenston's widow.

A gentleman Villiers had never met before floated the subject of the forgotten objectives of *Mayflower II.* Perhaps it was time, the stranger said to prod *Plimoth Plantation* to set up the charitable trust that had been part of the original plan. Villiers informed Hornblower that he believed the stranger was possibly Jewish, Hebrew or Israeli. *"I have a considerable experience of the Semitic countenance and manners from my time with other semites in those Indian dhows and elsewhere."*

Villiers guessed, correctly, that Warwick had persuaded one of his friends to befriend Mrs. Fenston, and raise the issue of long forgotten objectives of the *Mayflower II* project. However, it was a clumsy initiative that failed to bring Warwick any closer to *Plimoth Plantation.*

Hornblower promptly invited Mrs. Fenston and her husband's attorney, Sir George Bull, to *Plimoth Plantation's* annual meeting. It was time to set up a trust for Anglo-American projects they all agreed. Hornblower asked Mrs. Fenston to become an Honorary Governor.

ILLEGAL GAMBLING

In the mid-1960s, the magazine journalism of which Warwick had become a part, declined in the face of competition from television, but his financial fortunes took a turn for the better. The UK government recognized that illegal gambling - some of it for very high stakes, was getting out of hand and they determined to regulate it. Gaming was known to attract characters of doubtful moral standing and some *"bad lads"* from the American gambling world were eyeing new opportunities in Europe.

Judah Binstock

The owner of the Victoria Sporting Club.

Warwick persuaded him that he could not continue to own a licensed gambling casino.

Through a long time friend, Donald Williams, Warwick was introduced to Judah Binstock, one of the owners of the Victoria Sporting Club in London. Mr Binstock was concerned that new rules would be introduced, many gaming houses would be shut down and a very limited number of licences would be issued.

He desperately wanted to position himself and his club in the center of London to get one of those prized licences.

Warwick's unique combination of personal courage, contacts in high places, and an understanding of how to manage public opinion, made him tailormade for the challenge, which he approached with a comprehensive marketing and public relations plan, worthy of his *Mayflower II* effort.

Working in the Casino business suited Warwick for a very important reason. He was still unable, as an un-discharged bankrupt, to operate a bank account. The casino owners happily paid him cash. Warwick was able to use his wide network of contacts in government, to obtain a coveted licence for two different owners of the Victoria Sporting Club. The owners immediately recognized they needed some semblance of respectability in order to retain the right to rake in millions from London's wealthy high rollers.

In no time at all, Warwick had them sitting down to dinner in the gilded halls of Mansion House, the official residence of the Lord Mayor of London. He set up this slightly improbable liaison by organizing an annual competition to be sponsored by the Victoria Sporting Club. It was called the International Award for Valour in Sport.

Every year Warwick solicited names of sportsmen and women throughout the world who had shown exceptional courage. The finalists were invited to London for the presentation to be made at the Guildhall, the formal residence of the Lord Mayor of London. Warwick ensured that a member of the Royal Family, as well as leading politicians were included on the guest list. They all got to listen to the owner of the Victoria Sporting Club make the main speech of the evening - written by Warwick of course. Camera lights flashed, stories were written and the owner of the Victoria Club was seen in the company of the establishment of England. They couldn't be that bad.

Warwick would ensure that the winners came from a different part of the world each year. One year it was a group of Russians, another some Japanese, as well as Niki Lauda the Austrian racing driver and always some Americans. The winners always had a topical plus that allowed Warwick to milk the event for maximum column inches.

It was no coincidence that the Russians won during a period when Anglo-Russian relations were at a low point. There was serious doubt whether the Russian sportsmen would be given visas to attend the ceremony and it took the last minute intervention of Lord Carrington, Britain's Foreign Secretary, before the visas were finally issued. The drama of the quest for visas made a wonderful running story and once more the attention of the public had been captured.

Warwick also invited sportsmen and sportswomen, who were popular at the time, to attend the event. These included John Curry who, at the time, was the most popular sportsperson in the country and therefore certain to attract press attention to the event.

Several Americans were nominated for the award including Kathy Miller, an outstanding runner from Arizona, who won. Teddy Kennedy, the then 13 year old son of Senator Edward Kennedy was nominated. Among other things, the younger Kennedy had triumphed over cancer. He was escorted to London by his famous father and Warwick pronounced himself pleasantly surprised by Senator Kennedy's knowledge of British history and system of government. He also admired the way Senator Kennedy insisted on staying out of the spotlight - *"This is my son's week"*, he told Warwick.

Warwick became an expert on Casino administration and ghosted a book on the subject for Judah Binstock, the then owner of the Victoria Sporting Club. It was difficult to find Warwick's name in the book but his imprint is unmistakable. The challenge Warwick faced was to make Judah Binstock come across as a serious student of all the issues related to gambling and therefore, an ideal recipient of one of the precious few licences to be issued. The book had to be dry and dusty but it had to be interesting enough to be read, at least by a few senior politicians and civil servants.

So the first page offered a forward by the Right Honorable Lord Meston, Barrister at law at Lincoln's Inn and Middle Temple, while the back of the book contained 78 pages of charts, tables, bibliography acknowledgements plus a further 105 pages of tightly packed small print which constituted the entire Gaming Act.

In between, Warwick treated the reader to the views on gambling of Gefforey Chaucer, a great literary chronicler of English life in the Middle Ages; then he reproduced a report published in 1731 on gambling in a news sheet of the time, the Daily Journal, and of course he could not resist the temptation to quote his favorite man of historical action, Oliver Cromwell. The great of the past were mixed into the story with the possibly good of the present, members of Parliament like Raymond Blackburn, Government grandee Lord Hailsham and the entire directorship of the new Gaming Board of Great Britain, complete with their pictures.

It could be argued that Warwick's book on Casino administration is the longest ever application for a licence for anything - but it worked. Warwick was successful in obtaining licences to operate for Judah Binstock and after he sold the club the licence was renewed for new owners but not before

Warwick took care of some threats, both local and from overseas.

The local threat came from the people and businesses in the neighborhood. Public meetings were organized to give everyone a voice in the decision to allow a major gaming house in the district. The local member of parliament was involved. The meetings were sometimes lively but it was interest from overseas that threatened disaster.

Warwick was to display his sheer guts in the face of adversity.

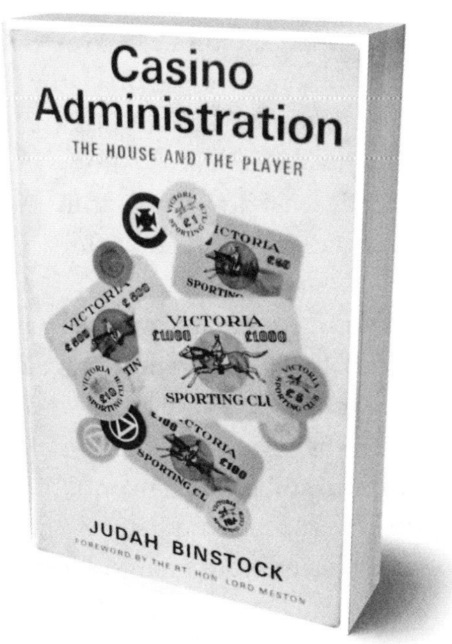

Warwick ghost wrote this book which had a significant impact on the gaming industry in the UK and his personal financial situation

BAD LADS

News of the success of the London Casinos had spread to the US and members of the mob decided to check out the action. Maybe they could get a piece of it. George Raft, the film actor with mob connections, flew into town as did several gentlemen with reputations for exerting violent control of their businesses. Warwick, and everybody else, knew that no licences would be issued to any casino that had even the hint of involvement with the mob.

Warwick went to meet them where they were staying in the penthouse suite in the Royal Garden Hotel near Marble Arch, a stone's throw from the Victoria Club in Edgware Road. He passed members of London's serious crime squad who were sitting in the lobby of the hotel and took the elevator to the top floor to speak to the American visitors. Warwick's daughter Vicki was sitting downstairs along with the police while her father was upstairs talking to the mobsters.

At one point, a young woman came down and sought Vicki out, explaining that the conversation upstairs had been getting heated and Warwick had asked her to leave the room. Vicki observed that she was wearing a strange outfit, which on close inspection turned out to be a rug from the hotel room. She had nothing on underneath and had apparently been dispatched with some urgency, as the conversation became intense.

Upstairs Warwick got straight to the point. *"You cannot stay. You have to leave. Now."* The amazed visitors demanded to know why, but Warwick refused to give an explanation. *"You have to go,"* he repeated. Then he volunteered to take them briefly to the Victoria Sporting Club to meet the owner, Judah Binstock who, he said, would repeat the instruction again.

As Warwick arrived at the Victoria Sporting Club with the mob members in tow, Judah Binstock dashed for his drink cabinet and downed a significant quantity of brandy.

Warwick allowed them to hear Judah mumble the same message that he had delivered - if a little less coherently. Then Warwick escorted some of America's most renowned and dangerous mobsters to London's Heathrow Airport and out of the country, with the police following at a discreet distance.

The Victoria Sporting Club's licence was safe and for a while five pound notes were falling out of Warwick's overstuffed pockets on a regular basis.

"My father showed more than raw courage," Vicki observed many years later. *"He pulled off a seemingly impossible task."* The Victoria Sporting Club was owned by Judah Binstock and other investors and Judah was being investigated by the police for illegal currency transactions that came under the exchange control laws of that time, since withdrawn.

Warwick persuaded Judah Binstock that he had to sell the business; that in order to satisfy the Gaming Act the ownership had to be squeaky clean with no foreign ownership, and that's how a man called Cyril Levan and his brother in law, Johnny Ashton, came to take ownership and the running of the club.

Cyril knew nothing about running a gambling club - he had made his money in a family run high street fashion business, but Warwick knew his clean record would satisfy the Gaming Board who would be issuing the licences.

Despite these problems Warwick succeeded in getting a licence for the Club, one of about only 147. Before the gaming act over 1500 clubs had been operating throughout the country.

"I don't know exactly how much money Warwick earned from investors in the Victoria Sporting Club back then," said Vicki years later *"But whatever it was, it wasn't enough. The club made millions. Individual gamblers, like members of overseas Royal families could bet up to a million pounds. My father just wasn't money oriented, it was getting the job done effectively that mattered to him."*

1970s. Warwick with his daughter Vicki, her children Suzanne and Nicola and Vicki's husband, Morton Ross. *Mayflower II* in background.

SOBER WITNESS

Warwick's marriage to his third wife, Marilyn, had broken down by the early 70's and she had returned to Florida with their three children Alex, Michael and Caroline.

In London Warwick met a 20 year old blue-eyed blond called Belinda Chapman. He was over 50. She was a bright young journalist working on a teenage magazine, edited by a friend of his. Even Warwick thought the age difference was a little alarming and the courtship proceeded for once at such a slow pace that one day Belinda seized the initiative in a taxi. The couple wound up at the Waldorf Hotel. Warwick ended up staying in the hotel for several days while he figured out a way to produce the cash to pay the bill. Before Belinda married Warwick, she encouraged him to give up alcohol and in the years to come he would be a sober witness at the funerals of many of his drinking friends.

Next, Warwick's career took another bizarre turn. American kids discovered skateboards. Through the Victoria Sporting Club Warwick got to know the new owner, Cyril Levan, who was also a property developer. Cyril wanted to do something with a large vacant lot in Torrance, Los Angeles. Skateboarding had become the latest American craze and Warwick suggested that they build the biggest and the best skateboard park in America. Warwick and Belinda went to L.A. to build it.

For three years, they operated out of an apartment on Hollywood's Sunset Strip and first built, then ran the park which they both enjoyed immensely. Warwick and Belinda were married in 1975 and this marriage endured until his death.

Warwick returned to England again and became involved in a number of new projects in partnership with property developers that he had met during his time in the casino industry. The developers challenged Warwick to come up with a use for a piece of industrial wasteland in Britain's Midlands, that was owned by the government Coal Board. It had been used for years by the mining industry to dump waste and now, with the demise of the coal industry, the land appeared both useless and valueless.

Warwick worked with architects and other professionals to develop a detailed plan to turn the ugly scar on the landscape, into a theme park called "Merrie England". Visitors would be transported back several centuries to the days of rowdy taverns, travelling entertainers and musicians, who would enjoy bacchanalian feasts, as was the custom prior to the adoption of plates and cutlery, in the company of lords, ladies and peasants.

The planning authorities were sufficiently moved by Warwick's imagination that they released the land for development. Soon after, the real estate developers received an attractive offer to sell the land for other, more mundane, purposes. Warwick packed up his small office in London, dumped his scale models and looked for the next challenge for his restless energy. He was to find it in the Middle East, back in Egypt, a country that he had got to know during the second world war.

Again, Warwick was approached by developers who saw an opportunity for this impoverished part of the world to grow its economy, by attracting tourists from northern Europe who were growing tired of package deal holidays in Spain. Once more, Warwick used his love of history and understanding of the country, to develop plans for a major new resort at Hurgada on Egypt's Red Sea. Yet again, Warwick's imagination was not matched by the investment community. A pattern emerged that, to Warwick's friends, looked suspiciously like he was being used to help property developers obtain land, which would later be put to more conventional and profitable use.

Other ambitious projects followed, including a theme park on the Isle of Man to be called "Vallhalla" that would recall the history of the Viking invasion of this tiny tax haven, sandwiched in the Irish Sea between England and Ireland. The history and design was meticulously researched by Warwick but once more his plans for this theme park never left the drawing board. A redevelopment in London's dockland called "London Gardens" suffered a similar fate.

However, although many of Warwick's "Walt Disney" ideas proved to be castles in the sky he earned enough from his writing and work with the gambling industry, to buy an interest in a faux castle, near Ringwood in Hampshire. And there was always *Mayflower II,* calling him back to the unfinished business of setting up Anglo-American scholarships.

WOUND HEALING

Twenty years after the arrival of *Mayflower II* in America, Andrew Anderson-Bell organized and paid for a reunion of the crew in 1978, but Warwick was excluded from the invitation list, at the suggestion of several members of *Mayflower II*'s crew. They remembered the tense affair ten years earlier, when Warwick and Alan Villiers had been at each other's throats.

Although Warwick was absent, Stuart Upham, the ship's builder who had not seen the ship for 20 years, made the trip to Plymouth, Massachusetts and was disturbed by what he saw. He made a thorough inspection of the ship and although he conceded that the *Mayflower II* was in pretty good shape, he worried that the modern paints used to protect the wooden vessel from rot, were not good quality. *"They don't make tar like they used to,"* he lamented. He worried about wood-rot, an observation that would be prophetic.

The anger between Alan Villiers and Warwick mellowed with the passing years. Villiers recognized the pressure Warwick had been put under to deliver the ship to *Plimoth Plantation*'s timetable. He went on to make the following observations about Warwick and John Lowe, two men whom he had dismissed as bastards.

"Give me a Ship to Sail," he had pleaded to Warwick. The ship had cost considerably more than the London promoters had foreseen, and the foregoing of revenues from further exhibition of the vessel before she left for America, was a serious loss.

"Had she been allowed to stay in Britain another 12 months she would have cleared all her costs. There were many of us, on both sides of the Atlantic, who regretted very much that this had not been done.

A vast amount of work went into straightening things out, and there was some criticism. However, it is to be remembered that, but for Mr. Charlton and his supporters, there would still be some oak trees growing in beauty spots in Devon but there would be no Mayflower II. They are not the first to fail to raise the full sum required for an enterprise. After all, the first Pilgrim Fathers were in debt to their promoters in London for many years....."

However, Warwick could not make his peace with John Lowe. He met his fellow *Mayflower* collaborator by chance one day in a London pub. John would not speak to him.

"I hurt John. I should have listened to him more. He had a much better business sense than me. He begged me not to rush off to America with the Mayflower. He put a lot of work into getting the OK for an exhibition at St. Katherine's Dock in London. We should have delayed, made money, paid all our bills. I just wouldn't listen. I was obsessed. John was right. . . . . "

Twenty-five years after the two partners had handed over *Mayflower II*, Brooks Kelly, the excutive director of the Plymouth County Development Council, estimated that the *Mayflower II* contribution to the local economy was "conservatively" in the order of $80 million.

George Hanlon, a local business writer wrote, *"Month after month they come. In cars, buses and tour groups. School buses by the dozen. In short, the missing link has been found, making the historic value of the visit to Plymouth that much more full. With its new concept as a living museum, complete with first person interpreters aboard the vessel, Mayflower II rounds out the solid Pilgrim experience being offered by Plimoth Plantation."* At least one member of Warwick's family was to get a first hand taste of the Ship's impact on Americans and the local economy.

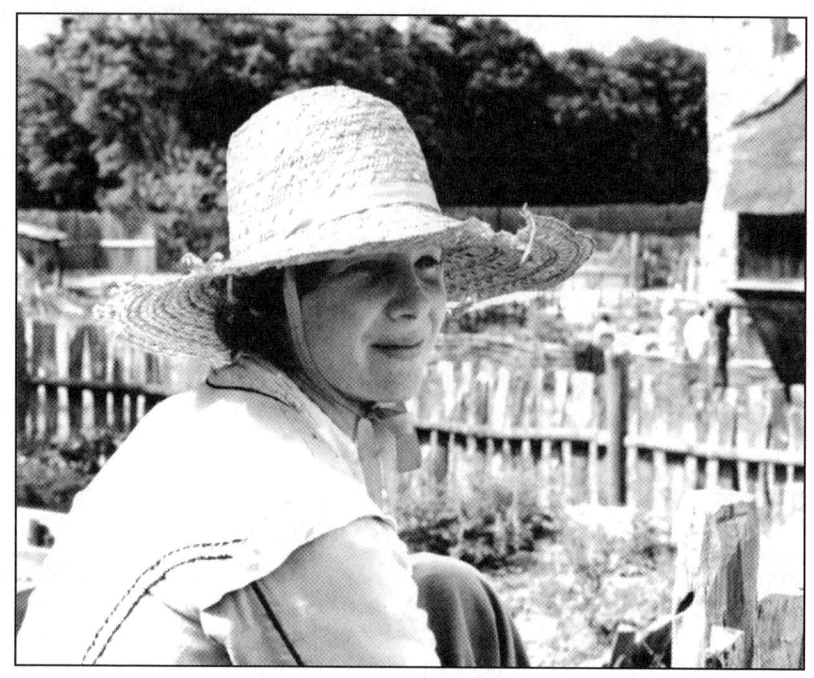

Rachel Charlton, one of Warwick's grandchildren, spent a year working at *Plimoth Plantation*

In 1984, Warwick's son, Randal, visited the *Plantation* and asked the executive director David Case to allow his teenage daughter Rachel to work at the *Plantation.* She became a "Living History" actress at the *Plantation* and worked there for a year before returning to England to go to university.

Family talk of the *Mayflower II* reawakened Warwick's interest in re-establishing his connection with the project. If the owners of *Plimoth Plantation* didn't want to deal with him, he would find someone else.

TIMOROUS MAN

In 1986 Warwick learned from a member of the crew, Andrew Anderson-Bell, that Henry Hornblower II, the Chairman of *Plimoth Plantation* had died. Warwick had not been notified or invited to the funeral but he got hold of a couple of press reports which contained eulogies. Hornblower had been praised at his funeral as

."... a proper Boston Brahmin stockbroker, historian, archaeologist, citizen, servant of good causes, founder of Plimoth Plantation, husband, father, brother, esteemed associate and good friend. He had been the driving force behind the development of one of the finest living museums of American history in the country. His legacy, with the help of his family was to show how the use of interpreters playing historical roles could bring dramatic life to any exhibit."

The October 31st, 1985 issue of *The Old Colony Memorial* noted Hornblower's part in the *Mayflower* project.

"It was Harry Hornblower, with the help of Plymouth High School history teacher Arthur G Pyle and the town - sponsored the Mayflower II reception committee, working closely with a group of Englishmen who brought the Mayflower II to Plymouth, on June 13th, 1957."

A few years later, Hornblower's colleague and fellow Governor, Bill Brewster, repeated his praise for Hornblower and noted that he had never heard his friend Harry say a bad word about Warwick Charlton, and was meticulously correct in his approach to business dealings.

Although Warwick's verdict on Hornblower was that *"he was a timorous man"*, he was undoubtedly dedicated and persistent, and there was, perhaps, more common ground between the two men than they realized or were prepared to accept. Both men were, in their different ways, romantics, prepared to take unusual measures to get what they wanted. Both men dreamed of re-building *Mayflower* at around the same time, after the war.

Over nearly ten years neither man made significant progress until they came together. Warwick displayed boldness of action as a normality whereas Hornblower was careful and relied heavily on legal advice; however, it could be argued that Hornblower pulled off an impressive piece of daylight robbery - the acquisition of *Mayflower II* at a tiny fraction of its cost without any obligation to comply with the conditions of the giver, hardly the act of a timorous man. He put the *Mayflower II* to extremely good use, but not the specific use that was intended for it and he was ruthless in ensuring that Warwick had nothing more to do with either the ship or *Plimoth Plantation.* He was also careful to exclude other members of his wealthy family from the *Plantation's* activities. This was one part of his life, at least, in which he exerted absolute control. If Warwick Charlton and Henry Hornblower had got on better, Disney might have had a rival and the history museums of America might have had a powerful pair of advocates.

Following Hornblower's death Warwick made another visit to Plymouth in 1986 in the company of his son Randal and granddaughter Lucy, who were both living in Connecticut. Warwick became visibly upset in the car park at *Plimoth Plantation* and his pent-up emotions exploded when the innocent lady at the ticket office asked him for his entrance fee.

Warwick walked around the *Plantation* in a state of high agitation; nobody there either knew or cared who he was. He left determined to take the *Mayflower II* story to a new, more exciting level.

RIVAL ATTRACTION

Warwick decided to build a rival attraction next door to *Plimoth Plantation*. It would be called *The Mayflower Experience*.

He made contact with a Boston property owner, who was trying to sell the Governor Bradford Hotel and the land adjoining the property as well as the Governor Carver Hotel. The asking price was $7 million. Warwick wanted the hotels because he thought they could be used to attract European property developers. His real interest however, was in the empty plot of land next door to the Governor Bradford.

There he would build a *Mayflower* theater and a geodesic dome. He had it all worked out; it would bring history to spine tingling life;

"The spectators will proceed inside the dome to walkways leading around and half-way up, perhaps with seating for 500-750 people. (They will see) the sky by day and night, the sun or the stars, scurrying clouds or the moon, projected around the top of the dome. Spectators look down at a mysteriously dark pool.

"Light, sound and music, the voices of the pilgrim fathers and mothers and their young people, at Plymouth England, 1620, at the quay-side ready to board ship for the New World.

"The main voice, our narrator and guide, is William Bradford who, aged 32, was the first governor of the Pilgrims.....as the spectators look down on the dark water it stirs, comes alive and then suddenly, the ship emerges, shaking herself free.....Bradford's voice takes us from Plymouth, England......the ship rides out a storm under bare poles.... a man is washed overboard then miraculously back again ...we are there with them at their arrival at barren Plymouth Rock...at the first

meeting with the Indians....the first winter...and half dead, they are sustained by their faith....

"The public would see, "images of the first settlers succeeded by images of all Americans that have been pilgrims since, to escape tyrannies (to find) freedom - English, German, Poles, French, Swedish, Italians, Vietnamese...finally the face of a contemporary young Bradford ends the story as he began it...

"Thus out of small beginnings....." the ship would sink out of sight back into the dark pool."

Warwick told his real estate investors that the show would last about 20 minutes. He figured that on a busy day the *Mayflower Experience* would comfortably deal with up to 10,000 visitors and would probably average about 3,000.

Although the project looked commercially viable, the money men did not share Warwick's imagination. They looked at the room rates at the two hotels on offer and the occupancy percentage and decided it wasn't for them.

CABIN BOY

Warwick went to the 1987 reunion of the crew, which was held in England at Rhodes College, Oxford. Thirty years after 17 year old Joe Meany served as cabin boy on the *Mayflower II,* he sat down to dinner with the man who intimidated the heck out of him. Joe, now an intelligent relaxed man in his forties, was enthralled with Warwick's insight into the politics of World War II. Joe felt much more at ease and accepted Warwick's offer to visit his home sometime. The two men had more in common than they realized.

Joe, like Warwick, had been virtually ostracized by *Plimoth Plantation. "I think that they had their own candidate for cabin boy,"* said Joe. *"Someone from Arthur Pyle's family. I was persona non grata."* But Joe, who married his childhood sweetheart and lived his whole life in Waltham, Massachusetts, took his children to nearby Plymouth from time to time, to see the boat *"that changed his whole life."*

Andrew Anderson-Bell, the city planner and sailing enthusiast, who had made his way from Ethiopia to England to win a place on the crew of *Mayflower,* stayed close to the ship for the rest of his life. Over the years he watched her become a big money earner for *Plimoth Plantation* but he looked on in dismay as the ship was allowed to deteriorate.

Money from *Mayflower* ticket sales was being diverted to help finance the new reception center at *Plimoth Plantation,* as the ship was allowed to rot. He was the one person who sailed on the ship, who was in a position to do something about it. He had settled down in New England, married a wealthy American, as he joked he would, and built a successful career as an architect and city planner. He became chief planner for Boston Renewal Authority.

The water color sketch of the *Mayflower II* was created by Peter Padfield, one of the crew members, some of whom signed the illustration and presented it to Warwick Charlton.

In the early 70's, after Henry Hornblower invited him to be a Governor, Anderson-Bell became the resident *Mayflower* bore at *Plimoth Plantation* committee meetings. He argued for years that a percentage of revenues should be set aside for the ship's upkeep. Finally, he arrived at one of the committee meetings with an armful of ice picks and gave one to each committee member. He took them to *Mayflower* and showed them how they could easily push their picks into the now soft wood. The committee were convinced, repairs were made, but the permanent solution of a *Mayflower* endowment was not put in place.

In the early 1990's as the *Plantation*'s financial position deteriorated, committee members began to talk about putting a diesel engine in *Mayflower II* so that she could be easily moved from place to place for promotional purposes. Anderson-Bell objected on the grounds that the ship was a national treasure, held in trust for the American people. Not so, said the managers of *Plimoth Plantation.* We own her and we can do what we like with her. In 1992 Anderson-Bell resigned in disgust. Anderson-Bell was not the only fan of *Mayflower II* who was horrified at the thought of giving her auxiliary power.

The interpreters and other staff who worked to maintain *Mayflower* reminded everyone how she could draw a crowd under sail. They learned to operate her sails and took the aging ship on the 30 mile trip across Cape Cod Bay to Provincetown and back. The trip drew crowds, the press and a great deal of fresh pictures and publicity for *Plimoth Plantation.*

In 1956, Freddie Pontiero spotted *Mayflower II* at anchor in Brixham harbor. He was at about 20,000 ft at the time, flying in an RAF Canberra plane along the English coastline on a photo reconnaissance mission, but he could not resist the temptation to put matters of national security to one side and use his expensive air force equipment to take this picture, which he has held onto for over 60 years.

RUSSIAN BOMBS

In the late eighties Warwick turned his attention in the opposite direction - to Russia. He had friends and connections even in Moscow. Ed Stevens, another wartime buddy, was the *Newsweek* correspondent for Moscow, and he introduced Warwick to politicians at the highest level of Moscow government.

The Russians took to this bear of a man, who knew more about their history than they did. Warwick worked on various real estate projects in Moscow, including the re-development of a new Hilton Hotel in Moscow's historic Kitai Gorod district. In the process, he dealt with Yuri Luschkov, the powerful teetotal mayor of Moscow and was asked to come up with a plan to get the city's casino industry under control.

In one long meeting with Yuri Luzkov, about the tortuous process of planning permission, a bored Warwick could not resist putting his business reasons for the meeting to one side. *"I have a solution to your economic problems"* he told the diminutive Mayor Luzkov, as he sat at a long table crowded with deputies, aides and translators.

"Yes?" Mayor Luzkov cocked his head.

"It's simple", said Warwick, *" Russia should announce that it is putting all its 20,000 nuclear weapons up for sale. Retain a high class firm of auctioneers like Sotheby's to do the job. At the same time you should tell the world that any bombs that remain unsold will be set off."*

Luzkov laughed. He loved Warwick's Russian mind but Warwick had a serious point to make.

The Western World was allowing its old war adversary to slide into economic chaos. The Russian people, who had been forced to suffer under 70 years of communism, were now being shown what it was like to suffer under capitalist freedom. The life expectancy of the Russian people was falling, the army was collapsing, the government appeared to have less power than the gangsters who had taken control of much of the Russian economy.

The possibility that Russians could be consumed by anarchy, posed massive threats to world peace. Somehow the complacent west needed a wake up call. It was sleeping soundly in the mistaken belief that the threat of nuclear war had been banished along with communism.

Between discussing hotel rights, Warwick poked around the city and discovered a small but unusually elegant building right next to the Kremlin that was closed and apparently not in use. He discovered that Ivan the Terrible had given the building to an Englishman, Sir Richard Chancellor, in 1556 for traders from Britain to use as they sought to do business with Russia. In 1649 the Russians had repossessed the property, angry that their English trading partners had beheaded their King Charles 1.

"Wouldn't it be wonderful", Warwick thought *"to refurbish the property and reopen it as an Anglo-Russian trading center?"* Warwick's enthusiasm for history and big projects infected the Russians, including his new friend Yuri Luzhkov, Leonid Varakin the chief architect of Moscow and Lydia Solovgaova the director of the Museum of Moscow. The Russians signed a joint venture agreement but Warwick was unable to persuade English investors to put up the $1.7 million needed to activate the 49 year lease that the Russians had offered.

Over the years, Warwick found several other grand schemes to occupy his restless energy and he made money, but he also made time to engage with his seven offspring and numerous grandchildren. His castle home became the center of attraction on high days and holidays and during times of family crisis.

Warwick could be delightful in the company of children, as he was when out walking one day with Sophie, one of his granddaughters. They passed someone selling helium balloons and on a whim he bought the entire bunch on sale. He then took Sophie into a toy shop, bought a teddy bear, tied it to the balloons and sent the bear on a journey up and away into the clouds.

"Warwick could be a very difficult person to deal with," his elder daughter Vicki observed. *"He insisted on everything being correct, particularly with anything to do with the English language. A letter, for example, had to be word perfect and he would rewrite it a dozen times or more if necessary. And he could not stand someone using bad grammar. I remember his flying into a fury when a family member kept using the word "nice." He would scream 'What on earth do you mean by saying this or that was "nice?"', and then go on to give a lesson in the use of the appropriate words."*

"Warwick's insistence on everything being historically correct made Mayflower II what it is; the insistence of using the tools of the 1600s, the old English in the insurance document, the particular dark red ink he used to print the thousands of copies of the Mayflower Compact.

"Warwick was also a great teacher. He once received a letter from my daughter Suzi, who had been on a school trip to visit the Mayflower II, and in it she wrote that her classmates could not understand how long ago the Pilgrims had arrived. Warwick wrote back postcards to all 31 of the 8-year old students in Suzi's class to explain the concept of a long time. 'Think about time and centuries by imaging the life of one

person, then the one person before that, then the one person before that and so on until you get to 1620. You will discover is was not that long ago - maybe six or seven people '. "

However, Warwick's love of history did not prevent him, on occasion, from imagining his own arc of events, as he did when he decided that the Wig and Pen Club at one end of Fleet Street *"was perhaps the only building in the neighborhood that survived the fire of London in 1666."*

"My father was full of contradictions," his daughter Vicki recalls. *"He was so shy that he would leave his own parties as the guests were arriving, only to return to hold center stage when everyone had had a few drinks.*

"He was also frightened of flying to the point where I remember one pilot asking him to leave the plane before it took off because he was unnerving everyone on board."

At the same time Warwick had no problem standing up to anyone whom he saw as a public menace no matter how young and large they were. In the early days of cell phones, he would routinely confront someone shouting down a cell phone on a train or bus by sitting opposite them and pretending, himself, to be speaking on a phone - only in reality he had nothing in his hand. On another occasion in his late 70s he coolly disarmed a young thug who had run off with a wallet stolen from a member of his family.

Warwick could be cruel to anyone whom he saw as pompous and ill informed. *"This could lead to self-destructive behaviour,"* recalls Vicki. She shudders at the memory of one dinner party where he could not help himself from the verbal destruction of a government minister. "*The minister didn't know what was happening,"* says Vicki. "*The poor man had only agreed to attend the party to help Warwick in one of his schemes."*

"Warwick had a lifelong problem with authority," she observed.

"It saddens me that Warwick was not recognized for what he was. He had a brilliant mind and had a truly astonishing list of friends at the highest level of the arts, entertainment, politics and business. He was a true visionary. Above all he was a great history teacher and what he wanted was to be involved in the history he had recreated with Mayflower II. For him, it was never about money. "

TOWN CRIER

At the age of seventy-six Warwick finally sought public office. His wife Belinda had been elected to the local council in the tiny market town of Ringwood in Hampshire. Warwick lobbied her hard to become the official town crier. Of course in 1996 it was a ceremonial job which meant Warwick had to dress up in the costume of a bygone age and parade around town, ringing a large hand bell. He was called to duty when there were important local events, like the illumination of the Christmas tree lights, and the Easter parade for the children of the area, or a special event in the Furlong Shopping Mall.

Warwick took the position very seriously. His parade ground voice was still very strong and only the deaf in the tiny market town in the New Forest could fail to hear the news he was announcing. Warwick valued the job because he was doing yet

Eventually Warwick sought low office - the job of unpaid Town Crier in the small English town of Ringwood. As always, he had an explanation based in history for his decision.

again what he was best at, spreading the word. *"Town Criers were the first source of information to the mass of the people"*, Warwick lectured anyone who showed the least interest. *"Before newspapers, before television, they brought the word down the dark streets of England's towns and cities that it was 5 o'clock and all was well."*

In 1996, he was contacted again by a member of the crew of *Mayflower II*. There were plans to organize yet another reunion - this one to celebrate the fortieth anniversary of the sailing of the ship. Warwick began to think it was time to do something special and he went down to Plymouth, England, in the late summer of 1996 to talk to the civic leaders about a new promotion to re-affirm Anglo-American relations.

The plan involved sailing *Mayflower II* back to Plymouth, England for a visit before returning home to Plymouth, Massachusetts. Of course it would involve obtaining the support of *Plimoth Plantation*. He would fly to America to see the Governors of the *Plantation*.

Soon after, his ex-wife Marilyn, became very sick. Warwick would delay his trip to America until Marilyn got through her health crisis.

SILENT WITNESS

Warwick Charlton had a grey look about him, that was due to much more than grief. It was October 1996. Now seventy-seven years old, he still stood impressively straight and although he weighed about 250 lbs., he carried his weight well. For once though, he was fading into the crowd with a deathly quiet that was quite uncommon. Belinda, his wife for the last twenty-two years, could see that he was not well, as could five of his children who were present as he stood by the grave. They had come to a green corner of a rural English churchyard in the market town of Ringwood, Hampshire to bury Warwick's third wife Marilyn.

As he stood by her graveside, he remembered how important the *Mayflower II* had been to Marilyn, how delighted she had been to take a tour of the ship as she lay at anchor in Miami harbor and how proud she had been, as an American, to have been married to the man who made *Mayflower II* happen.

Warwick was due to go to America two days after the funeral. He hated flying, in part because he found it difficult to fit his heavy frame comfortably into the cramped tourist class seats and partly because he couldn't understand how planes stayed up in the sky. Right then, the turbulence was all in Warwick's mind. Marilyn's death had brought back memories of the time they had together a few months after the arrival of the *Mayflower II* in America. Now, by coincidence for the first time in almost 40 years, he was being welcomed back.

True, it was an unofficial welcome, true it came from a relatively junior member of the staff of *Plimoth Plantation,* but it had been a positive contact. Marietta Mullen, who was a historian at *Plimoth Plantation,* was researching the history of the crossing of the *Mayflowe II* in 1957. She had written to Warwick - and the other men who sailed on her, for their reminiscences. Virtually all of those sailors were now either old or dead and Marietta wanted to get the stories of the survivors, before it was too late. It was a request Warwick could not refuse.

One of Warwick's sons called him after the funeral and pleaded with him to postpone his trip. So did his eldest daughter Vicki. "*You have had a difficult time*" they both said. "*You don't look well. Wait a while until someone can go with you for company.*" They both knew he planned to go to see the *Mayflower II* and the people at *Plimoth Plantation* and they both knew how much distress it might cause him.

Marietta Mullen

worked for many years as a guide to visitors who swarmed over *Mayflower II.* Eventually she decided to contact Warwick to get answers to questions that intrigued her.

Yes, Warwick assured them both, he would hold off going for a while, maybe until Belinda was free to travel with him. Two days later he boarded a plane for the United States. The *Mayflower II* beckoned. It was time to heal the bitter wounds of the last 39 years. It was time for everyone to come together again. He had an idea for making the *Mayflower II* an important part of the millennium celebrations. It would sail back to Europe to Plymouth, England where hundreds of thousands would come to see her. The leaders of Plymouth Council were enthusiastic and he had worked out a lot of the details, including the tricky question of insurance. He had promotional plans that would involve educational groups all over America.

All he needed at this stage, was to get the approval in principal of the managers and Board of Governors of *Plimoth Plantation.* Why wouldn't the Plantation's leaders agree? He would show them how they could earn several million dollars for the further upkeep of the *Mayflower II* and *Plimoth Plantation* itself. At the same time *Plimoth Plantation* would attract worldwide attention once more and perhaps finally, forty years later, the Anglo-American trust, which was a major reason behind the original exercise, could be endowed.

In New York, Warwick felt unwell and called his wife Belinda to say he was turning around and coming straight home, then, shortly after, he perked up again and sent a fax to his daughter Vicki. He was going to Massachusetts, as planned, to present his proposals to the people who looked after *Mayflower II*. His message was upbeat and optimistic.

MARIETTA'S MOVE

At Boston's Logan Airport, Warwick was met by Marietta Mullen and he immediately brightened up. Marietta had worked for several years on *Mayflower II* as an interpreter and had been inspired by reading Warwick's 1957 book, *"The Second Mayflower Adventure"*. He had an attentive, attractive audience of one which was the most he ever needed.

Marietta apologized for the state of the transportation she was providing for her VIP as he squeezed into her rusted-out 1985 Le Baron. Work on the *Mayflower II* was rewarding but not highly paid, she explained. Warwick, as always, was unconcerned. He had spent his entire life riding either in taxis or other people's cars and he was unconcerned by the quality of his transportation.

The only time he had driven himself was in the desert during World War II. Then, as a young officer, he had taken over from his driver who had immediately requested a transfer. Anything would be preferable to being a passenger in a vehicle driven by Warwick Charlton - even front line duty close to the sound of gunfire.

Warwick talked incessantly as Marietta drove him from Boston to Plymouth in her beat up old car, where he checked into the Governor Bradford Hotel. The hotel is just a short walk from where the *Mayflower II* was docked. Marietta suggested he rest, but Warwick couldn't wait to walk the decks of *Mayflower II.*

There, for two hours, he paced up and down the little icon of American history and released his pent up energy as he recounted the story of the building and sailing of the

Mayflower II to the interpreters whose job it was to explain to the public the voyage of the first American settlers.

Warwick brought back to life his simple story of *"water, wind, sun and sail"*, the time in 1957 when he felt close to the beat of the pulse of life. *"The breath of wind, the sway of the ship moving with the sea, the slow dignity of sunrise and sunset."* At first he confessed he viewed these things as an onlooker. *"But after a few days at sea I felt part of them."* He remembered how he laughed, and millions laughed with him, *"to see the sails conceive big bellied with the wanton breeze."*

His audience wanted to know how he built the ship and he told them how he found plans where none existed, how he found the money when no-one had anything to spare, how he found the right type of crooked oak in a time of timber rationing, how old cider barrels were used to make wooden nails, and how he persuaded an English shipbuilder to rediscover the lost art of constructing a seventeenth century sailing ship.

Warwick discussed early American history with experts on early American history and reminded them of the wicked side of the first Pilgrims. They were not above lust or adultery but they were magnificently ahead of their time. About 25 years before England would be engulfed in a bloody civil war, the first settlers had sought a new way of living; a life free from domination by the church, in which communities governed themselves, with leaders elected from their own number.

The next morning, Warwick was up early, dressed in suit and tie, pacing back and forth in the tiny hotel lobby waiting for Marietta and her rusty transportation. She drove him to the outskirts of Plymouth, to the replica of the original Pilgrim Village, to meet the managers of *Plimoth Plantation*.

The only person there to receive him was the senior historian, Mr. James Baker who appeared neither overjoyed nor impressed with the appearance of his visitor. Warwick noticed that Baker didn't even offer him a cup of coffee and he felt the old antagonism returning. He felt very unwelcome once more. The old wounds were re-opening.

Mr. Baker explained uneasily that it was a difficult time for the *Plantation*. Warwick really needed to speak to either the Executive Director or the Chairman but the Executive Director, David Case, had recently left and the Chairman wasn't available. None of the other Governors was around. Mr. Baker explained that the *Plantation* had brought in some management consultants to advise of the future management and development of the *Plantation* and *Mayflower II* exhibit. Money was very short. Times were hard.

"The same old story," thought Warwick. *"The same story Harry Hornblower used to tell me nearly forty years ago whenever I wrote to him."* Even so, this was one of the reasons why Warwick was there. Now was the time to put his ideas forward.

Warwick looked at the donnish Baker with his grey hair swept back into a pony tail and sandaled feet and decided it wasn't fair to expect him to respond. He was talking to the wrong person. It was unfair to unload everything on this gentleman who was merely doing his academic job.

Warwick was bursting to talk about the last forty years. Why had the *Plantation* staff ignored him, yet made his assistant cook an honored member of the *Plantation* ? Why had they avoided writing to him and made one of his crew a governor? Why had they made the widow of one of Warwick's backers an honorary governor and conferred the same honor on a junior public relations executive who had helped to promote the New York exhibition of *Mayflower II* in 1957?

Why had they done all this and not sent him as much as one annual report? If he had received annual reports, Warwick would have seen that the value of the *Mayflower II* had steadily increased in the audited accounts to $1,206,999 in 1994. More importantly, why had they ignored the debt they owed him and why had they broken the agreement to set up a trust to further Anglo-American relations?

That had been the sole basis on which he had transferred the *Mayflower II* to the care of *Plimoth Plantation,* on behalf of the American people. Warwick had been banished from Plymouth, much as some of the more wicked settlers had been over 300 years ago, after being found guilty of fornication, adultery or some other unlawful act. What, he wondered, was his crime?

He picked up some brochures on the *Mayflower II* and left Mr. Baker's office without getting the answer to any of these questions, and without explaining his new plan for bringing the *Mayflower II* back onto the center stage of the millennium celebrations.

Although Warwick went away disappointed from his visit to Plimoth Plantation, Marietta Mullen would eventually be recognized for her work in telling the story of *Mayflower II.* It would take time, but in 2003 she received the Hornblower award for her work in preserving the history of Warwick and the crew of *Mayflower II.*

Over a decade later, in 2015, she received the Award of Merit from the prestigious American Association for State and Local History. Shortly thereafter the Massachusetts State Senate endorsed Marietta's valuable historical contributions with an official citation congratulating her on preserving the story of *Mayflower II* for future generations to enjoy.

REAL Pink Gin?

The spirit of the NEW Elizabethans

Shades of Drake, Raleigh, Frobisher and Hawkins! Devon distils the spirit of the new *Elizabethans—in a gin of character for a people of character. Made to the centuries-old recipe that has been a Devon family's secret for generations, it has spread Devon's fame throughout the world. Now Plymouth Gin leaves the ancient Black Friars Distillery (where provisions for the Mayflower of 1620 were stored) on another historic voyage. In the new Mayflower it is, of course,* the *gin selected to be carried across the Atlantic. So drink success to the voyagers—in Plymouth Gin, Spirit of Devon!*

PLYMOUTH GIN

pink, plain or partnered

BOTTLE [illegible] · HALF BOTTLE [illegible] · QUARTER BOTTLE [illegible] · MINIATURE [illegible] U.K. ONLY

Plymouth Gin and the Plymouth City Council supported Warwick from the early days, right through until the late 1990's, when the city rolled out the red carpet for Warwick to stage a reunion of all involved in the *Mayflower II* project.

THE WHITE HOUSE

WASHINGTON

June 13, 1997

Warm greetings to everyone gathered in Plymouth, England, to mark the 40th anniversary of the sailing of Mayflower II to America.

In June of 1957, Mayflower II arrived in Provincetown, Massachusetts, after a transatlantic voyage that captured the attention of American and British citizens alike. The brainchild of Warwick Charlton, Project Mayflower highlighted not only the courageous voyage made by the Pilgrims in 1620, but also the strong ties still enjoyed between the United States and Great Britain.

Four decades after Mayflower II docked at Provincetown, it is as important as ever to celebrate the continuing friendship between our two countries. I am delighted to join you in observing the 40th anniversary of the Mayflower II project and in applauding the important role it has played in teaching millions of Americans about our rich past. Hillary joins me in saluting the members of the original crew of Mayflower II, and we extend best wishes to all for a truly memorable anniversary celebration.

Bill Clinton

Warwick received support from the US President for his planned celebrations in 1997.

HEART FAILURE

Two days later, after taking his leave of Marietta and the *Plimoth Plantation,* Warwick Charlton lay in a hospital bed at the Mayo clinic in Rochester, Minnesota, close to death. The doctors diagnosed chronic heart failure and prescribed a series of drugs designed to stabilize his blood pressure and prevent a stroke.

His son Michael, who was himself a doctor at the Mayo Clinic, called the family to report. He gave the bad news which included the likelihood that his father had a relatively short life expectancy. *"The good news is that the doctors have managed to reduce Dad's blood pressure to a lower level than it's been for most of his adult life."*

Warwick's blood pressure and his life expectancy could be improved if Warwick took the Mayo doctors' advice; if he took the right medication, lost some weight and altered his lifestyle. He needed to slow down and forget about the ship which had been the cause of so much stress in his life.

After a week in the Mayo Clinic, Warwick left for England determined to be a good patient. He would do everything he had been told - except turn his back on the ship. The Mayo doctors had given him the most compelling deadline of his journalistic life but Warwick Charlton had invested too much energy and emotion in the *Mayflower II* story to shy away from trying to write one last chapter. He would organize a reunion to celebrate the fortieth anniversary of the second *Mayflower's* voyage.

This reunion, the first he had organized, was to be a little different from the clubby affairs for the Captain and those who had sailed on the *Mayflower II*. Those still alive were welcome but Warwick tried to contact the people who helped him make the voyage possible; his former partner John Lowe, his office staff, the patrons, the men who worked in Upham's yard and those who gave or lent money. He wrote to Governor William Weld of Massachusetts and Senator Edward Kennedy as well as the mayor of Boston. He invited Marietta Mullen, of course, and other representatives from *Plimoth Plantation*. When Marietta protested that the *Plantation* couldn't pay her air fare, he found it.

He set out his purpose in a letter to President Bill Clinton dated March 18 1997, in which he asked for the President's blessing;

"We wish to rededicate ourselves for the millennium to one of the primary objectives of the project when it was founded; to strive to encourage Anglo-American relations of a similar (if less exalted) academic level of the Rhodes scholarship. Over half the crew have gone to the "watch below." All of us are bound to join them in the not too distant future, so this anniversary has special significance for us and we hope in the new millennium our ship will remain a reminder of the part our forebears played in the foundation of your great country."

The US president replied with a letter of support, and Governor William Weld of Massachusetts sent a proclamation recognizing Warwick's role in conceiving and funding the *Mayflower II,* and bestowing it on the American people. He declared June 13 - 14 1997 *Mayflower II* Commemoration days.

However as the fortieth anniversary of the Atlantic crossing of *Mayflower II* approached there was precious little to celebrate at *Plimoth Plantation*. David Case, the longtime president was gone, as was his number two man, the development director. As the governors spent months looking for replacements, drastic measures were taken to reduce costs. A ten hour, four-day-week, was imposed on the permanent staff throughout the winter of 1997 and all but essential expenditure forbidden.

The public relations department made the usual attempt to put a positive spin on draconian cost cutting, with a press release that contained the business speak that was fashionable in the mid-nineties. *"The 17th century living history museum is being positioned for the future"*, the release announced.

Over 509,000 visitors walked the decks of *Mayflower II* and toured the bare earthern streets of *Plimoth Plantation* in 1996, a 6.9 increase on the previous year. Revenues were also up by 6 per cent. The problem was that costs were rising faster mainly because the *Plantation* was saddled with too much long-term debt. The release omitted to say what many of the long term employees believed, that the future of both *Plimoth Plantation* and *Mayflower II* was hanging in the balance, threatened by impatient bankers who no longer had Henry Hornblower II to reassure them.

Some of the permanent staff were let go and not all the seasonal workers were re-hired but those that remained struggled to put together an exhibit that would continue to excite the imagination and stimulate interest in American history.

Mayflower II lay in Plymouth Harbor covered in protective sheeting. She was badly in need of repairs that the experts had calculated would cost $100,000 and take three years to complete. They would have to wait. The historians and interpreters planned a new exhibit for the spring opening in late March. For the first time Marietta Mullen and her colleagues would tell two stories to the visitors who came aboard *Mayflower II*. They would talk, of course, about the voyage of 1620 and all that meant to the settlement and establishment of a new nation.

But they would also talk for the first time, about the 1957 voyage. They would explain how *Mayflower II* was built and why; about the insistence on historical accuracy in the construction and in the details of the voyage that brought the ship from one Plymouth to another. They would also talk about the dreams of Warwick Charlton and the others involved in the project; Henry Hornblower, of course, the naval architect William Baker and the dozens of others who made a critical contribution.

The interpreters would also talk of Warwick's long-term goal to foster relations between England and the United States. Many of the listeners would be far too young to understand how millions of lives had been lost on both sides of the Atlantic in the twentieth century, in two great wars that were fought to preserve common beliefs.

Through the dedication of Marietta Mullen, who became responsible for telling the story of the 1957 voyage, Warwick reappeared in a central role at *Plimoth Plantation*. However, Warwick needed more than Marietta had in her power to give; he needed to be involved in setting up a trust to fund Anglo-American scholarships, a project that would use his restless mind and his love of history. He turned instead to outer space.

OUTER SPACE

Shortly before his 80th birthday Warwick embarked on a new project that encapsulated his lifelong fascination for space - a "Space Time" museum to be built in the city of Seville, in Spain. He secured the support of Professor Stephen Hawking, the world's most prominent and respected living expert on the universe and among many other things the author of a best-selling book about Time. Warwick went to see Hawking at Cambridge University where he has worked for years despite suffering from a body ravaged by debilitating disease which left him physically helpless, speechless and wheelchair bound.

Warwick pointed out that there was a need for action because neither he, at 80, or the wheelchair bound Dr Hawking had the prospect of much time to complete the project. Dr Hawking was as excited with the idea as Warwick. Although Warwick would live another four years, the project was never funded. However, Warwick's lifelong ability to ignore any setback is summed up in the letter he wrote to his son Randal. The letter also reveals Warwick's almost childlike wonder at the way the world works and of course his way with words.

Avon Castle, Ringwood 11 May 2000

Dearest Randal,

Here at last is the David Geffen book I promised. It arrived today just as I was beginning to give up - five weeks after it was ordered. I never quite trust the post - it has always seemed magical to me that you can entrust a letter or a parcel across a counter to someone you have never met and that it ends up, sometimes thousands of miles away, delivered to the person whose name you have noted on the parcel or envelope.

My visit to Spain-Seville has been delayed and I am in limbo - I was all keyed up anticipating the fun of the 2 and a half years work to open the Hawking Space Time Center. There is a problem about putting the funding jigsaw together: a mixture of private, city, provincial government, EC investment - a total of $10 million (dollars or Pounds?) I am of course determined to press on. In life on planet Earth we pass through different time horizons. When we are young they appear limitless. But now in my 80th decade I can see the last horizon, the singularity of my life, so before I drop off into the deep, dark, dark pool of oblivion I want to build a Space Time Center.

Love Pops.

DUSTY CHAMPAGNE

Warwick got up and put on his best country gentleman's green and brown tweed suit. He was due to spend the day with his daughter Rachel and Warwick was in good spirits as he left the castle that he called home, for the short drive to Ringwood. He was looking forward to parading around the Hampshire village where he was known as the eccentric town crier with the deep sergeant major's voice.

However, as he strolled down the main street of the picturesque market town his heart finally gave up on the task of servicing a body that had been full of manic energy for over 80 years. He collapsed on the pavement and finally shuddered to stillness on December 10, 2002.

The man whom many suspected was out to make a fortune from the *Mayflower II* and his other ideas, died without a bank account, virtually no cash and no other significant resources.

He would have loved what happened from this point on. Most of the famous people Warwick had worked with had predeceased him and although the local church was full of mourners most were family and local friends, with one exception, Patrick Skene Catling a great writer whom Warwick had got to know as a journalist on the Baltimore Sun. Stephen Hawking, the world famous Cambridge University physicist who had been a partner in Warwick's last great adventure, wrote a eulogy that recognized Warwick's *"special abilities."*

" Warwick's ideas were always on a very grand scale, but they were also inspirational with a down-to-earth reality which people from all works of life could appreciate."

Warwick would have been overjoyed to know that Marietta Mullen and Peter Arenstam from *Plimoth Plantation* had made the journey across the Atlantic.

Later, at Warwick's request, his ashes - at least some of them, were attached to an industrial strength rocket that was ignited and sent in the general direction of the outer space that fascinated him. The remaining ashes were saved for a trip to *Plimoth Planation,* in the summer of 2003.

On board the *Mayflower II,* docked as usual at State Pier, at 6 pm on May 31st 2003 a memorial service for Warwick took place. It was at the invitation of Nancy Brennan, the recently appointed Executive Director of *Plimoth Plantation.* Staff from the *Plantation* were present, including Warwick's longtime advocate, Marietta Mullen. So were several of Warwick's children and one or two of the crew who had sailed in *Mayflower II.*

Following speeches celebrating Warwick's life, his widow, Belinda, attempted to scatter the ashes overboard onto the water. But a firm breeze that suddenly picked up, blew virtually all the ashes back on board. Some settled as a fine dust that coated the champagne in glasses in the hands of the mourners. The rest landed on deck. Belinda gave up the challenge of the wind and put the funeral urn down.

After the dignitaries had departed, the crew picked up the urn, which still contained some of the ashes and went to the front of the ship between decks. They found a space between the boards where Warwick's remains could be deposited and remain undisturbed.

Later in 2003, with both Warwick and Henry Hornblower gone to "the watch below", *Plimoth Plantation* produced a 24 page color issue of *Plimoth Life,* that included a lengthy dedication to Warwick Charlton, British visionary and *"mover of mountains who founded Project Mayflower Ltd, that built Mayflower II in 1957."*

The concern about commercialism was forgotten, as Karin Goldstein celebrated the different promotions that were used by Warwick to raise funds to build and sail the ship. They included his newspaper *Mayflower Mail,* the oak chests sold for 460 pounds each and the 140,000 pieces of mail that were stamped on board and mailed on arrival.

Plimoth Plantation was now developing a collection of artifacts that demonstrated the early days of corporate sponsorship, the involvement and support of British companies including Carr's biscuits, Harvey's Bristol Cream sherry and Ben Truman beer - just some of the products donated for the voyage. The magazine carried a rare picture of Henry Hornblower shaking hands with Warwick.

On November 7th 2003, *Plimoth Plantation* named Marietta Mullen the winner of a Hornblower award because *"Almost single handedly she recognized and restored a unique relationship between our museum and members of the crew that sailed Mayflower II in 1957 including, pre-eminently, Warwick Charlton."*

By 2017 over 25 million visitors had walked the decks of the *Mayflower II* and she was being described as an American icon, a national treasure. However, the years since 1957 had taken their toll and she was sent to Mystic, Connecticut for extensive repairs. They are being carried out over three years at an estimated cost of $7.5 million. *Mayflower II* is being readied to resume her starring role in 2020, as the country celebrates the 400-year anniversary of the voyage of the first settlers.

In 2020 and beyond, Warwick's ashes, buried as they are, deep in the bowels of the *Mayflower,* will move restlessly as the ship sways and rocks in the water. And if you believe in ghosts, as Warwick sometimes did, it is not difficult to believe the apparition wandering the decks at night, restless and cantakerous as ever, seeking to deliver another history lesson; perhaps reciting the Mayflower Compact.

In the name of God, Amen. We whose names are underwritten, the loyal subjects of our dread Sovereign Lord King James, by the Grace of God, of great Britain, France and Ireland, King Defender of the Faith etc. having undertaken for the Glory of God, and Advancement of the Christian faith, and the honour of our King and country, a voyage to plant the first Colony in the northern parts of Virginia; Do by these presents, solemnly and mutually, in the presence of God and one another, convenient and combine ourselves together into a civil Body Politik, for our better ordering and preservation, and furtherance of the ends aforesaid: And by virtue hereto do enact, constitute and frame, such just and equal laws, ordinances, acts, constitutions and officers, from time to time, as shall be thought meet and convenient for the general good of the Colony; unto which we promise all due Submission and obedience. In witness whereof, we have hereunto subscribed our names at Cape-Cod the eleventh of November, in the Reign of our Sovereign Lord King James of England, France and Ireland, the eighteenth, and of Scotland the fifty-fourth, Anno Domini 1620.

Acknowledgements

It took **Warwick Charlton** less than two years to conjure *Mayflower II* out of nothing. However it took over 20 years to tell his story, even with his help. In the mid 1990s he submitted to two weeks of intense questioning and made all his records, which were not particularly well organized, available. He also submitted to many recorded interviews including a video set up by my brother **Alex Charlton**.

Plimoth Plantation, who at the same time, were going through a change of leadership, generously opened their records for inspection. Their senior historian, **James Baker** was particularly helpful, as was **Marietta Mullen,** who was largely responsible, along with **Peter Arenstram**, for resurrecting Warwick's role in building and sailing the *Mayflower II* to America. If anything, Marietta was almost as passionate and determined as Warwick in her efforts to tell the true story of the second *Mayflower* voyage. **Henry Hornblower's** neat hand-written notes following phone calls and Warwick's eloquent letters along with copies of contracts and internal memos brought the characters of those involved, vividly to life.

However, Warwick found his own story difficult to read and it was consigned to my basement until 2017 when my sister, **Vicki Charlton,** lacking reading material, picked it up and spent a sleepless night experiencing her father's incredible achievement and how it ended in financial disgrace and decades of personal pain and regret that he had not found a way to work with his partner, **John Lowe**, as well as Henry Hornblower and others on both sides of the Atlantic.

With 2020 on the horizon, Vicki thought it was time, finally, to tell her father's story. My friend **John Henley**, a magician and movie actor by profession and editor by inclination, has devoted months to reviewing the manuscript and giving advice. He has conjured a large amount of new material to support and validate Warwick's story and used his sharp eyes to suggest many ways, which, I believe, have helped to hone the narrative. John, who has also appeared in over 80 movies has brought his love of film to a review and repair of family film of Warwick Charlton and *Mayflower II*.

Thanks are also due to **Sue Atkinson**, the family historian who has spent many years tracing the extended family ancestry to which she and Warwick belong.

Thanks are due to my wife **Lee** and my daughter **Rachel,** both of whom have helped to clean up the various drafts and remind me of the correct use of the English language.

Warwick always acknowledged that in order to create *Mayflower II* he had to sail pretty close to the wind at times. With the help of the above mentioned people and many others, including Warwick's extended family, I hope we have sailed close to capturing the life and achievements of a self described Wicked Pilgrim.

Unless otherwise stated, pictures have been sourced by the author who acknowledges contributions from many members of Warwick's family including family historians Sue Atkinson and **Sally Morton** , as well as **Suzanne Charlton**, Victoria Charlton and of course Warwick Charlton and his widow **Belinda**. I also appreciate photographic contributions from non-family members including the family of **Joe Meany**, who was a cabin boy on board the *Mayflower II*.

We would also like to thank ***Plimoth Plantation*** for help in locating pictures (back in 1994).

Appendix A

Warwick Charlton and the cast of characters who were involved in the Mayflower Project.

Dr R.C.Anderson : British Maritime Museum. *76, 77, 82, 85, 91.*
Slim Arons : Yank magazine. *47.*
Winthrop Aldrich : American Ambassador to the UK. *74, 108.*
Andrew Anderson-Bell : Crew member. *185, 186, 234, 356, 372, 375, 379, 380, 381.*
Peter Arenstam : Manager Plimoth Plantation. *406.*
James Baker : Senior historian at Plimoth Plantation. *395, 396, 409.*
William Baker : Executive Bethlehem steel/ historian of wooden ship design. *91, 92, 111, 112, 196, 197, 334, 402.*
Lord Beaverbrook : Wartime cabinet minister and head of Express newspaper group. *70, 81.*
Miss Beck : Secretarial assistant Project Mayflower Ltd. *222.*
Paul Bird : New York businessman. *148, 181, 306.*
Herbert Boynton : Governor, Plimoth Plantation. *133, 134, 135, 170, 323.*
Dick Brennan : Manager of the Wig and Pen Club. *103, 104, 138, 140, 188, 246, 247, 268, 301, 353, 354, 356.*
Nancy Brennan : Chief executive, Plimoth Plantation. *406.*
William Brewster : Governor Plimoth Plantation. *93, 112, 113, 204, 214, 254, 323, 375.*
Scottie Burgess : Yank Magazine. *47.*
Sir Harold Caccia : British Ambassador to the United States. *248.*
Archie Calhoun : Aide to General Montgomery and distinguished academic. *64.*
David Case : Chief Executive, Plimoth Plantation. *374, 395, 400.*
Birdie Charlton : Mother of Warwick Charlton. *23, 24, 25, 64.*

Randal Thornton Charlton : Father. *20, 21, 22, 23, 24, 41, 83, 104.*
Lucy Haywood Charlton : First wife. *29, 30, 33, 326.*
Paula Charlton : Second wife. *299.*
Marilyn Charlton : Third wife. *318, 369, 389, 390.*
Belinda Charlton : Fourth wife. *369, 388, 390, 391, 392, 406, 410.*
Randolph Churchill : Son of Sir Winston Churchill, British Prime Minister. *36, 43, 97, 98, 211, 263.*
Sir Winston Churchill : British war time leader. *33, 36, 43, 44, 45, 51, 52, 53, 55, 61, 124, 125, 131, 211, 212, 343.*
Bill Clinton : US president. *398, 400.*
Bill Connor : Columnist of the Daily Mirror. 42, *69, 71, 72, 86, 108, 266.*
Joe Coral : Owner of the Wig and Pen club. *103.*
Frank Costello : New York Mob boss. *161, 162.*
Hugh Cudlipp : Later Lord Cudlipp, head of the Mirror Group. *42, 71.*
D'Arcy Edmonson : British Embassy, Washington DC. *171.*
Dominic Elwes : Son of famous painter. *73, 84.*
Emmwood : Daily Mail cartoonist. *124, 125.*
Felix Fenston : Real estate developer. *73, 74, 84, 88, 120, 121, 130, 131, 135, 136, 141, 199, 200, 201, 206, 213, 214, 215, 217, 270, 273, 277, 278, 279, 281, 284, 287, 288, 293, 294, 295, 298, 304, 322, 323, 327, 334, 336, 340, 356, 360.*
Ian Fleming : Author of James Bond novels. *97, 98.*
Ronnie Forth : Organizer of welcoming plans for *Mayflower II. 15, 173, 179, 180, 203, 247, 248, 249, 255, 272, 308, 338, 339, 340.*
Lord Fraser of North Cape : Distinguished wartime admiral. *98, 107, 149, 150, 154, 183, 193.*
Nigel Gaydon : British Embassy Washington, DC. *106.*
Laurence Gillingham : Director of Features BBC. *63.*
André Glarner : French war correspondent. *44.*
Fred Glass : New York businessman. *148, 306.*
Hughie Green : Host of TV talent show "Opportunity Knocks". *225.*

Commodore C.H.Grattidge OBE : Captain of the *Queen Elizabeth. 98, 129, 130, 131, 135, 136, 141, 149, 154, 336.*
Mrs. Grimmets : Secretarial assistant, Project Mayflower Ltd.
Fred Gullet : News editor of Daily Worker, UK communist daily paper. *68.*
Sir Francis de Guingand : Former chief of staff to General Montgomery. *17, 43, 57, 347.*
Sir Patrick Hannon : British Industrialist. *95.*
Peter Haddon : Actor, producer and collaborator with Warwick on two plays. *64, 65.*
Walter Haskell : Editor, The Old Colony Memorial, Plymouth. *92, 233, 234, 257, 307, 308, 309.*
Christian Herter : Governor of Massachusetts. *14, 113, 167, 168.*
Henry Hornblower II : Plimoth Plantation president. *11, 84, 85, 91, 92, 93, 112, 113, 120, 121, 128, 131, 133, 134, 136, 138, 140, 141, 153, 155, 156, 157, 158, 159, 160, 161, 177, 178, 200, 203, 204, 205, 206, 207, 210, 211, 213, 214, 215, 218, 228, 248, 249, 250, 254, 266, 271, 273, 274, 275, 277, 278, 282, 284, 287, 288, 292, 293, 295, 296, 298, 299, 301, 302, 303, 304, 305, 307, 308, 309, 310, 311, 317, 323, 324, 331, 340, 351, 353, 354, 356, 357, 358, 359, 360, 375, 376, 380, 395, 396, 401, 402, 406, 407, 409.*
Sir Edward Hulton : Chairman of Hulton Press newspaper chain. *70.*
Miss Jeans : Office manager Project Mayflower Ltd. *117, 222, 294.*
Audrey Jones : Head of BBC unit that employed Warwick. *63.*
Jan Junker : Third mate. *187, 194, 226, 227, 233, 241.*
Geoffrey Keating : Head of wartime photographic unit. *30, 38, 39, 55, 237.*
Harry Kemp: Poet of the Dunes. *12, 259.*
John F Kennedy : Junior US senator from Massachusetts. *14, 173, 248, 271.*
Reis L Leming : US serviceman who saved multiple lives in British flood. *165, 166, 167, 317.*

George Sanders : New York businessman. *148.*
Jack Scarr : Crew member. *233, 437.*
John Sloan Smith : CEO Aero Mayflower Transit company. *126, 128, 266, 267, 314, 315, 319, 346.*
Adrian Small : Crew member. *227, 233, 437.*
Harry Sowerby : Crew member. *233, 438.*
George Stewart : Insurance company executive. *145, 146, 147, 148, 163, 214, 297, 306, 327, 331.*
Doctor John Stevens : Ship's doctor. *194, 243, 244, 254, 437.*
Fiona McCrae-Taylor : Public relations executive for movie industry. *177, 204, 336.*
Dylan Thomas : Poet and BBC contributor. *63, 94.*
David Thorpe : Crew member. *233, 438.*
The Honorable David Tennant and Virginia Tennant : owners of the Gargoyle Club. *79.*
Stuart Upham : Boat builder. *88, 89, 90, 101, 102, 108, 109, 110, 112, 113, 114, 121, 126, 134, 136, 139, 141, 142, 143, 146, 147, 153, 154, 155, 157, 165, 170, 179, 184, 190, 192, 193, 195, 197, 199, 214, 217, 218, 224, 230, 254, 269, 336, 372, 400, 437.*
Alan Villiers : Captain *Mayflower II. 12, 117, 118, 119, 152, 178, 182, 186, 187, 188, 192, 194, 198, 209, 210, 211, 215, 220, 225, 226, 235, 238, 252, 257, 259, 264, 266, 267, 268, 271, 275, 276, 280, 281, 291, 292, 299, 304, 307, 308, 310, 321, 340, 360, 372.*
Lord Walker : Member of parliament and member of Prime Minister Thatcher's cabinet. *143, 144, 145.*
William Weld : Governor of Massachusetts. *400.*
Godfrey Wicksteed : First mate. *224, 292, 437.*
Wendell Wilkie : President Roosevelt's special envoy to North Africa. *47.*
Lieutenant Commander D.K. Winslow : Family ancestors sailed on the original Mayflower. *109, 110.*
Lothrop Withington : Henry Hornblower's attorney. *9, 92, 278, 293, 296, 297, 300, 332, 354, 357.*

Appendix B

Warwick Charlton's life.

Warwick Charlton born March 9, 1918 - died December 10, 2002.

Warwick's Family:

Lucy Haywood Charlton.
Children: Randal and Victoria.

Paula Theedom Charlton.
Children: Rachel and Thea.

Marilyn Russell Charlton.
Children: Alex, Michael and Caroline.

Belinda Chapman Charlton.

His creative milestones.

Plays.

Tomorrow Is A Lovely Day.

Stately Homes.

Projects.

Mayflower II 1957.

The English Court, Moscow.

Merrie England.

The International Award for Valour in Sport.

Valhalla.

The Space and Time Museum 2000.

The London Docklands English Gardens Project.

Russian Hotel Project 1994.

Redesco, a leisure development on the Egyptian Red Sea.

Skateboard World Park in Torrance, Los Angeles, California.

Wartime Editorships.

ME Middle East poetry collection 1940.

Eighth Army News.

The Crusader - Eighth Army News Weekly

Tripoli Times.

Syracuse News.

Phoenix.

War correspondent.

The Times of Malta.

Peace time correspondent.

Daily Express.

Daily Sketch.

Sunday Graphic.

Sunday Dispatch.

Daily Herald.

Magazines.

John Bull.

Picture Post.

Everybody's.

Today.

Consultancies.

Consultant to the British Gaming Association, responsible for co-ordinating a report that led to legalization of gaming in Britain.

Consultant to Norwich Enterprises Ltd. owners of the Victoria Sporting Club in London and Gateways Ltd. a merchandising company specializing in television and movies.

Consultant to the Mecca organization on the development of a 500 acre Theme park to be called `Merrie England`.

Chairman of Second Opinion Ltd. a research and development company dealing with joint ventures in the Soviet Union.

Books.

"The Second Mayflower Adventure".

"Stephen Ward Speaks".

"Casino Administration, The House and the Player".

Radio.

BBC "Meet the people".

Military rank and awards.

Major, Africa Star and Oak leaf, Burma Star. Mentioned in dispatches at El Alamein.

Citations.

Honorary citizen,

Honorary sheriff and other recognition for *Mayflower II* endeavour from the following cities;

New York NY, Boston MA, Harrisburg PA, Phoenix AZ, Portland ME, Miami FL, San Antonio TX, Houston TX, Dallas TX, Philadelphia PA, Raleigh NC, Indianapolis IN, Pittsburgh PA, Cincinnati OH, New Orleans LA, Hartford CT.

Town Crier : Ringwood, Hampshire, England.

Appendix C

The following sources are acknowledged and thanked.

Charlton, Warwick, private files including the files of Project Mayflower Ltd. Up to 1996.

Plimoth Plantation, public documents, files and correspondence including all records relating to Mayflower II up to 2003.

Bradford's Journal.

The Street of Adventure, Phillip Gibbs.

Fictional story with Randal Charlton represented as the character Christopher Codrington.

The Pageant of the Years, Phillip Gibbs.

Randal Charlton pp 61, 68, 69, 70.

Biography of Randal Charlton.

https://bearalley.blogspot.ca/2016/12/randal-charlton.html

Letters from Alan Villiers. National Library of Australia. Monty, Master of the Battlefield 1942 - 44 Nigel Hamilton.

Charlton, Warwick; editor Eighth Army News and Crusader p79-83, 179, 374; Victory parade Tripoli 138; and Robertson 180, 221; Axis Troops, 372, 373; and Mountbatten 373; and Monty's personality; 374, 473, 480; and Patton, 374.

Monty and Rommel: Parallel Lives: Peter Caddick-Adams.

The Men behind Monty: Richard Mead.

Combat and Morale in the North African Campaign: The Eighth Army and the path to El Alamein: Jonathan Fennell.

Patton, Montgomery and Rommel: Masters of War: Terry Brighton.

Cabinet Government and the 1956 Suez Crisis by Paul Duckenfield 1995.

"This Somewhat Embarrassing Ship": The British Foreign Office and the *Mayflower II,* 1954-57. Ted R Bromund, New England Quarterly Volume 72, No1 March 1999 pp 42-60.

Suez 1956 by Chris Leininger (c11@acussd.edu) Chris Leininger review of crisis and reasons for poor Anglo-American relations.

The Western Morning News.

April 13th 1957. Showing an objective of the *Mayflower II* was the implementation of scholarships for US and UK Exchange students.

***Life* Magazine June 17,1957.**

Full report on voyage of Mayflower II, pages, *Life* Magazine June 17,1957 vol 42 number 24.

Charlton, Warwick promoter of Mayflower II; leeches died after feeding on Warwick's blood p 36 *Life* magazine, June 17, 1957.

National Geographic 1957.

Decription of voyage of *Mayflower II* by Captain Alan Villiers.

***Time* Magazine May 1, 1944.**

Monty's fighting editor p86-89.

***The Times of Malta,* Tuesday July 20 1943 page 2.** With the British Infantry in Sicily by Captain Warwick Charlton Editor Eighth Army News.

The Second *Mayflower* Adventure.

Charlton, Warwick, Little Brown and Company 1957.

Lloyd's Log March 1957.

Lloyd's insurance policy p11,12,13,14 *Mayflower II* insurance policy.

***Today* Magazine** September 7 1963 Bankrupt by Warwick Charlton.

Description by Warwick Charlton of his bankruptcy process.

Casino Adminstration, the House and the Player. Judah Binstock.

Ghost written by Warwick Charlton.

Stephen Ward Speaks, by Warwick Charlton.

Walking on the Water, Hugh Cudlipp Autobiography of Lord Cudlipp.

Charlton, Warwick, p152.

De Guingand, Major-General Sir Francis.

Charlton, Warwick 383-384.

From Montmartre to Tripoli.

André Glarner - French War Correspondent.

Swaff , The life and Times of Hannan Swaffer, Tom Driberg.

Charlton, Randal 53, 59, 61, 219 Charlton Warwick x 219, 221.

Parade magazine March 11, 1944.

Frontline Headlines army papers reviewed by RJ Gilmore.

The New York Times, December 21, 2002.

Obituary of Warwick Charlton.

The Guardian January 3, 2003.

The man who brought the Monty out of Montgomery. Obituary of Warwick Charlton by Patrick Skene Catling.

The Pilgrim John Howland Society.

Warwick Charlton and *Mayflower.*

Appendix D

A Timeline of Warwick's *Mayflower* Adventure

****

His Life before *Mayflower II*

1918 Born Warwick Michael John Charlton to Randal and Birdie Charlton.

1937 Joined London Daily Sketch.

1939-1940 Joined Royal Fusiliers as private, later commissioned as second lieutenant.

1940-1944 Major in British Army. Served on personal staff of Field Marshall Montgomery, Editor of Eighth Army News, Crusader and multiple other papers for British and foreign troops.

1940-1944 Produced two intelligence publications for widespread distribution to troops.

1944-1946 Served on the personal staff of Lord Mountbatten , Supreme Commander, South East Asia.

1947 Consultant to Tate and Lyle, major sugar manufacturer under threat of nationalization by British Government.

1947-1955 Writer for London Daily Express. Broadcaster for BBC.

March 27, 1952 First night of *"Stately Homes"*, play by Warwick Charlton and John Audley, Embassy theater, London.

1949 Wrote play *"Tomorrow is a Lovely Day"* with Peter Haddon .

1954 Established Public Relations Company in Partnership with John Lowe.

Mayflower II: Life during

March 30,1955 Initial agreement to collaborate project Mayflower Ltd. and *Plimoth Plantation* memorandum of heads of agreement between Project Mayflower Ltd. and *Plimoth Plantation* inc. setting out intention to build *Mayflower II* and responsibilities of each party. Memorandum stipulates establishment of a trust fund with objective of providing academic and cultural exchange scholarship facilities for American citizens to study in thc United Kingdom and to further research on the Pilgrim period.

July, 1955 Keel laying ceremony at Brixham boatyard.

July 26,1956 Suez Crisis creates serious political conflict between US and UK.

Aug 15,1956 Memo to Mr Lothrop Withington from David Freeman, *Plimoth Plantation* stating that it was agreed to revise the heads of agreement of March 30 in two particulars. There would be no need for a separate trust fund and it would be more practical to establish a special restricted fund of the *Plantation*. Also the committee - made of a majority of American members and a minority of English - would have maximum flexibity in the use of the funds.

Sept 22,1956 Official launch of hull of *Mayflower II.*

Sept 26,1956 Agreement as to procedures. Sets out transfer to *Plimoth Plantation* not later than November 1957. Project *Mayflower* to be responsible for necessary expenditures up to the time of handover. After handover of *Mayflower II* to *Plimoth Plantation,* the *Plantation* is responsible for all costs and revenues.

It is agreed that the plan for the trust fund for fostering Anglo American relations to be cleared subsequently by mutual agreement.

Feb 25,1957 Senator John F Kennedy of Massachusetts agrees to serve on *Mayflower II* reception committee with Senator Saltonstall and other members of congress.

March, 1957 Nationwide shipbuilders strike shuts down all work except completion of *Mayflower II.*

April, 1957 Almost finished *Mayflower II* launched, and lists to over 30 degrees but stays upright.

April, 1957 *Mayflower II* sets sail for America.

June 13, 1957 *Mayflower II* welcomed at Plymouth, Massachusetts.

Aug 16, 1957 Ministry of Transport consents to export of *Mayflower II.*

Aug 22, 1957 Warwick and John Lowe sign document transferring ownership of *Mayflower II* to The Mayflower Foundation Incorporated, a non profit they have set up for this express purpose.

Sept 7, 1957 Letter from Warwick Charlton to *Plimoth Plantation* confirming transfer of ship to Mayflower Foundation Inc, a Connecticut corporation.

Setting out terms of transfer which include the payment by *Plimoth Plantation* of all debts existing on September 11, 1957. Any surplus to be used for the purposes of the Anglo-American trust.

Sept 11, 1957 Warwick Charlton confirms terms of transfer to *Plimoth Plantation.*

Agreement giving *Plimoth Plantation* the right to retain all income from the ship for a period of three years, thereafter a percentage of the gross income to applied to the Anglo-American trust. The organization of the trust is set out.

Sept 12, 1957 Transfer of *Mayflower II* to *Plimoth Plantation* for $1 written in English of the 1600s.

Sept 16, 1957 Confirmatory bill of sale to *Plimoth Plantation,* a private company.

Sept 17, 1957 *Plimoth Plantation* attorneys confirm approval of all sale documents.

Mayflower II: Life after gift

Nov 21, 1957 Agreement by Henry Hornblower on behalf of *Plimoth Plantation* Inc on how and when outstanding creditors will be reimbursed.

Nov 27, 1957 *Plimoth Plantation* Inc. hold official public ceremony to announce acquisition of *Mayflower II.*

Nov 28, 1957 Warwick publishes his account of the voyage, "The Second *Mayflower* Adventure".

Nov 29, 1957 *Plimoth Plantation* take over agreement to partner with Mayflower Ltd., a New York corporation regarding New York exhibition.

Jan 1958-1960 Lecturer in USA on the first and second *Mayflower* Adventure.

June 28, 1958 *Plimoth Plantation* Inc. signs agreement with *Mayflower* Ltd. regarding revenues for exhibitions in Miami and Washington DC .

1960 Returns to the UK, and resumes career in journalism.

April 1, 1996 Marietta Mullen of *Plimoth Plantation* contacts Warwick Charlton to say the *Plantation* would like to tell his story of the 1957 crossing.

Dec 10, 2002 Warwick Charlton died aged 84.

May 31, 2003 *Plimoth Plantation* hold Memorial Service for Warwick on *Mayflower II.*

Nov 2004 *Plimoth Plantation* produce magazine celebrating his central role in building the *Mayflower II* and the innovative ways he used to raise funds to build the ship.

2020 *Mayflower II* is refurbished at a cost of $7.5 million and is slated to form the centerpiece of celebrations to mark the 400 year anniversary of the first settlers arriving in New England.

Appendix E

Index of Photos used in book

Sources.

Page

5	**Author,** Randal Charlton	*Randal Charlton*
6 - 7	*Mayflower II* sails into New York harbor	*National Geographic*
8	Warwick Charlton	*Charlton family archives*
10	Bill of Sale for $1	*Charlton family archives*
11	Telegram announcing handover of *Mayflower II.*	*Charlton family archives.*
12	Signing of the Compact	*Associated Press*
19	Warwick Charlton.	*Charlton family archives*
20	Randal Charlton, Warwick's father	*Charlton family archives*
23	Birdie Courtney, Warwick's mother.	*Charlton family archives*
33	Captain Warwick Charlton	*Charlton family archives*
36	Randolph Churchill.	*Public Domain*
37	General Bernard Montgomery.	*Public Domain*
40	Eighth Army News.	*Public Domain*
42	Hugh Cudlipp, head of the Mirror Group.	*Alamy stock photos*
43	Sir Francis de Guingand.	*Public Domain*
44	Tripoli Times.	*Public Domain*
45	Winston Churchill, Britain's Prime Minister.	*Public Domain*
48	American Sherman tank.	*Public Domain*
50	American air force volunteers scrambling.	*Public Domain*
54	Eighth Army newspapers.	*Public Domain*
57	The Crusader: Eighth Army Weekly.	*Public Domain*
59	Warwick and musicians.	*Charlton family archives.*
62	Warwick broadcasting during the war.	*Charlton family archives*
67	Tate & Lyle's "Mr Cube" .	*Tate & Lyle*
72	Bill Connor and Warwick Charlton.	*Charlton family archives*
73	Felix Fenston.	*Project Mayflower Ltd*
74	Winthrop W. Aldrich, US Ambassador.	*Public domain*
76	Warwick Charlton and John Lowe.	*Mayflower Mail. Ltd*
78	The Gargoyle Club.	*Undefined source*
79	John Lowe, Warwick's partner.	*Project Mayflower Ltd*
84	Henry Hornblower II.	*Plimoth Plantation*

Appendix F: Businesses behind *Mayflower II*

Over 200 British businesses supported Warwick Charlton's Mayflower Project in a variety of ways.

This included equipment and services for the ship, food, drink , medicine and supplies for the journey of *Mayflower II* and the purchase of space in the Treasure chests that made up the cargo. Many are alive and well today in one form or another and some are among the biggest companies in the world.

A

H.R.Aulton & Co.
Anglo Dutch Gold and Silver Manufacturing Company
Ash Bros. & Heaton

B

Bairnswear Ltd.
D. Ballantyne Bros & Co. Ltd.
Barrie & Kersel Ltd.
Barr Lamb Ltd.
Benger Laboratories Ltd.
The Bentley Engineering Company Ltd.
Berketex (Overseas) Ltd.
M.Berman Ltd
Messrs Beswick
House of Bewlay
Blackstaff Flax Spinning Co. Ltd.
Erven Lucas Bols
Boulton Bros. (Glovers) Ltd.
Braemar Knitwear Ltd.
E.Brain & Co. Ltd.
British Jute Trade Federal Council
British Ropes Ltd.
British Schering Ltd.
The Briton Brush Co.Ltd.
Brixham Urban District Council
Broadway Damask Co. Ltd.
Messrs H. Bronnley
J. Buck & Son Ltd.
Buckden Hosiery Co.
Burnyeat Ltd.
Burroughs Wellcome & Co.

C

The Carborundum Co. Ltd.
Carrs & Co. Ltd.
Carsons Drinking Chocolate
Messrs Carter, Stabler & Adams
Messrs Casimer
Joseph Cheaney & Son
The Chemical & Insulating Co. Ltd.
Chivers & Sons Ltd.
C. & J. Clark Ltd.
Coates & Co (Plymouth) Ltd.
D. & H. Cohen Ltd.
Colgate-Palmolive Ltd.
Thos. Cook and Sons Ltd.
Cooke, Troughton & Simms Ltd.
Cooper & Roe Ltd.
Susie Cooper Pottery Ltd.
Corgi
Coventry Climax Engines Ltd.
P.B. Cow & Co. Ltd.
Messrs Cox Moore
Crompton Parkinson Ltd.
Cross & Blackwell Ltd.
Culmak Ltd.

Cussons

D

Dalmas Ltd.
Davison, Newman and Co Ltd.
Down Bros. & Mayer & Phelps Ltd.
Direct Manufacturing Supply Co.
Duncan, Flockhart & Co. Ltd.
Dykehead Horn Products

E

Chas. Early & Co. Ltd.
Joshua Ellis & Co. Ltd.
John Emsley Ltd.
English China Clays Ltd.
Enicar
Escoffier
Ethicon Ltd.
Evans Medical Supplies Ltd.
Wm. Ewart & Son Ltd.

F

Fabric Combiners Ltd.
J.K.Farnell Ltd.
Fassbender & Evans Ltd.
Thos. Ferguson & Co. Ltd.
J.Florsheim Ltd.
Josiah France Ltd.
Messsrs Fuller & Hambly

G

W.T.Glover & Co. Ltd.
George Goodman Ltd.
Glengair Ltd.
Glen Har Ltd.
Glenmac Knitwear
Glennae Knitwear
Goldcroft Glove Co. Ltd.
Gourock Ropework Co. Ltd.
Wm. Green & Son Ltd.
John Griffiths & Son Ltd.
Guinness Exports Ltd.

H

C.W.Hall
Messrs Hall Brothers
John Harper & Co. Ltd.
John Harvey & Sons Ltd.
G.J. Hayter & Co. Ltd.
Healey Marine Ltd.
H. J. Heinz & Co. Ltd.
Highfield Productions Ltd.
John Hill Ltd.
Hillsborough Linen Co.
George Hogg & Sons Ltd.
Wm. Hollins & Co. Ltd.
Hollins Brush Co. Ltd.
Hudson's Bay Company
Huntley & Palmers Ltd.

I

Illingsworths Snuffs Ltd.
Imperial Chemical Industries Ltd.
International Paints Ltd.

J

James Johnston & Co. Ltd.
Jarrett, Rainsford & Laughton Ltd.
N.C.Joseph Ltd.
Justerini and Brooks Ltd.

K

Kalamazoo Ltd.
Kaymet Company
Kelvin & Hughes Ltd.
T.W.Kempton Ltd.
G.B.Kent & Sons Ltd.
James Kenyon & Son Ltd.
Kid Knitwear Mfg. Co. Ltd.
J. Kohnstam Ltd.

L

Lafarge Aluminous Cement Co. Ltd.
Alex Lawrie & Co. Ltd.
Lee, Howl & Co. Ltd.

Leppington (Cutlers) Ltd.
S. J. Lethbridge (Plymouth) Ltd.
W.Liddell & Co. Ltd.
Linesw Brothers Ltd.
Lissco Products Ltd.
R.A. Lister (Marine Sales) Ltd.
Lloyd Attree & Smith Ltd.
Lloyds of London
Lyle & Scott Ltd.

M

JohnMackintosh and Sons Ltd.
Marconi International Marine Communication Co. Ltd.
Alfred Marsh Ltd.
W. & J. Martin
S.Maw Son & Sons Ltd.
Samuel McCrudden & Co. Ltd.
William McNaughton
Thomas Mercer Limited
J. & J. Minnis Ltd.
Mobil Oil Co. Ltd.
Molmax Ltd.
Munster, Simms & Co.

N

National Wool Textile Export Corporation
The Nestlé Co. Ltd.
Newarke Co. Ltd.
Newton Shakespeare Ltd.
J.Scott Nichol Ltd.
F.Norton & Son Ltd.

O

Old World Inn Industries
Onsa Watch

P

Parker Pen Co. Ltd.
Parnall and Sons Ltd.
Patrician Art Products Ltd.
Patterson & Stone
D.Payn Ltd.
Peak Frean & Co.
W. O. Peake Ltd.
Pearce Duff & Co. Ltd.
W. Pearce & Co. (Northants) Ltd.
Pfizer Ltd.
John Player & Co. Ltd.
Plymouth Gin
James Porteus & Co. Ltd.
Priestleys Ltd.
Robert Pringle & Sons Ltd.

R

J. & J. Randall Ltd.
W. Reik Ltd.
Ridgeway Potteries Ltd.
James Ritchie & Co.
J. A. Robertson & Sons
Rosina China Co. Ltd.
G. & R. Ross
Thos. Ross & Son (London) Ltd.

S

Thomas Salter Ltd.
Seaboard Lumber Sales Co. Ltd.
Searchlight Products Ltd.
Shell-Mex Ltd.
R. Silcock and Sons Ltd.
Silvro Manufacturing Company
Messrs A. Simpson
Simpson, Wright & Lowe Ltd.
Sindall Bros. & Co. Ltd.
Smedley's
Smith & Nephew Ltd.
T. J. & J. Smith Ltd.
Southampton City
J. W. Spear & Son Ltd.
Spence Bryson Co. Ltd.
Stevenage Knitting Company
Andrew Stewart & Co. Ltd.
Stewart & Maclennan
Stewart, Smith & Co. Ltd.
Robert Stocks & Co. Ltd

Strelitz Ltd.

T

Talbot Tool Co. Ltd.
Taunton & Thorne Ltd.
Taylor Law & Co. Ltd.
Theo. Taylor & Co. Ltd.
Richard Thomas & Baldwins Ltd.
Wallace Thorn Ltd.
Thring & Luffman Ltd.
Trentham Bone China Ltd.
Truman, Hanbury, Buxton & Co. Ltd.
Turner Rutherford Ltd.
Tyrrell & Green

W

John Waddington Ltd.
H.Wald & Co. Ltd.
Waller & Hartley Ltd.
Watts Fincham Ltd.
Webb & Co. Ltd.
Francis Webster & Sons Ltd.
Wellworthy Ltd.
Whitby Bros. Ltd.
John White Footwear Ltd.
Thos. C. Wild & Sons Ltd.
David Williams & Sons Limited
Herbert Williamson Ltd.
Windsor & Sons Ltd.
H.H.Winter Ltd.

Y

Yates Brothers
York Street Flax Spinning Co. Ltd
.

Z

O.Ziegler Ltd.

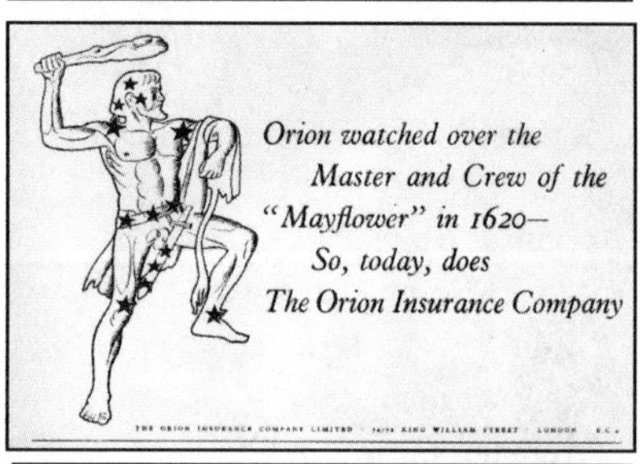

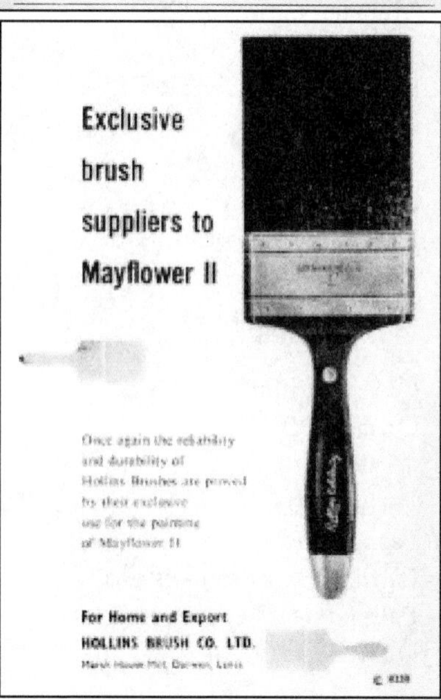

Appendix G: The Crew

1. Captain: **Alan Villiers:** Oxford, England. Trustee of National Maritime Museum.

2. Super-Cargo: **Warwick Charlton**: Kennington, London, England. His ancient title meant he had responsibility for all commercial activity in relation to the ship and its contents.

3. Caulker: **Stuart Upham:** Brixham, Devon, England; Builder of ship. The title of caulker means he was responsible for keeping the ship watertight.

4. First Mate: **Godfrey Wicksteed:** Cambridge, England. Schoolmaster. He received leave of absence from Cambridge Education Committee. Second in command to the master of a merchant ship.

5. Second mate: **Adrian Small:** Solihull, Birmingham, England

6. Third mate: **Captain Jan Junker:** Copenhagen, Denmark.

7. Bo'sun: **Ike Marsh:** Berry Dock, South Wales. A ship's officer in charge of the equipment and crew on board.

8. Bo'sun's mate: **Joe Lacey:** Bristol, England.

9. Ship's Cook: **Walter Godfrey:** Romford, Essex, England

10. Mariner and Cook: **Richard Brennan:** London, England

11. Cook's assistant: **Jack Scarr:** Oxford, England.

12. Surgeon Seaman: **Dr John Stevens:** Ipswich, England

13. Wireless operator: **J.D.Horrocks:** Southport, Lancashire, England

14. Ship's carpenter: **Edgar Mugridge:** Brixham, Devon, England. Was on the team that built the *Mayflower II* in Brixham.

15. Cabin Boy: **Joseph M. Meany:** Waltham, Mass, USA. He was chosen in a nationwide competition to represent the Boys Clubs of America.

16. Cabin Boy: **Graham Nunn:** Corby, Northants, England. He was chosen to represent the National Association of Boys Clubs

17. Crewman: **John L Goddard:** Woking, Surrey, England.

18. Crewman: **H.C. Sowerby:** Piccadilly, London, England.

19. Crewman: **F.E Edwards:** West Derby, Liverpool, England .

20. Crewman: **Joseph Powell:** Beak Street, London, England.

21. Crewman: **D.M. Cauvin:** Forest Hill, England.

22. Crewman: **Beric Watson:** Horsforth, Yorkshire, England.

23. Crewman: **John Winslow:** Kew Green, Surrey, England.

24. Crewman: **D.C. Thorpe:** Ewell, Surrey , England.

25. Crewman: **M.J Ford:** London, England.

26. Crewman: **A. Anderson Bell:** Edinburgh, Scotland.

27. Crewman: **P.L.N.Padfield:** Weybridge, Surrey, England.

28. Crewman: **Charles Church:** Nova Scotia, Canada. He was in the Royal Canadian Navy

29. Crewman: **Andrew Lindsey:** Biddeford, Maine, USA.

Chroniclers:

30. *Life* magazine Photographer: **Gordon Tenney.**

31. *Life* magazine Reporter: **Maitland Edy:** Martha's Vineyard, Massachusetts, USA

32. Project Mayflower Movie Cameraman: **Julian Lugrin.**

33. Transatlantic News Photographer: **Lee Israel**

The Captain and Crew of the *Mayflower II*

1957

Photo by courtesy of WickedLocalPlymouth.com

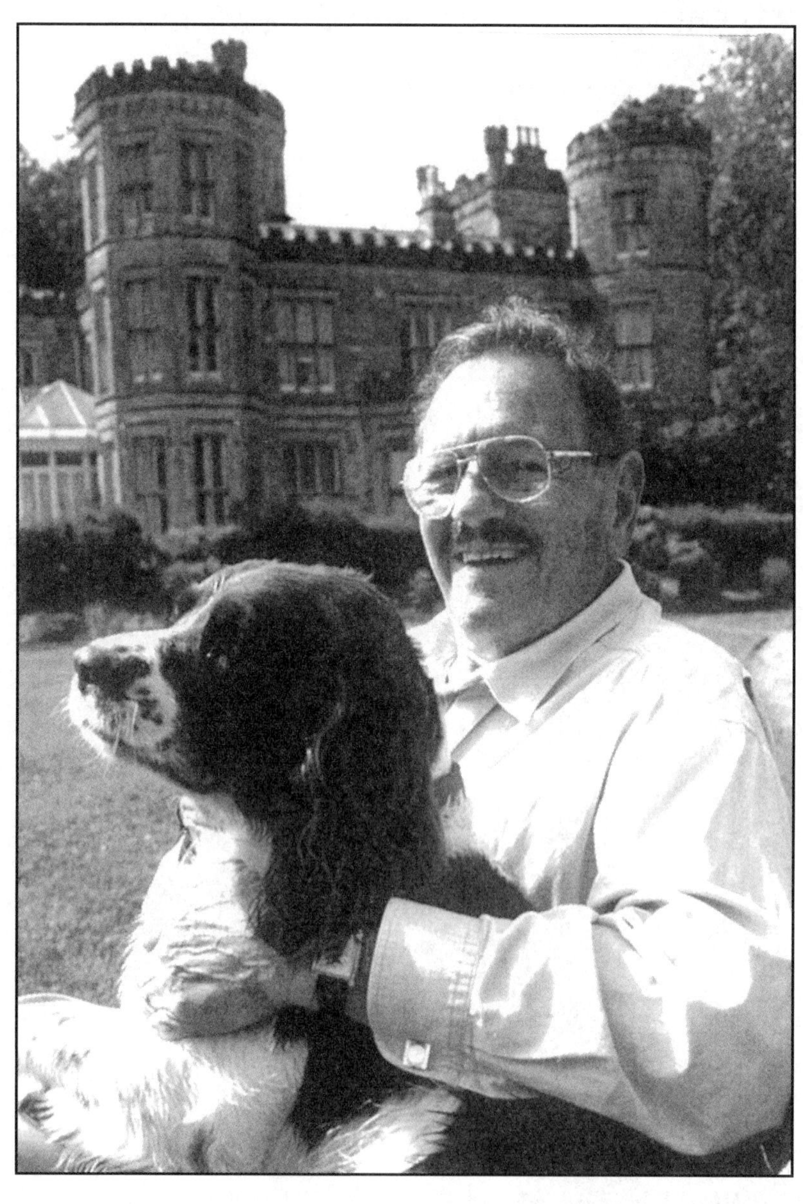

Warwick Charlton with his dog, Oliver Cromwell, in the grounds of his English home.